Praise for *Business Is About to Pick Up!*

"Some of the most electrifying and iconic moments in the history of pro wrestling (including many of my own) have been called by legendary Jim Ross. Jim's masterful play-by-play commentary has always been driven by his passion, deep wrestling knowledge, and, most of all, his ability to make the audience FEEL the action of the wrestling match."

—Dwayne "The Rock" Johnson

"Jim Ross doesn't just call a match, he makes you believe. He has the ability to take less-than-stellar writing and elevate it to something unforgettable (trust me, I know)."

—Brian Gewirtz, Hollywood writer, producer, and former head writer for WWE

"If you were to ask my generation, 'What are your greatest memories as a wrestling fan?' I have no doubt that most were elevated in that moment by Jim's call. It's in these moments, we remember where we were, what we were doing, how his enthusiastic delivery excited us—or made us sad, or made us laugh, or made us feel compassion when we perhaps otherwise wouldn't have. Jim hasn't just been the narrator guiding us along our journey in pro wrestling—he has become the voice synonymous with wrestling. It's been the greatest honor to have experienced his work as a fan, and to also have benefitted by working alongside him in AEW."

—Kenny Omega, former IWGP and AEW champion

"Jim Ross has an incredible ability to identify grit and inner character. Through the years, he has been not only the voice of some of the greatest stories ever told in sports entertainment, he has identified and helped a great number of successful professionals. Jim was a strong advocate for me when very few were and I'm extremely grateful for all his guidance through the years."

—John Cena, sixteen-time WWE champion and member of the WWE Hall of Fame

"On countless occasions throughout my career, I would visualize big moves and big moments—ways to make a lasting impression on wrestling fans. On most of those occasions, I would also imagine the type of call Jim Ross might make for those moves and moments. With his inimitable announcing style and unmatched passion for pro wrestling, Jim Ross has the ability to turn a good match into a great match, and a great match into the stuff of legends. For an entire generation of wrestling fans, Jim's immortal calls were part of the soundtrack of their lives; eclipsing wrestling itself to become an indelible part of popular culture."

—Mick Foley, three-time WWE champion and member of the WWE Hall of Fame

"When I look back on Jim Ross, I can think of few men who truly impacted the wrestling profession more than he did leaving his own indelible yet unseen thumbprint everywhere going back to the mid-80s. Jim was often right there in the room during the most crucial years when so much was happening. Jim Ross has always spoken the truth to me. His deep-rooted love and passion, first as a fan, then announcer, and eventually as a booker were always visible from the start from Mid-South, WWE, and now AEW. To my memory, Jim was the greatest play-by-play wrestling commentator there is, was, and ever will be; simply said he was the Excellence of Execution. He brought TV's greatest wrestling matches to life, and the many unforgettable memories that come involving each superstar on each telecast, taking you there word by word, guiding you carefully to the finish for one more wild ride. Jim's unique ability to translate wrestling theory and logic, as well as his down-to-earth analysis made so many rich memories for fans all over the world. That gift was making something worthy to carry all one's lifetime as a cherished moment unlike any other. I know wrestling wouldn't have been the same without his unique ability to simply spell it out. I have no doubt he has much to say about all things wrestling, shedding light with honesty, passion, and a splash of zesty southern humor."

—Bret Hart, five-time WWE champion and
member of the WWE Hall of Fame

BUSINESS
IS ABOUT TO
PICK UP!

Also by Jim Ross

Slobberknocker

Under the Black Hat

J.R.'s Cookbook

Can You Take the Heat?

BUSINESS
IS ABOUT TO
PICK UP!

50 YEARS OF WRESTLING IN 50 UNFORGETTABLE CALLS

JIM ROSS
WITH PAUL O'BRIEN

BenBella Books, Inc.
Dallas, TX

BenBella Books, Inc.
10440 N. Central Expressway
Suite 800
Dallas, TX 75231
benbellabooks.com
Send feedback to feedback@benbellabooks.com

BenBella is a federally registered trademark.

Printed in the United States of America
10 9 8 7 6 5 4 3 2 1

Library of Congress Control Number: 2023947914
ISBN 9781637744642 (hardcover)
ISBN 9781637744659 (electronic)

Editing by Leah Wilson
Copyediting by Michael Fedison
Proofreading by Ashley Casteel and Rebecca Maines
Indexing by WordCo Indexing Services
Text design and composition by PerfecType
Cover design by Pete Garceau
Cover photo © All Elite Wrestling, LLC
Printed by Lake Book Manufacturing

Special discounts for bulk sales are available. Please contact bulkorders@benbellabooks.com.

To a lifetime of fans, from a lifelong fan

CONTENTS

INTRODUCTION

Professional wrestling.

You say those words to people and it'll probably elicit a myriad of different reactions. Some might throw out their favorite Kenny Omega match, some might try an eyebrow from The Rock, while others will shake their head and tell you it's not real. Me? I have loved professional wrestling my whole life—long before it ever became my career. I was drawn to the irony of how the friction on my TV could bring people together. I loved that, at its core, wrestling fulfilled a human desire to see conflict have a satisfying conclusion: good versus evil, right versus wrong, heel versus babyface.

In looking back to write this book, I'll never forget how lucky I was as a small-town farm boy fan to break in at all, and how blessed I continue to be to stay in. I found my way in at the most unlikely time, in the most unlikely place, with the most unlikely chance of lasting. I wasn't connected to anyone who would protect or vouch for me. I didn't have any of the undeniable attributes that wrestling coveted, like a sculpted body or freakish athleticism. In a world of sequins and showboats, I was just a chubby guy in a polyester suit.

But once I found my voice, I found my place.

In 1974, I left my parents' home in Oklahoma for a summer job in wrestling, but that summer ran into Christmas, then another year came, then a decade, then another. I was Dorothy who found herself a long way from Kansas—but the difference for me was, I didn't want to find a way home. I was happily lost in a world of tough guys, kind souls, weary travelers, grifters, sweethearts, liars, and friends. From all parts of the world, we arrived backstage through many paths, from many places, but come showtime we all waited together behind that curtain to entertain and excite. Didn't matter our nationality, age, sex, or beliefs, we were bonded by the live reaction, and judged by the dollars we drew and the ratings we garnered.

From the outside, professional wrestling can present itself as a glamorous and alluring proposition, but it can also be a cruel machine that constantly needs to be fed with fresh faces, stories, and personalities. Thousands and thousands have come and gone while very few build a decades-long career, but somehow, throughout the various twists and turns in history, I managed to do just that. I worked across several companies through several eras, giving me a front row seat to all the major start-ups, mergers, signings, and takeovers that led wrestling itself to grow into a multibillion-dollar business.

My wonderful wrestling odyssey has led me from regional crowds of tens of people to a global audience of millions. As the business grew, changed, and thrived, I was right there with it, watching, narrating, evolving from role to role, company to company, talent to executive, and back again. And I did it while making mistakes, trying to be decent, failing, climbing, struggling, and calling my heart out.

Over the last fifty years, I have kept my passion for professional wrestling—and thankfully maintained a fan base who wants to hear me call it. Now, I'd like to take you with me, across my half century in the business, as I drop in to some of wrestling's biggest events, happenings, and history-making moments, narrating the action the way I have my whole career: with the words that left my mouth at that moment, at that time, in that place.

And just as I've crafted my words at the announce desk over the years, I'm excited to do so here now.

So sit back and relax as we journey back through the last fifty years of professional wrestling using calls you may have heard, some you may have forgotten, and others that might be completely new to you—each of which meant something in the context and era in which I had the privilege to say them.

Ladies and gentlemen, business is about to pick up!

"ATTENTION, WRESTLING FANS!"

To understand my fifty years in wrestling, you might need to first understand the years that came before it. Right up front I'm going to say something that would have earned me an ass-kicking when I broke into the business: professional wrestling is entertainment. And like all entertainment, it has always only been as potent as the vessel that carried it. Whether it was the first pressed record, or the birth of the cinema, or the first TV satellite launched into space, the entertainment industry has always strived to develop better, more efficient ways of bringing its products to the masses—and the wrestling business is no different.

In the beginning, wrestling was 100 percent a live-ticket business that thrived or died on its ability to promote itself locally. Whether it was the carnival barker outside the tent, or flyers around town, converting attention into ticket sales was what led to either a good night at the box office or a bust.

So in the 1940s, as wrestling became a proven moneymaker and began popping up all across the US, a business pact was reached to carve up North America (and other parts of the world) into regional territories that would act as independent fiefdoms. This arrangement meant each promoter would respect the boundaries of their colleagues' territory and not trade on their turf, while also adhering to the other rules and business practices set forth by a new collective governing body known as the National Wrestling Alliance.

The NWA consolidated all the titles across the regions into one, crowning one recognized and touring world champion. The working theory was—having *the* world champion come to your town and wrestle your local hero boosted your ticket sales considerably, *and* built up your hero to become a box-office draw in his own right.

This privilege, of course, would cost you a percentage to the NWA—which usually made financial sense, until it didn't.

You see, the NWA wasn't an independent body, but a select pool of the most powerful promoters it was supposed to oversee. And those promoters wanted what people who sit around political tables *always* want: what's best for themselves. So even with full control of where the world champion wrestled—and the outcome of the match—the spoils weren't always shared equally across the territories.

As time went on, the "lesser" territories knew they couldn't rely on the champion stopping by to keep them alive. It was every territory for itself. They needed to understand their local audience, give them what they wanted—and then find a way to do the same in the next town, the next week.

What worked in one place might get booed out of the building in another. Southern parts of the country enjoyed a more realistic, rough-and-ready flavor of wrestling, while WWE's northeast region preferred the larger-than-life spectacle. But as far-flung as one promoter might have been from another, they all shared the same common problem: how to put an ass every eighteen inches. After all, the greatest wrestlers in the world, having the greatest matches, didn't mean shit if nobody knew about it. So, no matter the time period, or the territory, gaining exposure was still the key to making money.

It was no surprise, then, that when along came TV—the greatest vessel for entertainment the world had ever seen—wrestling hit its first boom.

Heading into the 1950s, when regional promoters could only hit hundreds of eyeballs, television reached twelve to fifteen million people across the country. The American Broadcasting Company (ABC), the Columbia Broadcasting System (CBS), the National Broadcasting Company (NBC), and the DuMont Television Network were looking for cheap "event" programming to occupy those same eyeballs—and paying a wrestling promoter who already had their own ring and wrestlers was a whole lot cheaper than paying a Hollywood producer who had to hire writers, actors, a director, crew, and pay for sets, props, and on and on.

So, in the age of Superman and Lucille Ball, in strutted a lightning rod from the wrestling world called Gorgeous George. By God, Gorgeous George made people from San Francisco to New York City *feel* something. And when the people *feel* something, they become invested; they stay tuned in; they spend their money.

Now, it just so happens that most of the feelings they had toward George were those of rage and anger—but that's the beauty of wrestling: the anger was induced by design. In a time of tough guys and wise guys, Gorgeous George glided into America's homes with dyed platinum blond hair and sequined robes; as manservants misted the audience with perfume, valets threw rose petals at his feet.

George Wagner was a good amateur wrestler who understood what was needed to become a great professional wrestler. And as Gorgeous George, "the Human Orchid," he became a household name across the country.

He became the toast of Hollywood, as all the top stars wanted to be seen at his matches. He wrestled for the NWA, and other less powerful promotions like the American Wrestling Association. Originally a depression-era small-town carnival wrestler, his star finally shone so bright that he was able to command half the box-office returns while wrestling in all the major cities, working with whatever promoters could afford him, making George not only the highest paid wrestler of the time, but the highest paid athlete, period. Many other famous names were influenced by him, including Muhammad Ali, Bob Dylan (weird, I know), James Brown, and just about every pompous blond wrestler who's come since.

All boats rose together, and wrestling became hotter even in the smaller territories where George didn't wrestle. But, like any boom, the "Golden Era" went bust as, at the end of the 1950s, *overexposure* took hold and the numbers fell. As wrestling's national TV time dwindled, the business mostly retreated back to its regional roots, where the promoters waited for a pathway to national exposure once again.

And that's where this chubby farm boy drops into wrestling's timeline in Oklahoma, 1974—a long time after any boom, and a long time after any Golden Era.

Now, how does a fan like me with no connections to the notoriously closed-off business get inside? I tell the promoter in my region that I can bring his company free exposure, that's how. I mightn't have been NBC calling, and I sure as hell wasn't promising national exposure, but I was a college kid who could reach people in their homes in our area, and tell them about the matches that were coming to their town.

Now, 1974 wasn't just a different time; it might as well have been a different planet. Richard Nixon was forced to resign as president of the United States; Muhammad Ali and George Foreman beat the living shit out of each other in Zaire. It was the year that Matt Hardy and Rey Mysterio were born, and legends like Ricky Steamboat and Jesse Ventura debuted. In the northeast territory, Bruno Sammartino was on top in what was then called the World Wrestling Federation (now WWE, World Wrestling Entertainment), who were separate from but friendly to the NWA, while Jack Brisco ruled the National Wrestling Alliance proper as their world's champion.

And somewhere right at the very bottom of that giant, golden ladder of greats and greatness, I sat in Tulsa, in my flared pants and standard-issue haircut, and explained to NWA Tri-State's co-owner, the huge, no-nonsense "Cowboy" Bill Watts, just how I could be of help to *his* territory.

I was twenty-two years old, married, working three jobs, and close to graduating college. And it was in that same college that I had access to a pipeline that had somehow never been used in an Oklahoma wrestling promotion before: radio.

If we co-promoted some shows as charitable events, I told Cowboy, I could get radio spots for free by making them public service announcements. That word, "free," was all that the budget-conscious Watts needed to hear. It was a no-risk situation for him, and if I managed to pull it off, he'd have a powerful tool in his arsenal for no money down.

I was immediately given the green light.

So I sat in my college radio booth at Northeastern State University, Tahlequah, Oklahoma, knowing that as long as I stayed useful, wrestling might keep me around—and that the second I wasn't, I was back to the farm.

That feeling is something that has never left me, my whole fifty years in wrestling. If I wanted to stay in, I had to constantly figure out ways to reinvent, to recalibrate, and most importantly, to evolve with wrestling's ever-changing nature.

That bright dusty day in my college booth, I pulled the microphone to my lips and first said the words I knew would either sink me or give me passage.

And how fitting they were:

| *"ATTENTION, WRESTLING FANS!"* |

"Hello, everybody, and welcome to another exciting hour of wrestling. My name is Jim Ross and I'll be your host . . ."

1975
Tri-State Championship Wrestling
KTBS Studios
Shreveport, Louisiana

I sometimes walk backstage in my role as a broadcaster for All Elite Wrestling, just like I did in WWE and WCW before it, and I think of all the roads people took to get where they ultimately ended up. What decisions did people make, or not, to get to where they ended up? What did a decision-maker see in them, or not, for them to get to the place they're at? Out of all the people we've seen come and go, why did this particular group of people make it to "the show" and not others?

How does a water delivery guy become AJ Styles? How does a bail bondsman become Big Show, or a limo driver become John Cena? I mean, I know he was John Cena back then, too, but he wasn't *John Cena*.

Some paths are easier to trace, like pro baseball player Randy Poffo following his father's footsteps into wrestling to become The Macho Man, or Paul Bearer going from being an undertaker to managing The Undertaker.

I guess the thing about wrestling and life in general is, you just never know where it's going to take you, or who you'll be traveling with.

My radio ads were such a hit that Bill Watts offered me a job with NWA Tri-State as soon as I finished college. The shows I had promoted on-air sold out, and Watts got a sense that I could be a low-cost, high-reward hire. In other words, he could pay me little and I would work a lot—and standing right at the edge of my dream job, I was happy to take that deal. So I did what I tell people looking to get into our business not to do: I left college right there and then. With just a few credits left, I wished my school all the best in its future endeavors and joined what my father described as "the circus."

Little did he know that wrestling was more like a nonviolent mafia. Cash business, no contracts, secret deals, bribes, bosses on top of each region, and once you were in, you never talked about the inner workings of the business to anyone outside the business. And I say "nonviolent," but there was plenty of blood, broken bones, and pulled guns along the way. But because it was mostly in-house and between the wrestlers (The Boys,) law enforcement never really got involved.

On my first day "inside," I had the same feeling in my guts as I had on my first day of elementary school: that I might not be cool. Or maybe the word is *welcome*—that I might not be *welcome*. This feeling was, you can imagine, a sharp adjustment to make. I went from the bosom of acceptance in school to the backside of rejection in wrestling.

I've since learned that a big part of longevity in the wrestling business is having the ability to stand out. And in 1974, I sure stood out. Among the toughest, coolest guys on the planet, in seas of beer, clouds of smoke, and miles of mustaches, I looked like a guy who had stumbled backstage to sell them aluminum siding.

I mean, it's hard to impress upon those of you who weren't around in the '70s just how sweaty and hairy that decade was. It was a time of war, inflation, and oil crises, civil unrest, and our president embroiled in a historical scandal. (Actually, I'm guessing you do know what those things feel like, as history has a funny habit of repeating itself.)

Our entertainment went from *Happy Days* to *Taxi Driver*, music swung from ABBA to Led Zeppelin, and the wrestling business was a dark, stripped-down affair with no music, no lighting—and if you can believe it, no baby oil.

And there I stood in the middle of it, the former vice president of the Future Farmers of America, dutifully being ignored by world champions and childhood heroes alike. In my cheap suit and bowl haircut, I began to wonder just how I was going to be earning my $125 a week. I hoped it was at least a role that would put me in the trenches with The Boys, so I could show them I was there to get my hands dirty and . . .

Nope, I was going to be working directly with the owner.

Well, that was nice. After all, nothing helps the guy who was just president of the student body fit into the notoriously paranoid wrestling business more than walking in the door and immediately becoming "the office."

(Little did they know my "office" job was really just driving the blind majority owner, Leroy McGuirk, from town to town while making sure he had enough sustenance to keep him going. And by sustenance, I mean cigars and whiskey.)

So I started in quite the hole in the eyes of The Boys backstage. But over the course of the next year or so, I worked tirelessly to dig myself back out again. I drove the wrestlers from town to town, too (for two cents a mile), so they could relax (get drunk) on their downtime; I joined the ring crews; I refereed the matches to earn extra money for my young family.

Once I got talking, the wrestlers began to understand just how much I loved the business, and how I was in it for life—just like them—if I could find a way to stay there that long.

I began to learn all sides of the business—from talent to booker and back again. Driving every day with Leroy, and every night with the wrestlers, I was in a rolling classroom. And I began to understand why "having the ear" of the boss was a coveted position for wrestlers, because back then your money was aligned with where you found yourself on the card, and where you found yourself on the card was the sole decision of the boss. Politics led to pay. If you weren't picked to work, you didn't earn.

It was as simple and as brutal as that.

I did job after job, I was free whenever I was needed, and I took on any extra work that people had for me. In a small touring company like ours, you did whatever was needed to get the show up on its feet every night—even if that meant filling in for the vacationing announcer on very short notice.

I guess I have a scheduling oversight to thank for my start in broad-casting. The regular announcer, Reeser Bowden, was given time off, and nobody seemed to notice until a couple of hours before the taping was to begin. I guess because I showed adaptability, I was asked if I'd do it, and sitting at that announce table did something to me that none of the other jobs I'd done in a business I already loved had.

It made me nervous that I might not get to do this for the rest of my life.

I felt like a million bucks in my fifty-dollar suit as I sat at the announce table beside the owner—a blind man, remember—to call my first match in wrestling. I thought about rehearsing some lines and practicing some catch-phrases, but it just wasn't me. All I wanted to do was to finally introduce myself. To the business, to the wrestlers, to the fans in the seats, and to the audience at home.

And that's what I did.

With Leroy by my side, and in front of seventy-five fans in KTBS Studios, Shreveport, Louisiana, I picked up my first television microphone and let the people know who I was.

> *"Hello, everybody, and welcome to another exciting hour of wrestling. My name is Jim Ross . . ."*

And just like that my career took off.

That's not true.

I was back off TV again just as fast as I got on.

And then back on again.

Then off again.

And, you guessed it, back on again.

And off again.

I quickly understood that my road to longevity in this business wasn't going to be straight, smooth, or without heartbreak. But I was willing to do almost anything to make sure I'd get my chance again. And when I did, I knew I could show a little more of what I brought to the table.

In the meantime, I was just feeling lucky, and broke as hell, but mostly lucky that I got to be in this company, on this learning curve, at this time, working the towns, studying the business, and managing all the personalities that came along with it. I didn't know it then, but the education I was getting then in small towns for no money, with no Golden Era in sight, helped get me ready for what was to come.

All the paths I took then as Jim Ross helped lead me to where I am now as JR. And while it was hard, and there were bad, bad times along the way, I'm so happy I stayed the course.

I guess I don't really know all the decisions and sacrifices that John Cena made, or what it took for all the others to get where they ended up. But I know what my journey was filled with: hard work, selfless mentors, hard bosses, and a big streak of luck to hold it all together.

"Everywhere I go . . . people are talking about Mid-South Wrestling."

March 20, 1982
Debut on Mid-South Wrestling
Irish-McNeil Boys' Club
Shreveport, Louisiana

Working in professional wrestling is almost like a relay race, where those of us who work in it get on the track and run for as long as we can before passing the baton to the next person to keep it going. The difference for us is, the race is never-ending, and sometimes the hand that's passing you the baton doesn't want to let it go.

But, thankfully, it wasn't like that for me.

I had been picking up pockets of broadcasting experience here and there in NWA Tri-State. But each time I sat at the commentary table there, Reeser Bowden would come back a match or two later tanned and relaxed, and the position, rightfully, would return to him.

Then along came the '80s, when transition was in the air.

The territories—and the system that tied them together—were in the midst of change, thanks to expanding national cable TV coverage. The iron grip of ABC, NBC, and CBS was slipping, and as more channels came from more places, the promise of cable TV sounded a dinner bell to all the ambitious and savvy promoters across the territories. A new national race began in wrestling to see who could dominate these new national pathways first.

The year 1982 gave the world Nike Air Force 1, the Commodore 64, *Blade Runner, E.T.*, "Thriller," and Bud Light. It was also the year my future boss at All Elite Wrestling, Tony Khan, was born, and the year my former WWE boss, Vince K. McMahon, bought the World Wrestling Federation from his father and promptly sought a weekly national telecast on the USA cable network, which debuted the following year.

Vince was new, but already defiantly and directly challenging the old-school way of doing business, as he split from the NWA (his father had split from them in 1963 before rejoining in 1971) to build his own national brand. McMahon's aggressive strategy involved immediately crossing the boundary lines into other wrestling territories while trying to buy up their syndicated programming.

Back home in Oklahoma, change was also coming fast down the pike, and with the old ways beginning to creak, change was a hard pill for the lifers to swallow. None more so than NWA stalwart Leroy McGuirk.

Before he ever booked a match, Leroy had a stellar career as the longest reigning light-heavyweight NWA champion in history. And he did it all with one eye, as he'd lost sight in one eye as a kid, before a car crash robbed him of sight in his other eye as an adult. After blindness forced him into competitive retirement, Leroy found his power as a promoter and higher-up in the National Wrestling Alliance. But even though he was the majority owner of NWA Tri-State, the overall direction of the company was handled by his forward-thinking booker, and minority owner, "Cowboy" Bill Watts.

Cowboy had been a top heavyweight draw for McGuirk before leaving to headline for the New York and Minnesota territories. When Tri-State's business fell off, Leroy asked Watts to come back home, and Bill, the ever-working businessman, saw a path to making about the same money for a lot less travel. He would return, but not only as a wrestler; he also wanted to be paid for running the shows as the booker, and get a slice of the overall company, too.

Leroy knew his shrinking ticket sales were inviting the wolves to gather outside his company door, so he and Bill shook hands on a deal. And, boy, it worked. Watts did what he said he would do and turned those shrinking numbers around. He created buzz, amassed a stellar roster, and put asses every eighteen of those precious inches. And Leroy never forgave him for it. This led McGuirk to meddle so much that Bill left again in '79 to go wrestle in Georgia and Florida before returning with an offer to buy Leroy out completely in '82.

And that's when Mid-South Wrestling was born.

And to my surprise, Watts also had an offer for me at that time: to be his full-time announcer. In between him leaving Tri-State in '79 and coming back in '82, I had been working on getting all the experience I could in broadcasting, even handling the arena interviews for the first team rodeo concept for ESPN. I knew I wanted to work in this area more than any other, and Cowboy handed me that opportunity.

With McGuirk gone, Watts immediately withdrew from Leroy's beloved National Wrestling Alliance. Watts simply didn't want to kick up 7–9 percent for the sole "luxury" of having the NWA champion come to his territory. Especially because he knew he'd still have to pay the champ 5–7 percent directly for that same booking, too.

Bill had the world champion's number; what did he need the NWA for?

He told the old wrestlers and promoters who ran the NWA office that paying them a percentage didn't make sense because the NWA didn't promote, publicize, or put one extra ass in one of his seats. But like all good breakup artists, he did give the NWA a reason to feel better about the split.

"When the government comes knocking on the NWA door, asking about a monopoly in professional wrestling, you can now use me as an example of how it's not," Watts told them. "Because I'm going to book your champion directly, and you're going to 'let' me do it."

And so he did.

On top of business, almost everything else changed and improved in quality under Bill's watchful eye—me included. Bill wanted every segment and match on a show to build someone up, and it was the commentator's job, he told me, to help that building process happen.

I guess that that lesson finally clicked for me during my very first Mid-South taping, as I got to experience firsthand what Bill wanted from his commentators when longtime announcer Boyd Pierce helped build my credibility for the people back home.

"You'll notice on my left a new face here on Mid-South Wrestling," Boyd began. "He's our guest. I know some of his background. He's educated from Oklahoma State University, and Northeastern State. His name: Jim Ross. Jim, we're glad to have you with us. But to continue his background: the only person, the only referee, in amateur ranks to referee in the state of Oklahoma: basketball, football, and baseball. That's really something. And he's a national commentator for ESPN rodeo professionally. He has his own TV wrestling commentary shows in many areas.

"And, ladies and gentlemen, he called me up and he said, 'Boyd, wherever I go people are buzzing and talking about the enthusiasm and great grapplers you have on Mid-South Wrestling.' And asked could he come here to watch it in person. I was only too glad. I invited him not only to come here, but he will be our guest commentator."

The veteran turned to me, the first-day rookie, looked me in the eye, and said, "Jim, we welcome you wholeheartedly."

And, man, he meant it. Boyd used his years of trust and capital with our audience to help build me up and launch my career.

I took his lead and, in turn, began to build the product up. Whether "everyone" was actually talking about Mid-South or not, it was our job to make the new company in town seem like a happening. MSW would go on to be a successful territory, but at this point everything was new and rising.

Much like myself.

"Well, thank you very much, Boyd. It's a pleasure to be here in this great state. Everywhere I go, it's really the truth: people

> *are talking about Mid-South Wrestling—the wrestling in the*
> *Mid-South area. I know many of you people see wrestling from*
> *other parts of the country on the cable and other overlapping*
> *television systems. And I think that the proof is there. The*
> *greatest wrestlers, the greatest matchups of competition,*
> *are right here in the Mid-South area, and I'm very excited*
> *about this great card that matchmaker Grizzly Smith has*
> *prepared today. Some faces will be new to me, but many of*
> *them I've seen before, and it should be a very exciting hour."*

But Boyd wasn't finished building me up *or* guiding me through what to say, and which parts of the storyline to focus on: "Jim, before we get into the actual matches, I'm just a country boy, and all our viewers will tell you, I love them and I appreciate them all. But you can break it down with your knowledge that you've attained. You're a lot smarter than I am. I want you to tell them about the recent surgery of Ernie Ladd. Break it down and explain to them in ways I'm sure they'll understand it."

His last sentence stuck with me, because that was the whole job. To break it down and contextualize what people were seeing in brief, memorable sound bites. And in the process, to build people up, just like Boyd had gotten me over in his introduction of me to his audience.

After eight years as a referee, a ring-crew guy, a driver, a literal pair of eyes for our blind co-owner, and a sometimes host and broadcaster—watching Boyd pass me the baton in such a gracious and enthusiastic manner made Cowboy's mantra—that everything we do is to build something, or someone—click.

I finally realized what a commentator's role in the machine was.

And it was a role that was now mine.

"Jerry, this one started off like a house afire, just like we knew it would."

December 24, 1983
Jim Duggan vs. Krusher Darsow, Mid-South Wrestling
Irish McNeil Boys' Club
Shreveport, Louisiana

I have no idea where working chemistry comes from. I have seen it in people who like each other, and people who don't. I have seen it in odd-couple partnerships and people who could be family. Two of the greatest WWE Champions of all time, Bret Hart and Shawn Michaels, famously did some of their best work together at the height of their bad blood. Chemistry doesn't seem to have any rhyme or reason, but we all know that once it comes around, you'd best appreciate it.

I've been one half of a duo, or part of a threesome (easy, tiger) my whole career, and building those relationships has been tricky at times, but nearly always ultimately rewarding. In the high-pressure, big-payoff trenches of live TV, you learn to cooperate, accommodate, and gel with the people who are in it with you.

Down through the years I've had the privilege to work with some of the greatest of all time: Monsoon, Heenan, Savage, Cole, Schiavone, Taz,

Heyman, Excalibur, and others—but I'm proudest to have worked with my longest TV partner, Jerry "The King" Lawler. And I'm even prouder that he's still my friend today.

As a matter of fact, he just spent the weekend at my place in Florida, where we caught his beloved Cleveland Browns playing the Jacksonville Jaguars, while eating BBQ and talking about the old days. In a business wrought with jealously, paranoia, and transactional friendships, I'm so happy that Jerry and I made it through—and built a couple of Hall of Fame careers along the way.

Most readers might remember "King" and "Good Ol' JR" from the "Monday Night Wars," where WWE went head-to-head with World Championship Wrestling in the ratings (more about that later), but Jerry and I first shared the booth a long time before that.

In 1983, the year Michael Jackson introduced the Moonwalk to the mainstream and *Return of the Jedi* stormed cinema screens across the world, Jerry Lawler walked into Shreveport, Louisiana, as the special guest of Bill Watts. At that time Jerry Lawler co-owned the Memphis territory with Jerry Jarrett, and both Jerrys were in the building to make a deal with Cowboy to reinvigorate their respective companies. Then, like now, the key to ongoing success was "new," and with small local pools to pull from, things could start to feel stale. Watts understood that wrestling fans liked surprises and new faces to cheer and boo, so he used the "regional curtain" between territories as a way to feed that want, by making deals with other companies to trade talent.

Nowadays there's little difference between Oklahoma and Memphis in terms of travel, TV stations, or general communication—but back then our territories might as well have been on opposite sides of the moon. And that separation brought opportunity.

Simply put, because Oklahoma didn't get Memphis TV—or vice versa—the trading of talent kept both territories fresh and gave wrestlers who needed a new coat of paint somewhere else to go. Sometimes, a great magician doesn't need new tricks, he just needs a new audience to dazzle. The same was true for a lot of professional wrestlers, who were touring the same towns week after week, year after year. So the Jerrys had come to look at the meat on the hoof before shaking hands on a new trade deal.

Over the years, I'd heard of Lawler through Bill Apter's writing in various "kayfabe" wrestling magazines at that time. Before the internet, or national wrestling television, the only real way to keep up with wrestling outside your territory was to buy these magazines, which treated the storylines as if they were happenings. Although Bill never owned any of the magazines—he just edited and wrote for them—such was his name value back then that any publication he was attached to became known as an "Apter mag." And Jerry was media savvy enough to understand the reach Apter had, and how that reach could translate Jerry's other position in Memphis, as heavyweight champion—a *territorial* heavyweight champion—into *national* interest.

It was Bill's reach that led to Jerry's biggest national exposure, when Bill's friend Andy Kaufman asked Apter about possibly getting into the wrestling business. Bill introduced Kaufman to Lawler, and the two new acquaintances came up with a massive storyline that erupted on the legendary *Late Show* appearance with Dave Letterman where King slapped Andy, in a moment that's remembered as one of *Time*'s Top 10 Best *Late Night* Moments Ever.

I remember watching from home in awe of what a great piece of business that interview was, and just how perfectly everyone played their part. So I was aware of Jerry, but I'd never been in his company, seen him wrestle, or even spoken to him before Watts suggested Lawler sit beside me in the booth in 1983—a suggestion that came only minutes before airtime.

And that separation brought opportunity.

Jerry simply shook my hand, and live in front of our TV audience, The King and I quickly discovered we had "it."

Chemistry.

Can't buy it.

Can't teach it.

But right from the moment we began, I knew we had it.

It was December 24, 1983, and the match was "Hacksaw" Jim Duggan, the red-blooded American, versus "Krusher" Darsow, the Soviet sympathizer. Don't you just love paint-by-numbers wrestling angles, folks?

> *"Here with me at mic-side is 'The King,' Jerry Lawler. And Jerry, this one started off like a house afire, just like we knew it would."*

"King" and I called four matches back to back that day, and even though he'd never seen most of the talent he was commenting on, our fans would never know it. Jerry brought a quiet intelligence that only someone who put together wrestling shows could have. He knew what to ignore, what to praise, and most importantly, what to highlight for the fans.

With only minutes' notice, "King" felt right at home.

> *"We have a winner, and the winner is Hacksaw Jim Duggan, and then a peer-six brawl ensued. Thanks very much to Jerry Lawler for being here. And, wrestling fans, we'll be back with more wrestling action after this word from the Mid-South Wrestling Television Network!"*

As the taping wrapped up, I understood what all the fuss was about in terms of Jerry "The King" Lawler down in Memphis. It was easy to see he was the real deal. He carried himself like a star but was humble to all around him.

The fact King walked into a brand-new territory and killed it on commentary shouldn't be a surprise to anyone now, because Jerry is as versatile a performer as anyone who has ever been in our business. Like the legendary Bobby Heenan, King could fit any role, on any card, in any building in the country—and still shine the brightest.

And if anyone can understand my want to keep moving forward in the business, it's Jerry. He's also a fellow retirement-age holdout who is still on the road every weekend wrestling—and by God, he's winning, too!*

I will never forget the time King came to Mid-South, because I met a future brother, and a lifelong friend. (If only my dating apps were as successful in finding such a compatible partner in my romantic life.) But King coming to Mid-South signaled something more than just a talent trade. It was a sign to me that the territories—once self-sufficient and independent—needed each other more than ever. The power of regional fiefdoms was waning, as a seismic shift in leadership and approach up north in New York was changing.

---

* Since I wrote this chapter, "King" suffered a stroke and is recovering well. His wrestling days might be numbered (never say never with King), but we're hoping to hit the road once again soon on an autograph tour!

"Reed is walking tall and he's whipping them all!"

August 3, 1985
Butch Reed vs. Dirty Dutch Mantell, Mid-South Wrestling
Irish McNeil Boys' Club
Shreveport, Louisiana

The creative DNA of Mid-South was "realism." That meant Bill Watts wouldn't let good guys and bad guys be seen in public together; wouldn't let talent injured on his show go out without their bandages or casts on. He especially wouldn't let someone who was beaten in a bar fight continue to work in his territory. And it also meant that my commentary had to be "real" at all times. I was never to wink at the audience with cute insider terms, nor was I ever to shit on talent, as if me pointing out someone was the shits meant Bill was the shits for hiring him. Watts wanted all parts of his promotion to be believable, and it was my job to support that vision.

Cowboy and his booker, the great Ernie Ladd, blended real with scripted every chance they got, as both men coveted realistic, shocking, bloody angles over everything else. While the young Vince McMahon up in New York wanted his talent draped in sequins, Watts wanted his draped in blood.

25

In 1985, the year we got New Coke (RIP, New Coke), it seemed the country in general was ready to literally open up a little, as air travel was becoming cheaper and more accessible, and TV was expanding out through cable and down from satellites.

This general connecting of the country brought equal challenges and opportunities for our business. Just a couple of years after buying out his father, Vince McMahon's World Wrestling Federation was blazing a trail with their "guy," the perma-tan giant Hulk Hogan. The then-WWF had formed a working relationship with a new music channel called MTV, and was using one of its megastars in Cyndi Lauper in their top angle.

The new "Rock 'n' Wrestle" era felt vibrant and alive.

Vince's WWF was making the NWA nervous about what was coming, and the territories quickly began to collapse, merge, or solidify as they looked for a response to the thunderbolt national expansion coming out of New York. It didn't help that McMahon was making it clear that he wasn't going to play by the rules of an alliance he was never going to be affiliated with. He wasn't coming to join the territory system; he was coming to compete against it.

In Mid-South, we might not have been working with the world's most popular music stars, but we were still rocking in our own right. When it came to our business model, we weren't clinging to what used to be, and we were all the stronger for it. Hell, I even got a bump in my wage packet when Cowboy made me head of marketing on top of my broadcasting duties. For about a hundred grand a year (long way from my $120 a week starting money), I would call the action on TV, and then behind the scenes be responsible for Mid-South's expansion across as many regional TV stations as I could muster. Because it became very clear: if you weren't growing, you were dying.

With that kind of motivation, inspiration as to which regions to cultivate next came from strange places indeed—including a Southwest Airlines flight book.

Up till then, Mid-South was a car territory, whereby any new ground we broke had to be reachable on wheels. But with the sky now becoming more of an option through cheap flights and expanding markets, I told Bill we should build our territory around the low-cost airline's newly expanded flight routes. So with the Southwest flight book as our treasure map, I began plotting a new course for Mid-South.

But while we were forward thinking in our business approach, we still had a ways to go in our booking sometimes.

Mid-South and a lot of "Southern Wrasslin'" was reality TV before such a thing existed in the mainstream. And in 1985, it was some of the philosophies about what professional wrestling was, and wasn't, that made it feel like we were a business straddling two eras. The promise of the future was right there, but some booking tropes of the past persisted. And like with all entrenched systems of thought, change is a slow, hard, painful road.

When I was a boy, my hometown was overwhelmingly white, and because we were too poor to travel, I never interacted with many people outside of my community until I went to college—and even then people with varied backgrounds were few and far between. I came to learn that a lot of our audience was just like that, too. They were white, less traveled, and living in small-town echo chambers.

For me, that was a huge part of why I wanted to join the circus of professional wrestling—to broaden my worldview, meet new people, expose myself to new ways of thinking and understanding.

However, when I finally got into the business that was going to show me the diversity of the world, I learned it had only one rule when it came to people of color, and that was "one per show." One Black person was all the old-time promoters were willing to put on their card, and even then only as an "attraction." I heard Cowboy being told more than once by the Good Ol' Boys of the NWA that he was ruining the business by having more than one "of them" on his card. Thankfully, Bill didn't listen to any of that nonsense; he went on to hire Ernie Ladd, who happened to be Black, as his booker—and put "Junk Yard Dog," who also happened to be Black, on top of his card.

And he did it because they were the best at what they did.

Professional wrestling was slowly—very slowly—beginning to drag itself out of its carnival mindset, where tropes and stereotypes and racial bias and general ignorance were the ceiling on which a lot of non-white, non-American performers would bump their head. Wrestling was never shy about using racial, nationalistic, and xenophobic prejudices as part of its presentation. The aim was to get the audience to cheer or boo in as few steps as possible. As we toured town to town, we didn't have an hour to set up character arcs in each feud, so putting an All-American against a Soviet defector told the fans who was "good" and "bad" the second they walked through the curtain.

TV was a little different. There was more time on TV to build out why someone was "good" or "bad." But most bookers still relied on simplicity because they wanted new channel-hopping eyeballs to understand what was happening no matter when they joined us. This led to a lot of angles that just wouldn't be done today, and stand out now in large part because they didn't stand out then.

Like on August 3, 1985, when "Dirty" Dutch Mantel, a hairy-backed, whip-carrying heel, went up against "Hacksaw" Butch Reed—and attacked him before their match even began. Butch was being built up as a babyface hero to get behind, and Dutch was using the most heinous actions to help Butch do it.

> *"We got action already and the bell has not sounded. Dirty Dutch Mantel has attacked Hacksaw Butch Reed . . . And Mantel is like an enraged animal. And he's lashing Reed with that whip!"*

The visual of a white man whipping a Black man didn't raise one eyebrow in 1985. Maybe it was because a proud African American veteran, Ernie Ladd, put it together, or maybe it was because our Black hero, Butch Reed, overpowered his attacker and whipped him worse in return.

Ernie wanted a Black man to take back his power and triumph in the end. Which he did. And he wanted to do it in the most visual way possible in the heart of the South. Everyone was onboard. Everyone knew their role. And the audience ate it up when Reed began to fight back.

> *"Reed is just too powerful, and Reed is hammering him. And now Reed's got the whip!"*

The storytelling of the past doesn't always stand up to the rightful scrutiny of today. But what I am most happy about is that we have taken long and significant strides toward fixing that over the years. Wrestling isn't perfect, but I know that in AEW diversity is hugely important to our boss, Tony Kahn, and to Senior Vice President and Chief Legal Officer Megha Parekh. We're always trying to do better, be better, and represent people's complex backgrounds within the company.

Because with nothing more than a level playing field, the cream will always rise to the top.

AEW's most dominant, longest-serving champion in the company's history is a Black woman, Jade Cargill. In 2020, Nyla Rose became our first transgender women's champion. More recently, in 2023, Anthony Bowens, one half of our most popular tag team, was faced with a crowd chant about his sexuality—but maybe not in the way you would think. "If ya told me years ago, I'd have an arena chanting HE'S GAY at me in the most POSITIVE of ways, I'd say you're crazy," he tweeted after. "It's pretty cool to see how far we've come. Still more work to do. Happy Pride #AEWRampage."

Like Anthony said in his tweet, still more work to do, but fifty years in, I've thankfully seen a lot of much-needed change moving massively in the right direction.

> *"Reed is walking tall and he's whipping them all! There is a supreme athlete and he's ready to go to war. What a man, Hacksaw Butch Reed. Yessir! . . . And we'll be back with Captain Redneck right after this."*

> **"Both men fatigued. They've beaten each other senseless in this confrontation for the heavyweight championship of the world."**

November 26, 1987
Ric Flair vs. Ron Garvin, Starrcade
UIC Pavilion
Chicago, Illinois

If we don't take it seriously, then the audience won't either. It's true of any form of entertainment. Why does that song hit you a certain way, or that scene resonate? Because they're delivered to you in such a way that it makes you empathize, and makes you *feel*.

And not just in the ring.

Back in the old days, the top guys would take the art of selling up a level by making it present not just in their ring work, but in their overall presentation. It was their job to make you believe that their whole life would be made or broken based on the outcome of their next match.

And some did it by convincing themselves first.

You look at Steve Austin during his Stone Cold run, and you could see in his eyes that he believed every single thing he was spitting down the camera. "Superstar" Billy Graham couldn't wait to find a microphone to amplify his braggadocious rants. They weren't "playing" who they were. They were who they were. Or, at least, a version of who they were.

It's been said that it's harder to sell a product you don't believe in. Well, in our world, you're the product you're selling. And your performances on weekly TV, and in airports, bars, and driving around towns are all opportunities to sell, sell, sell.

That's never more the case than when you're the world's heavyweight champion. And on a late November night in Chicago, with me about to call my first-ever pay-per-view main event, the one man who was most obsessed with being—or becoming yet again—the world's heavyweight champion was about to make his entrance.

BOM, BOM, BOM, BOM, BOM, BOM, BOM, BOM . . .

In 1987, the lights hit; the music most synonymous with the NWA main event spot blared over the speakers in Chicago. Some might know the arrangement as "Also Sprach Zarathustra," but we wrestling fans know it as the calling card of "the Dirtiest Player in the Game."

From a cloud of dry ice, a silhouette appeared, walked into focus— white robe with gold trim. Loud attire, but a steely stare. The audience tried to make contact with The Man as he walked that aisle to the ring like only he could. He was focused, his legendary loud mouth shut, his platinum blond head bowed slightly in concentration. One twirl for the audience to drink him in, and he entered the cage just as his music peaked.

This was the "Nature Boy" Ric Flair, and nobody believed it more than he did. Nobody felt it more than he did. Nobody sold it more than he did.

We cut to a wide shot of him in the center of the ring—bathed in strobing lights, surrounded on all sides by legions of fans. He was ready to wrestle in the main event, and I was ready to call it. This was a step up for me and my skills, and I knew it. This was Ric Flair versus Ronnie Garvin for the NWA World Heavyweight Title.

> *"Both men know the price it takes to win; what you gotta do to get your hand raised. And never has a match had more importance than the match the fans around the world are about to see right here live."*

In 1987, *The Simpsons* first appeared on our screens, Guns N' Roses released *Appetite for Destruction*, and *Three Men and a Baby* owned the box office. In wrestling, Owen Hart won *Pro Wrestling Illustrated* Rookie of the Year, and WrestleMania 3 cemented wrestling as a pay-per-view behemoth with the historic Hulk Hogan versus Andre The Giant main event.

It was that new model of PPV that WWF's competitor—and my new employer, Jim Crockett Promotions—was keen to chase. Not only could wrestling companies now charge those in attendance for wrestling cards; they could also charge anyone at home who wished to see the action on their TV. The market size moved from how many people could you get to watch in a building to how many homes could you get to watch around the country.

That evening, we were at the end of a whole night of firsts, as "Starrcade"—NWA's first-ever pay-per-view offering—rolled into its final match. Everything Leroy and Bill and my years calling studio matches taught me, I was here to use. This was national, this was the NWA World Title, and it was on pay-per-view.

Bring it on.

You're probably wondering what happened that I ended up calling NWA. Didn't Mid-South go national? Are you still wearing awful suits on TV? Well, the answer to those questions is yes and yes.

You see, in '87 there were only a couple of national slots airing professional wrestling. Vince McMahon already had one of them, on USA Network, and he wanted the other, on Ted Turner's Superstation TBS. Back then companies bought time on the networks, rather than today's practice of the networks paying companies for the rights to air their shows. But when McMahon made an offer to Turner to buy Georgia Championship

Wrestling's time slot from under them, Ted wouldn't budge. It turns out that Ted was a longtime wrestling fan, and he already had his tried-and-true programming airing in that coveted two-hour slot, with the NWA territory Georgia Championship Wrestling.

That should have been the end of that, but the aggressive McMahon simply figured if he couldn't buy the time slot from Turner, then he would buy the company that contractually owned the time slot—so he took his offer directly to GCW instead, and they accepted.

With that, not only had McMahon locked up both national slots, but he was going to be using one of them against the wishes of the guy whose name was literally in the station call sign.

So, stuck with Vince on his network, Ted Turner called Bill Watts to put Mid-South on TBS as an alternative to the invasive "Yankee" New York wrestling. And all of a sudden, not only was Mid-South on national TV; it was also pulling in a higher rating than WWF.

The southern audience didn't want Vince's brand of wrestling—with wrestlers who they didn't know. His first day on the network became known by fans as "Black Saturday," because their beloved GCW was canceled for a wrestling show they didn't like or ask for.

Vince was losing money courting a dwindling fan base and could also see that Turner was lining up the better-rated Mid-South for his time slot, so the New York promoter sold his TBS contract to rival promoter Jim Crockett for a million dollars. McMahon couldn't make good of the TBS airtime? Well, now neither could Turner.

Even though Vince knew Crockett was trying to assemble all the NWA territories under one national banner to rival WWF, McMahon needed the money to finance the birth of a little idea he had going on called WrestleMania.

This left Mid-South needing to expand faster than ever to try to compete with Crockett and Vince, who were both chewing up all the stations, buildings, and talent they could stomach. But as we over-leveraged ourselves trying to scale, a sudden recession in our key markets left us vulnerable.

With the writing on the wall, I brokered a deal for Crockett to buy Watts's company. As part of the deal, our new owner wanted to keep our titles, some talent, and . . . me.

So that's how I ended up at Starrcade, my first time working a PPV, my first time working with the NWA, and my first time in the booth with my now longtime good friend and fellow AEW announcer Tony Schiavone. (I can't confirm it, but looking back at the video of that night I'm pretty sure Tony was in a booster seat, as he's a foot taller than me sitting down, when he's a foot shorter than me standing up.)

> *"Ric Flair is very resilient, he has a very high*
> *threshold of pain, but when you talk about pain,*
> *Ronnie Garvin takes you to a different level."*

Another one of the "firsts" that night was also, in my opinion, an error of judgment on the part of management. This was the first Starrcade event held outside of Greensboro, North Carolina, and maybe a sign that my new company was more focused on chasing new national audiences than it was in serving the audience who already loved it the most.

But they were paying me to call what I saw in the ring, in the best way I could. And, man, what I saw that night was magic.

> *"Both men fatigued. They've beaten each other senseless in this*
> *confrontation for the heavyweight championship of the world."*

I was thirty-five years old, and even though I wasn't nearly as good as I thought I was, I was trying with everything I had at that time to match the intensity and passion I saw playing out in the ring. Both champion and challenger chopped the hell out of each other. Flair bounced all around the canvas, while Ron walked him down, never backing up; never giving an inch.

And after fifteen minutes of war—both men now bloodied and beaten from trading chops and pinning attempts—finally, with the crowd in the palm of their hands, Flair launched Garvin headfirst into the steel support that held the cage around the ring.

Skull on metal, Ron went down hard.

And just like that, with WWF firmly in their sights, Crockett and the NWA made the strongest move they could make: to give their biggest draw, best worker, and most recognizable face, Ric Flair, the World Heavyweight Championship once again in front of a rabid crowd.

> *"The Nature Boy has just become the five-time heavyweight champion of the world in one of the most physical battles in the history of this sport!!"*

When the red light went off, I was exhausted. Tony and I had gelled well, and the talents in the ring gave everything they had, but I knew I was still learning how to sell that emotion that I was genuinely feeling back to our audience back home. I wanted them to feel what I felt, but I wasn't all the way there on just how to make that happen. I had the pieces, and they were coming together for me, but as happens in life, I still had a ways to go.

In the ring, I saw Flair could do it. He could sell just about any emotion to the people in the stands. And I knew that's where I wanted to get to. I knew I wanted to be able to reach them at home the same way.

After all, selling isn't just the job of the hero of the story; it's also a vital tool for the narrator, too. And, boy, was I trying.

"They're trying to put his eye out! They're sticking that spike right in his eye!"

November 26, 1988
Dusty Rhodes and The Road Warriors, World Championship Wrestling
TBS Studios
Atlanta, Georgia

Blood has always been a tool used to heighten storylines in wrestling. Hell, I was even involved in stories myself where my blood was drawn to further heighten a program. (I didn't cut myself; I let "Stone Cold" Steve Austin do the honors because I had no idea what I was doing.)

But like all storytelling tools, you want to make sure you're using the right one for the job or its effects are lessened, or downright useless. And depending on what company, in what era, the frequency of allowing wrestlers to cut their own flesh to draw real blood has varied hugely. In the past it wasn't uncommon for the front row to go home with some wrestler's blood on them, but now, with all we know about blood-borne viruses, and just having more common sense, the use of blood has lessened a lot.

In 1987, I was ringside calling a brutal match between my dear friend Steven Williams, known as Dr. Death, and Big Bubba for the Universal Wrestling Federation World Heavyweight Title, where it got real bloody,

36

real fast. And I remember looking down at the monitor, doing my job, only to sense them getting closer to where I was. I had recently started wearing glasses, and I made the mistake of glancing up just in time to get a Jackson Pollock–like smattering of Bubba's blood right across both lenses. I still, to this day, can feel how weird it was to wear another man's blood on my face, as I sat there calling his match. It was a different era, with very little known about the associated risks of something like that, so I didn't know how dangerous that could have been.

I just wiped my face, took off my glasses, and kept going.

During the anything-goes Attitude Era of the 1990s at WWF, Vince had a soft spot for guys who felt they needed or wanted to do color for their angles, so it was an item on the menu for a long time there. Back then, we found ourselves in a position where we felt as a company, and as individual performers, that we needed to do whatever we could to keep our show and brand edgy and Attitude Era–ish. We knew it was that approach that kept the money coming in and had raised the company to heights it had never experienced, making more millionaires backstage in the locker room than I'd ever seen before. Now, it certainly wasn't *all* down to blood, but there were some guys who felt having that open palette to create with was essential to preserving that edge.

But as time moved on, and the culture began to change once again, the sponsors got involved and said they didn't want their brands associated with blood and guts. WWE at the time I worked there was moving past "getting color" and being overly sexual, shocking, or attitudinal to becoming a more family-friendly brand and show. That meant that blood was used very, very sparingly.

And that's the thing about blood anyway. If you don't overuse it, it can still be used for great dramatic effect.

It's like a match we had in AEW in 2021, between Britt Baker and Thunder Rosa, where blood was used to shock and get people talking—and mostly in a good way. The color red in that match helped highlight the violence and the aggression that both women had endured and put each other through. It was hugely effective.

Listen, when it comes to Texas Death Matches, First Blood Matches, and other variations on that theme, the use of color as a creative medium is something I have no problem with whatsoever. As long as the wrestlers are okay with it, and everybody is safe and tested, I say let it be an occasional cameo in our storytelling.

But all blood isn't spilled on the mat. Behind the scenes there was corporate "bloodshed," too.

In 1988, I packed everything I owned into a Lincoln Continental and left Oklahoma as a newly divorced man and a newly hired broadcaster. I had neglected my home life in pursuit of my wrestling career, and it caught up to me and my then-wife. I take full responsibility for that. It's one of the few things I wish I could go back and change in life. But all you can do is move forward, which is what I was attempting to do when I left my home state for a new role at Turner Broadcasting System, as they began to rebrand their newly acquired property, Jim Crockett Promotions, as World Championship Wrestling.

So, to recap, Georgia Championship Wrestling had sold their TBS time slot to World Wrestling Federation, who'd sold it to Jim Crockett Promotions, who'd bought the Universal Wrestling Federation, who ended up selling their company to Turner Broadcasting System, who proceeded to name their new company after Georgia Championship Wrestling's old TV show: World Championship Wrestling.

After McMahon came on the scene in 1982, Jim Crockett, a several-time NWA chairman, had tried to grow his territory nationally, too, which caused him to neglect his core fan base in the Carolinas while running half-empty shows coast to coast in a blind effort to expand before McMahon got too big.

Crockett tried in vain to use the once-powerful might of the NWA to corral other promotions together, in an effort to stand more united against WWF's rapid and aggressive expansion. But due to disputes over money, and who got what, when, those alliances and pacts soon fell apart.

The fall of Jim Crockett Promotions happened across a few different areas of the company at the same time. JCP was spending well outside its means on jets and limousines, while the company's creative squandered top storylines that could have driven it forward. And in 1988, with JCP under threat of bankruptcy, TBS, the parent company of Ted Turner's Superstation, bought it for under ten million dollars.

So, after all the territory carnage and closures across the country, it looked like two viable national companies were left standing. And I was going to be lucky enough to broadcast for one of them.

Not too long after I arrived, the newly reshaped World Championship Wrestling wanted to get their momentum going with something that would resonate and grab people's attention. Their booker was the legendary "American Dream," Dusty Rhodes, and Dusty was feeling the heat to come up with something big and fresh and bold to separate WCW from their rival, WWF.

Now, I kinda figured the second I saw Dusty on my monitor that day wearing a white shirt that red was sure to follow, because red and white go together in our business like peanut butter and jelly. But even I had no idea just how red that white was about to get.

In a small soundstage in the belly of TBS, Dusty rolled into the ring looking for a fight, and by God, Road Warrior Animal was quick out of the dressing room to give him just what he wanted. The crowd picked up immediately in reaction to the sudden acts of aggression taking place in front of their very eyes. Punches and kicks flew everywhere, and the people loved it!

> "Road Warrior Animal and 'The American Dream'
> Dusty Rhodes. It's like a street fight here!"

And it was just like a street fight, until Animal's tag team partner, Hawk, jumped in the ring and made it a two-on-one affair. Dusty was quickly overpowered and outnumbered—so much so that Animal was able to break away from the brawl to remove one of the large steel spikes from his entrance-gear shoulder pads and whack "Dream" right in the head with it.

Dusty went down hard, and then Animal turned Dream right into the camera and . . . stabbed the spike directly into Dusty's face.

> *"They tried to blind him! They stuck*
> *that spike right in his eye!!!"*

Blood poured from Dusty's face and covered his white shirt as the crowd looked on, genuinely horrified at what they saw.

It was certainly the shocking and headline-grabbing moment that Dusty was looking for, except not for the reason he wanted. TBS Standards and Practices had made us all aware, long before the angle happened, that the company didn't want any violence that led to blood to occur on their screens—and that there'd be consequences if it did.

> *"Rhodes is bleeding! You can hear him screaming!"*

Even back then, as I was calling it, I couldn't figure out why Dusty did it. He was as shrewd an operator as the business had at that time, and fully knew the consequences of violating such a concrete policy.

But I guess Dream was a classic example of an old-school guy who saw blood as being as fundamental to a main-event storyline as rings and ropes were. I'm guessing he felt that if he could spark an angle big and ratings-grabbing enough, the brass on top, who knew nothing about the wrestling business, would see the reward and figure the road to get there was justified.

Unfortunately, that's not what happened. Instead, Dusty was fired. The angle was so shocking and graphic that all the higher-ups in Turner-land saw the clip, too. So, just as I arrived to WCW, my good friend Dusty Rhodes was gone. And the booking in that company never really recovered.

Dream isn't with us anymore, but I can't help but imagine him somewhere in heaven, cutting promos with a glint in his eye, if you wiiillll, because of all that white around him.

"You can hear them breathing. You can hear them exerting every ounce of energy in their athletic bodies, as a battle for the world's title in the NWA is on the line . . ."

February 20, 1989
Ric Flair vs. Ricky Steamboat Trilogy
UIC Pavilion
Chicago, Illinois

There're times in life where you're kinda forced into finding out what you're made of. In 1989, I felt I was good at my job, but I had reservations about my work, like I still do to this day. I'd felt myself grow in Mid-South, but in the back of my head, I always wondered where my voice might lead me on the national stage. I guess what I'm saying is: now that the guide rails were off, I wondered how good I really was. I was a part of WCW during a year when the legendary Ric Flair versus Ricky Steamboat trilogy put my thoughts of where I was at to the test. This was a series of matches so perfect, so ahead of their time, that they're still talked about today as the benchmark when it comes to wrestling trilogies.

And all the ingredients were there from the start.

In life, contrast creates friction, and friction creates heat. Same thing in wrestling. Ric Flair was a brash, flashy loudmouth and Ricky Steamboat was a humble, quiet Everyman. Ric was a ladies' man; Ricky was a family man. Ric was fighting for ego and lifestyle; Ricky was fighting for pride and legacy.

The two men looked different, talked different, were different—and just happened to be two of the most talented professional wrestlers in the world.

And I was made lead broadcaster on their program.

Because I'm a fan of wrestling, first and foremost, I knew calling Flair–Steamboat was going to be something special, and I just felt blessed to be at the right place at the right time to get the chance.

The whole Chi-Town Rumble card was pretty darn good, with the young bleach-blond Sting standing out as being majorly over with the crowd. He was clearly on the rise, and it was a great sign for WCW that another young, talented, and hungry babyface was growing in popularity.

But when it was time for the main event, the atmosphere in the building changed. I was on the headsets that night with Magnum TA, who, had he not been seriously injured in a car wreck a few years prior, would have almost certainly been a main feature in the NWA main event scene himself. We had good chemistry together, and the stage was set for something special.

And Flair started it all off with a kiss.

He entered the ring accompanied by six beautiful ladies, kissed one, and then threw roses to the crowd.

> *"The champion certainly travels in fast company.*
> *I think that would distract me, but, uh . . . I*
> *guess he's used to it. I certainly wouldn't be."*

Steamboat, however, was steely focused, ready for business.

And so was I.

I wanted to set the stage, bring the audience inside the emotion and weight of the match at hand. I was raised on radio sports broadcasting, and I can see a little of that visual storytelling in my work that night. Feel free to read along with the commentary sections in my voice if that helps. Use a "BAH GAWD!" to ease you into it if you'd like.

> *"One-hour time limit for the World Heavyweight Title of the World. And this is what we've waited on. The first NWA champion was crowned in 1905 . . . There has been two title changes in Chicago since the inception of the NWA. One in 1961 when "Nature Boy" Buddy Rogers upset Lou Thesz, and one in 1987 when Ric Flair regained the World's Heavyweight Championship from Ron Garvin . . . Ricky "The Dragon" Steamboat, five-eleven, two-thirty-five. Ric Flair, six feet, two-forty-two . . . Neither man will have an advantage as far as the size is concerned in this one. The finest official in the sport, Tommy Young, has been assigned this very important contest. Collar and elbow tie-up. Flair and Steamboat. It's Flair with the advantage. Steamboat retaliates with a side headlock. This one will be quick, I can assure you. Football tackle! Steamboat right down. 1 . . . 2 . . . and Flair kicks out! What a surprising move! Hey, The Dragon doesn't work by the hour, I've been told . . . He has proved he can beat the champion, but can he do it with a belt on the line? That is the question."*

And that's how we got this thing rolling. The history. The spectacle. The players. The stakes. The stats. All of it building to a question this match needed to answer: Could Steamboat beat Flair when the bright lights of history were burning down on his back?

Well, we were about to be taken on a twenty-three-minute journey of pure passion, ability, and heart to find out. And personally, I wanted to know if I could keep time with the men who were, back then, the two best in the world. I needed to find out if my lyric could hang with the music they were providing on the fly, live, in front of an enthralled crowd.

> *"You can hear them breathing. You can hear them exerting*
> *every ounce of energy in their athletic bodies! As a battle*
> *for the world's title in the NWA is on the line . . . Another*
> *chop by The Dragon. The number-one contender is*
> *fighting this one for his family, for his young son, for every*
> *working-class person in America. He's giving it his all! Oh,*
> *the clothesline—The Dragon came out of nowhere!"*

I wanted to remind our viewers of the contrast between the two wrestlers once more, and that, in the buildup to the match, Flair had insisted on repeatedly insulting Steamboat's family and his integrity. Well, as another great sportsman once famously said: Steamboat took that personally, and he repaid Flair repeatedly with heavy hands.

> *"Ric Flair is in trouble. The Dragon reaching down.*
> *You gotta think he's got that young son, The Little*
> *Dragon, right in the front of his mind. He's up top.*
> *THE DRAGON WILL FLY. He nailed . . . oh, Tommy*
> *Young went down. He's got Flair pinned, but Tommy*
> *Young, the referee, down . . . Oh, I hate . . . this is*
> *terrible. I hate for something like this to happen . . .*
> *Tommy Young is not physically able to make the count.*
> *They wiped him out. Wait . . . Steamboat's going back*
> *up top! This match is still going on. Steamboat flies, and*
> *he missed it! He missed the flying body press off the top,*
> *and now Flair has turned the corner! He twists the leg,*
> *inside . . . wait a minute, inside cradle. CAN HE HOLD*
> *HIM?! . . . YES HE CAN! RICKY THE DRAGON*
> *STEAMBOAT HAS WON THE WORLD TITLE!!"*

Steamboat—stunned, beaten, and exhausted—held his title up as the Chicago crowd lost its mind. Flair looked devastated, a bad loser. He cursed the call, the referee, the crowd, and anyone and anything else in his path. Naitch, always smart and always "on," was already laying the bricks for his and Steamboat's next two encounters.

The intensity in Chicago had been unbelievable. But their second match a couple of months later, while it was another classic, had a completely different vibe.

The atmosphere in New Orleans for their Clash of the Champions VI rematch was strange, because the Superdome seated around sixty thousand fans and we only had around six thousand fans in the building. But that didn't stop Ric Flair walking to the ring in style while the company misspelled the name "Rick Flair" behind him in neon letters.

I'd never seen a more WCW thing in my life.

The match was a two out of three falls match with a sixty-minute time limit. And it was a bruiser.

> *"They have no regard for their own bodies,*
> *and even less for their opponent."*

After almost an hour of a classic encounter, which was more methodical and strategic than the first, but maybe even more thrilling, the men were tied one to one. Flair back suplexed Ricky, but the ref counted Ric's shoulders on the mat even though he shouldn't have, because The Nature Boy's foot was in the ropes.

The controversial call meant both men would have to meet a third and final time to decide the fate of the world title once and for all.

As we moved toward match number three, I felt honored to have called two already, as through their changes in style and storyline across the matches, I felt like my game was evolving. My work was getting sharper and more distinct as I went along for the ride.

And then we rolled into Nashville, Tennessee, for the third and final match. The Nature Boy came ready, walking in with forty women this time. He might not have been the champion, but he was more brash, more arrogant, and more confident than ever before. It was quite the visual to see Flair surrounded by a parade of sequins, lipstick, and peroxide blonde, while Steamboat walked to the ring with his wife, both of them helping their young son ride in on a pony.

Needless to say, Flair and Steamboat had another absolute match for the ages. The chemistry between Ric and Ricky was so perfectly mixed that I believe it would have been impossible for them to have a bad program.

But it helped tremendously that all three matches they had were unique, with Ric and Ricky determined to change it up between bouts. Sometimes their matches were technical, sometimes wild, sometimes they were targeting body parts, and other times it had the feeling of a brawl. But it's no surprise, when you have two artists in there who paint like Picasso, that you end up with something great, no matter the tone or tenor of what they're producing.

> *"Steamboat fights back; boy, what a heart the champion has.*
> *What character. Eww, what a chop by Steamboat. And a*
> *karate kick! Perhaps it was out of desperation, but what a move*
> *by the champion, whose left leg is virtually useless in the ring.*
> *Steamboat's got him up . . . a slam . . . but Flair inside cradle.*
> *1 . . . 2 . . . HE DID IT. STEAMBOAT'S LEG BUCKLED.*
> *AND FLAIR HAS DONE IT. FLAIR HAS DONE IT!!"*

It's a great memory for me. I've never called three better matches in a series. Kenny Omega versus Kazuchika Okada is up there; Rock versus Austin at WrestleMania is up there. But for me, it was this trilogy, back when I was fifteen years in and finally feeling like I was beginning to come into my own.

"And he says hit me again! And hit me again! And the champion is doing it."

July 7, 1990
Ric Flair vs. Sting, The Great American Bash
Baltimore Arena
Baltimore, Maryland

This book, in part, is about longevity in a business that doesn't always allow such a thing. There's only a handful who have been in the wrestling business for decades. And the guys I can think of all managed it by switching careers midstream. Most of the time, anyone who makes it past a couple of decades has invariably gone from being a wrestler into a backstage role as a "lifer."

My time in wrestling has primarily been spent on the headsets, in the booth, calling wrestling matches—while also fulfilling other duties. I've always said the key to longevity in wrestling is adding more strings to your bow; the more useful you are, the less likely you are to be let go. It just makes sense to be as skillful as possible in your chosen area, and once you become good at that, look for another "area" to get good in.

Our business has always been full of people who double or triple job—ring announcers who are on the ring crew, announcers working in the office, top stars being bookers—and I can name many people who have mastered the art of longevity in our business. But there's only one I can think of who has done it by wrestling at the top of his industry for his whole near-forty-year run.

That man is Steve "Sting" Borden.

Now, there are other wrestlers who have had in-ring careers that spanned decades, but usually not at the top level, and they certainly didn't spend all their years on top always being the good guy. Everyone else who has clocked up impressive mileage like Sting—take Undertaker, for example— has kept their presentation fresh and relevant by jumping from the dark side to redemption and back again—many, many times.

But despite having a cup of coffee as a heel in Mid-South, Sting arrived in the *national* spotlight as a babyface and never crossed the line in the fans' eyes into being a bad guy—even when WCW tried to force the issue in 1999 against Hulk Hogan. The audience back then still cheered Sting, and booed Hogan, so the company kinda just let the Stinger stay a hero and never touched his presentation in that way ever again.

But anyone who has watched Steve's career from the beginning will tell you just how special he is, and was, in that protagonist role. As I write this, he is currently still active in AEW, where he has surprised many with just how great his contributions in the ring have been—even though he's sixty-four and approaching four decades in wrestling.

It's perfect symmetry that we both might finish our long careers in AEW, because I was there when he debuted in 1985, in the same regional promotion as I did in 1974. And just like I was ringside when he debuted in Mid-South, I was also working ringside the night he won his first WCW title in 1990.

> *"The young man people say will dominate the '90s*
> *against the man who has dominated the '80s."*

Giving Sting the world title was a decision that was long past due. In wrestling you have to have the instincts to tag in someone who is hot—and in WCW at that time, Sting was as hot as they come. So of course they waited years to pull the trigger on a can't-miss guy. The head of WCW at that time was Jim Herd, a corporate hire who was out of his depth, with no product knowledge. He liked the ripped and tanned Lex Luger as the next challenger for the world title, because Luger looked like the kind of wrestler that Herd knew Vince McMahon loved. And by Herd's thinking, if ripped and tanned was good enough for Vince, then it was good enough for Herd, too. He felt we needed our own Hulk Hogan—a tanned, jacked, huge head-turner—and that kind of thinking was one of the many dumb reasons Sting had been put on the long finger to become our world champion.

The guy who held the title at the time, Ric Flair, was already a made man. He didn't need the belt to solidify who he was, or what he was. But as a younger, up-and-coming contender, Sting needed some big wins to maintain all that fan attention and enthusiasm, or the audience would lose interest. So, naturally, they had the red-hot, young, and hugely talented Sting challenge for the title and lose.

Ugh.

With the fans clearly behind Sting in a huge way, and Luger not fulfilling the promise of his presentation, the reasons to not pull the trigger on The Stinger were getting smaller by the day. So, after a lot of dithering, an injury, and previous failed attempts to win, Sting got his world title match yet again, this time at the Great American Bash, 1990.

I can still remember the visual of Sting, with stars-and-stripes face paint, standing face-to-face with Naitch as the crowd roared with excitement before the bell even rang. The energy in the building had the distinct tone of cautious optimism; the fans were desperate for Sting to finally win the big one, but after almost two years of him *just* missing time and again against the same cheating world champion, they were unsure to say the least.

But maybe tonight was the night?

They could feel it was shaping up that way. But it was my job to add a little doubt by bringing up Sting's real-life knee surgery earlier in the year. The more doubt I could add, the larger I could make the mountain seem, the bigger the pop for the new champion when he finally overcame and triumphed.

Backed by the full house in Baltimore, Sting dug deep down and finally won the big one!

> *"Sting has upset Ric Flair to win the heavyweight championship of the world. The Stinger has done it! The Stinger has done it! . . . Fans, there's nothing we can say right now. Take a look at this crowd, and take a look in the ring . . . The crowd here standing. They have seen history here at the Great American Bash!!"*

What a night, and what a memory.

Sting and I have watched each other get older, and I'm thrilled we both ended up in AEW several decades later. Sting is a devout Christian now, has a whole new point of view on the world that he wants to pass on to the new blond, face-painted, fan-favorite babyface in wrestling, AEW star Darby Allin. Steve is a perfect no-drama mentor to the entire roster at AEW, as a lot of the wrestlers in the company grew up as Little Stingers.

Even in his sixties, Sting has remained an attraction, as AEW owner Tony Kahn doesn't overbook the legend—not that the smart veteran would ever allow that to happen. And we are lucky to have him now, just as WCW was lucky to have him then.

"I don't know the condition of Abdullah The Butcher. And I don't see anyone rushing to give him mouth-to-mouth resuscitation."

October 27, 1991
Chamber of Horrors, Halloween Havoc
UTC Arena
Chattanooga, Tennessee

One can't shine shit.

That's what my dad used to say.

And in 1991 I found his proclamation to be true. More than once.

There have been many awful matches in professional wrestling. There have been many awful gimmick matches in professional wrestling. But I don't know if any one match started off with so much promise but ended so terribly as WCW's first and only Chamber of Horrors match.

The storyline on-screen started with Sting going up against Foley in his deranged Cactus Jack persona, and it ended with a large "Sudanese" man being "electrocuted" in front of a PPV audience.

It all began when Ric Flair and WCW parted company, after Ric received a new contract offer that was straight up insulting to the man who had carried the NWA on his back for so many years. Nature Boy warned management that if they didn't rethink and present him a fair offer, he would leave their ranks for the first time in his career. Of course, WCW, showing its growing dysfunction, decided instead to strip Flair of his world title and fire him.

That move alone showed me the state the company was in, and how little vision it had at the top. They thought about the situation with their top star and pulled heartily on the worst lever available to them, gifting their biggest asset to WWF. And while WCW might have stripped Ric of the world title, Flair took the world title belt itself with him to WWF.

This move caused WCW to threaten a lawsuit, only to find out that Flair actually owned the world title belt due an agreement he signed with Crockett before WCW bought the company. And Ric proceeded to parade around WWF television wearing the WCW world title while calling himself "the Real World's Champion."

So, now, not only had WCW lost their marquee talent, but the NWA title was vacant for the first time in almost five decades, too. They had to literally buy the title back from Flair, for a huge number, just to get it back on their TV.

But it wasn't just the NWA title that was irreplaceable. It turned out Flair was, too, and the company began to blindly step on one rake after another. A mix of bad management and bad booking left WCW millions in the red, and without any franchise name on top. On top of that, our fans began to revolt in the arenas as they chanted for Flair to come back.

It was a hard year to be a part of WCW, to say the least, and I had a feeling it wasn't going to get any easier as time rolled by. I knew, for my own mental health, that I needed to move outside that negative bubble and remind myself just how lucky I was to be in the business I loved.

I needed a distraction, and an outlet away from the viper's pit that WCW had become. So I looked to start my own wrestling radio show, where

I could interact with our fans and remind myself why I loved this business so much in the first place. I had a feeling it could be a great success—and so did the general manager of WSB 750 AM out of Atlanta. I was already in discussions to call Atlanta Falcon football games on WSB, so I pitched their general manager on a weekly call-in show for professional wrestling, too. I wanted to host the first mainstream wrestling radio show on the national airwaves. I knew that fans of any sport liked to vent and sound off about their teams—and wrestling fans were no different.

Not to mention how, at that time, WCW was giving their audience no end of strange and illogical moments and matches to sound off about. The latest of which was the Chamber of Horrors match.

Now, anyone who knows me knows I love Mick Foley. So, when I saw his deranged character, Cactus Jack, getting into a program with the hugely popular Sting, I had high hopes for his chances of finally getting that main-event run he so richly deserved. Maybe it was a sign that WCW, too, was turning a corner and realizing they had compelling workers who could deliver compelling storylines if given the shot.

Nope. Instead, the central, compelling story of Mick and Sting was muddied up by adding *six* other wrestlers: the Steiner Brothers, El Gigante, Big Van Vader, Abdullah The Butcher, and Scott Hall, all of whom had to face each other at the same time in a match so ridiculous that I find it hard to comprehend how it even got out of the idea stage. But somehow, someway, the Chamber of Horrors match was born.

As the match started, our ring announcer tried to fill the audience in on what the rules were before I hit the mic to call what was coming next. He said, "This special attraction will involve two teams, each team consisting of four team members. The match will be confined to the Chamber of Horrors, which is equipped with several Instruments of Torture. The object of the match is to put a member of the opposing team in the Chamber of Horrors' Chair of Torture, and then to pull the Fatal Lever, which will render one of the teammates helpless.

"Now, the participants in our electrifying first contest."

Then came the entrances of the poor, poor wrestlers who had to work the match—some genuine all-time talents caught in a bad situation in a bad part of history.

You just know it's going to be one of those matches when a random, masked man pops out of a coffin just so Scott Steiner could beat his ass, and never mention him again.

> *"Someone came out of one of those caskets. The*
> *referee has a camera mounted on his head."*

The only good thing about the match was that I had my good friend Tony Schiavone on the call to get through this with me. But even Tony couldn't work enough magic to make this one palatable. As the electric chair dropped from the cage and spooky music played over the speakers, we tried our best to call this one just like we'd call any other match. I really tried. Tony really tried. But I want you to remember what my father said.

> *"And now the focus will go on this small cage. It contains*
> *the Chair of Torture, as it's being called. The objective*
> *now is to get a member of a team in there. And when*
> *the lever is pulled, which is mounted on the side of*
> *the cage, at that time someone is going to get a rather*
> *shocking experience and this match will end."*

I mean, we had Sting, Mick, Vader, the Steiner Brothers, and a young, jacked Scott Hall in there, and we stopped them from doing anything creative by lowering a large cage into the ring so they had nowhere to work. And then several men dressed as orderlies walked out and just stood there on the ramp. They had white faces for some reason.

Mick was busted open, Abdullah was busted open, we had coffins and suplexes, and lots and lots of punching. The end drew near as Abby ended up in the electric chair, and as Mick waited to pull the large switch downward to start the, I guess, murder, the switch fell down all by itself to the clearly marked "ELECTROCUTE" position several times, which we all just pretended didn't happen.

The match was supposed to end with Mick's partner Abdullah knocking Rick Steiner in the electric chair, and then Rick reversing his and Abdullah's positions last minute so that, when Mick pulled down on the lever, he accidentally shocked Abdullah instead. So, when Mick saw that moment coming, he turned his back on the action so he wouldn't see Rick reverse Abby's attack.

However, after Rick reversed Abdullah, it took so long to get Abdullah hooked up to all the prop electrocution elements that poor Mick had no choice but to just stand there for an uncomfortable amount of time with his hand on the lever, pretending he didn't see anything, before finally and mercifully "accidentally" pulling the lever on his own partner.

> *"What a wild matchup. Even the ring is on fire. They used sticks, they used steel. A lot of blood was spilled."*

It's never for a lack of effort on the talent's part that these kinds of matches don't turn out the best, and I felt bad for Mick in particular. Just horrible. I tried to sell the match as I normally would, but the situation and stipulation made this one unsalvageable.

> *"I don't know the condition of Abdullah The Butcher. And I don't see anyone rushing to give him mouth-to-mouth resuscitation. Maybe Cactus Jack will take that assignment."*

Cowboy always told me that you have to be careful not to ask your audience to suspend their disbelief any more than pro wrestling already does. And this one did that, and more.

It's not that I don't love a good gimmick match. But just a few days later, WWE would deliver on the biggest match in pro wrestling with Ric Flair vs. Hulk Hogan at a live event in Madison Square Garden, and I would've been lying if I said I didn't wish I could call matches like that, in that kind of atmosphere, instead of matches like the Chamber of Horrors, in the growingly toxic atmosphere of WCW.

One can't shine shit.

I mightn't have succeeded that night, Dad, but I sure tried.

"He's now on top of the mountain!"

August 2, 1992
Ron Simmons vs. Big Van Vader, WCW Main Event
Baltimore Arena
Baltimore, Maryland

1992 was a mixed bag of a year, man. The first Mall of America opened, Bill Clinton won the US presidential election, Johnny Carson hosted his final *The Tonight Show* episode, and Whitney Houston terrorized us all with "I Will Always Love You."

Across the pond the Premier League debuted, and sports in general were demanding more of our time and money, with "sports packages" a growing option on cable.

As Nirvana, the internet, Hurricane Andrew, and "Achy Breaky Heart" all vied for our attention, widespread rioting broke out in Los Angeles after several police officers were acquitted of "excessive force in arrest" after they were videotaped savagely beating Rodney King near the Hansen Dam.

In the wrestling world, there was a seismic shift toward smaller, more technical wrestlers that led to Bret "Hitman" Hart winning his first world title from Ric Flair. And hell froze over when the real King of Memphis, Jerry Lawler, did the "unthinkable" and joined WWF.

I was still working in World Championship Wrestling, where I found myself trapped in a cocoon of self-inflicted misery. Unusual for me, I know. I'd heard my broadcast partner—and the future governor of Minnesota—had the cheek to work less than me, and get more pay. Somehow, I twisted Jesse Ventura's good deal into a personal slight. I was dumb, my thinking was dumb, and "The Body" had only done what I wished I had the clout to do: get a better deal for myself.

But I knew a big pay raise didn't seem likely. All of WCW's major markers were plummeting. TV ratings were down, PPV buys were down, and the live event business was collapsing.

And it wasn't just us.

Up in Stamford, World Wrestling Entertainment was experiencing record decline in their TV and PPV numbers, as well as having to cancel house shows due to lack of demand.

The wrestling business was moving in the wrong direction, as both national companies were plagued with stale ideas, hokey "characters," and a general sense of un-coolness that was hard to shake. Outside of our bubble, the world was rapidly changing, and our business was struggling to keep pace. After the Rock 'n' Wrestle peak of the '80s, wrestling was becoming a forgotten destination in pop culture again.

Truth was, we were floundering to find something different.

Something that reflected the world around us.

Something new.

So, WCW turned to what all great innovators turn to in times of need. A raffle.

But let me rewind here a little, before we get to that.

Back in the territories, "I already have one" was the answer some promoters would give whenever a Black wrestler sought bookings in a territory where another Black wrestler already worked. At the time, my boss and mentor, "Cowboy" Bill Watts, was having huge success in Mid-South Wrestling with Junk Yard Dog, a charismatic African American ticket-selling machine, and simply having a Black man as a headliner compelled other promoters to tell Watts he was "killing the business"—to which Bill would simply reply, "My favorite color is *green*."

I mention this again because, in 1992, Bill was now the booker for WCW. After years of WCW losing significant money, Turner Broadcasting was tired of it, so they brought in Watts, who had a reputation for running a wrestling company with an iron fist.

Turner brass didn't understand, or care, that there's a difference between blind accounting and accounting. I know the numbers need to work in any business, but in wrestling, your way to the bank is through creating and retaining stars. Unfortunately, 1992 WCW had a nasty habit of investing in, creating, and then losing those stars to the better-paying WWF, just as they had with their franchise player, Ric Flair.

So, like every year in WCW's existence, something needed to change creatively in order for it to survive. It was a frustrating time for me in that regard, as the company never settled into a rhythm, and was always two steps from disaster. So, after a small parade of different faces failed to right the WCW ship, in came Watts to do it his way. And like most bookers in wrestling history, Cowboy wanted to revisit the formula that brought him the most success in the past. He wanted to reimage his run with Junk Yard Dog in Mid-South. All he needed was the right star to position in the JYD role.

All of this was the backdrop against which former Florida State all-time great Ron Simmons found himself, as he toiled in the mid-card for WCW.

In college, Ron wasn't your traditional football player. He wasn't a monster in size, didn't have a huge height or weight advantage for his position. But when all was said and done, he ended up as one of the greatest defensive linemen in history, with his jersey retired by FSU and membership in both the Orange Bowl *and* College Football Halls of Fame.

It was during Ronny's college football days that I first saw him, as he dominated the defensive line at "just" 240 pounds. Anytime he came to play my beloved Oklahoma Sooners, I told the coaching staff, who were friends of mine, that if we were to have any success, we'd have to control

Ron any way we could. Chop him, tackle him, hit him late. Whatever we needed to do to win the game.

Simmons was that commanding, that good.

When Ron left football and entered wrestling, the business was still stuck in a lot of its old-school thinking when it came to people of color. Simmons was cast for several years in predictably stereotypical storylines that were designed to play up all the old racial undertones that wrestling of that time flirted with nonstop.

But one night in 1992, when "The Icon" Sting got hurt and had to be pulled from the main event, Watts saw an opportunity to switch things up *and* to build a new star. Three things Cowboy loved in a top guy were authenticity, physicality, and athleticism—and Ron Simmons checked all three boxes significantly.

So, at a live event in Baltimore, Maryland, the headline of Vader versus Sting got switched to Vader versus Ron Simmons, after Ron "won" a rigged raffle to get a world title shot—WCW's creative way of getting an unlikely-to-the-fans challenger in place quickly and decisively.

It was a hard-hitting match that ended when Ron slipped out of a powerbomb attempt and caught the big, all-conquering, four-hundred-pound champion with a power slam out of nowhere.

> *"He got the power slam! He got the power slam, and . . .*
> *he got it! Simmons got it! Simmons has won the belt!*
> *Simmons is the champion. Simmons has won the world*
> *title! . . . He has realized his dream to become the best in the*
> *world, and indeed, he is now on top of the mountain!"*

The crowd loved it, the TV audience loved it, and I loved it, too.

I remember hoping Ron's run would help chip away at some of the backward thinking that had plagued our business when it came to race. I knew that it would still be a long road—and more work will always be needed—but that Ron Simmons's shoulders were wide enough to carry the weight of becoming the first Black WCW World Heavyweight Champion (and, most would argue, the first recognized Black heavyweight champion, full stop).

It was a helluva sight to see, and moment to experience.

Nowadays the AEW roster is packed with people of all colors, and genders, and sexualities, and religions. Prejudices still exist, and the only people who can fix that is us. But things are changing, and I'm happy to say we've come a long way as a business since the days of "we've already got one."

As I reach the back nine in life, I am proud to be "an old guy" now who wanted change then, and is still trying to be part of that change today. I might stumble to find the right terminology here and there, but that's because I want to be respectful when I put my voice to people's unique stories. I sometimes get the words wrong, because I so desperately want to get them right. I want to be a part of the change—the modernization of our business, and the overall reckoning in our society.

Ron Simmons becoming world champion didn't "cure" or "fix" what was broken in our business, but having Ron Simmons, the man, in our locker room, I would argue, helped more than any title run ever could have.

In 2021, on the *Stories with Brisco and Bradshaw* podcast, Ron said of his career, "I'm often asked a lot about racism and coming up with racism along the way. Of course I encountered racism along my way there. But guess what? I handled it the way it should be handled; I handled it right then and there. To me, as a man, if I couldn't earn your respect as a man, then I didn't want it, and I didn't need it, okay? So, when I look at myself in the mirror, I feel absolutely proud of the way I've done it and the things that I've accomplished. 'Cause I did it the right way."

What better legacy can a world champion leave behind?

"Hannibal used elephants in many wars..."

April 4, 1993
WrestleMania 9
Caesars Palace
Las Vegas, Nevada

I've seen guys get lost on the road. Sometimes literally, but more times personally. Over the course of the long miles and endless nights, people can forget who they are without family and friends around to set them right.

While crisscrossing the country, and the world, I've seen families made and families broken over the demands of the wrestling business. I, myself, have been divorced twice because of my obsession with my job. I was wrong, and I take full responsibility. I think a big part of it is the nature of being "in the circus," as my father called it, means distance. Whether it's through the weekly grind of airports, car services, hotels, and city traffic— or through following a whole company to another part of the country.

A lot of times, in people, distance creates distance. Before the internet and FaceTime and all the other ways you can keep in contact with loved ones nowadays, we used to arrange calls back home from pay phones. Sometimes people made those calls and sometimes they'd miss them. Sometimes they made an effort to make them, and sometimes they'd make an effort to miss them—it just all depended on how solid a relationship was before the circus left on tour.

When you put young people, who are in great shape and earning great money, miles from home, they can become different people than the ones their parents raised. I know I've made my own fair share of mistakes on the road. I've seen plenty of others make them, too.

And the thing is, we were never off the road.

I sometimes think about why some of us survived and thrived, when many thousands of others did not. What was the common denominator between those who became "lifers" in the business and between those who fell by the wayside? And all I can think of is, those who "made it" were the ones who understood the power of adaptability, both on the road and in a business that never stopped changing. Those who didn't get that became either bitter or unemployed.

One of my biggest adaptability tests came in 1993, when Meat Loaf would "Do Anything for Love," Bill Clinton became president, and *Jurassic Park* tore it up at the box office. It was also the year that led me to embark on another move cross-country to another company—to a new life in Connecticut to work for WWF.

When I first left home in 1987 to work for Crockett, I moved to Dallas where I bought a house, only to have to sell it again a few months later for a thirty-thousand-dollar loss to move to Atlanta because Crockett sold to Turner.

Unfortunately for me, losing that much money on a home came at a time in my life when I didn't have that much money to lose. So another move put me in serious financial trouble, and tested just how much I wanted this job and this business to be my life.

But the Big Top moved, so I needed to move with it.

And that's when I learned that in the wrestling business, those who can roll with the punches the quickest usually survive the longest. It turned out that I loved living in Atlanta. Being in a new place with new people, starting a new job and a new life, didn't faze me one bit. I loved the variety of broadcasting for World Championship Wrestling and the Atlanta Falcons while also having the highest-rated show on the same radio network as my new Falcons gig. It was a dream come true for me, and it meant that I was working every day, and most nights, on one of various projects.

It also meant I was chewing up the road, with both my wrestling gig and my football gig, which could disorientate a person if they weren't careful. But I wanted this more than anything. I wanted to run the miles and do the work and be wherever the itinerary sent me.

Now, don't get me wrong, I don't love traveling one bit, but I do love where that traveling brings me. So, for me, the miles were worth it.

But as things played out over the years in WCW, after several changes of management, it became clear that I wasn't in the plans there. Even though I'd worked my way up to become their head of broadcasting, I was considered "a Cowboy guy," so when Bill Watts was ousted as executive vice president and the incumbent Eric Bischoff came into that top spot, he wanted his own hires in high places. I had a three-year deal, so they couldn't fire me, but my role was changed, and they took me off TV. I could have sat home and collected my money, but I wanted to work, and I knew I had a lot to offer, so I decided to make a run for the top of the mountain by making a call to the WWF.

And what a fruitful decision that turned out to be.

I was invited to meet Vince McMahon, which turned into a three-hour conversation, the result of which was another move, another company, and another world to navigate—this time farther from home than I'd ever been.

At that time I'd been in the business for nineteen years, and I'd gone from driver, to referee, to ring crew, to ring announcer, to syndicated salesman, to broadcaster, to executive, to radio host, and back again. I knew I was good at adapting, and one more time sure wasn't going to break me.

So, with no guarantees, no solid plan, and nobody by my side, I packed up from Atlanta and moved to Connecticut to join WWF—where my first live assignment was the biggest event of the year: WrestleMania.

As soon as I arrived backstage at Caesars Palace, I found myself surrounded by "Macho Man" Randy Savage, a herd of elephants, the Undertaker with a buzzard on his shoulder, Cleopatra getting her hair styled, Hulk Hogan with a mysterious black eye, a seven-foot-four guy getting abs sprayed on his bodysuit in the corner—and I was dressed in a toga. Talk about being a long way from the farm I grew up on in Oklahoma—but, by God, I knew I'd made it where I wanted to go.

Vince said to me, "I wanna ask you something. I know you're a serious broadcaster and I like that. But this is kind of . . . this here's the Palace, so I need you to wear a toga, but if you're not comfortable wearing a toga we'll move your debut to King of the Ring or wherever or one of the syndicated shows."

Now, here I am, nineteen years in the business, so no overnight sensation, and I'm coming out of a very dysfunctional family split in Atlanta with WCW. I knew I needed to be accepted again; I needed to prove that I could still do my job and to show those decision-makers in Atlanta who thought I couldn't that they were wrong.

But I could also picture the so-called wrestling "traditionalists" shaking their heads at someone like me doing the "WWF bullshit" because I came from the blood-and-guts realism of Southern Wrasslin', where the mission statement was still to try to convince the audience that wrestling was real—and if we couldn't convince them, then, by God, we'd break our asses trying.

In my new job at WWF, I was surrounded by lots of glitter and animals, and ladies wearing not much, and guys looking pretty instead of looking legitimate. And the thoughts of those same "traditionalists" almost got to me. I worked my way up through the territories; I paid my dues in the harshest environments, and learned a whole lot along the way.

But I figured when anyone said anything about WWF being the cartoon, sanitized version of what "wrasslin'" was supposed to be, I'd comfort myself knowing that they were saying it from a half-full bingo hall, and I was about to call the first-ever outdoor WrestleMania at *Caesars Palace*.

Gimme the goddamn toga and pass my golden microphone!

> *"Indeed, it will be a day of firsts, ladies and gentlemen.*
> *My very first WrestleMania. First time that yours truly,*
> *from the great state of Oklahoma, has ever been in a toga*
> *myself. This is quite an impressive outfit, and I could get*
> *used to this. What do you think of these gold shoes? How*
> *would those play in Tulsa? . . . Over sixteen thousand fans, a*
> *worldwide television audience. What a day it's going to be!"*

I knew I had the best gig in my field. My first assignment was technically a challenge to an old-school, "serious" broadcaster like me, but nobody watching saw that challenge in my performance—not when the elephants came out, not when the buzzard showed up, not when Cleopatra came out to wave. What they did see was a man living his dream, calling his heart out, and making the decision to adapt and not be frozen in time or ideology.

I left home and moved across the country to work, and to try to put my voice to what I hoped would be some of the most vivid wrestling moments of all time. I was at WrestleMania, and I did then what I believe I still do now: move with the times, adapt, and overcome.

And back then I had no idea that my best calls were indeed ahead of me.

"It's good to be back and feel that electricity in the air!"

July 11, 1994
Bret Hart vs. The 1-2-3 Kid, Monday Night Raw
Fernwood Resort
Bushkill, Pennsylvania

In pro wrestling, it doesn't matter who you are or where you find yourself on the ladder: you're going to feel the effects of momentum—upward or downward. In wrestling, just like in life, sometimes you feel the tide rolling with you, and other times it's dragging you under.

I guess the same can be true for a company, too, because in 1994, my new employer, WWF, the once mighty leader in our space, was in a downward spiral. WCW had recently promoted Eric Bischoff from executive producer to executive vice president, and he saw the WWF was on the ropes in a way it hadn't been since Vince took over. So, Bischoff began to make moves to compete in a way WCW hadn't done before—starting with signing Vince's biggest draw, Hulk Hogan.

It was a mega money deal, and Hogan's first in-ring PPV immediately broke WCW's existing records. World Championship Wrestling would still have many, many challenges ahead, but this was definitely a moment when I could feel the tide rolling with them.

On our side, McMahon was getting dragged under in a legal battle with the federal government on charges of steroid distribution. And not only was it weighing heavily on him personally, but it was also taking a huge toll on the company that he usually dedicated every waking moment to.

WWF was only four years removed from their massive Hulk Hogan versus Ultimate Warrior main event at WrestleMania 6, but even inside the company, iconic matches like that felt like a million years ago. Business was sinking, Vince's top stars were aging out or leaving, and the WWF's profile in mainstream pop culture was all but gone.

Even in the face of distinct challenges, though, the WWF was grinding. And it was the new main event names like Bret "Hitman" Hart and Shawn Michaels who were pulling the wagon, even when the heavy son of a bitch had zero momentum.

I guess I could relate. I had about the same amount of momentum myself at that time.

Even though I was only in my second year in my dream job at WWF, it had already been a whirlwind of good news/bad news. I got hired; got married to my angel, Jan; got my first of three bouts of Bell's palsy; got let go; and then got rehired again when it became clear that Vince's attention would be focused on the trial and they needed a voice to fill in for him.

Even though it was only a short-term contract, I wanted to show the world that I could come back from Bell's palsy, which had partially paralyzed one side of my face, affecting my ability to speak properly.

It wasn't a great hand for anyone to be dealt, but it was all the more devastating for a person who makes their living talking on TV.

I've never once felt entitled to a single day in this business, so I was willing to persevere. Because whether due to illness, change of creative direction, or just being plain fired, I have circled the drain more than most. But I've always managed to not only survive, but thrive, in the end.

My experience told me that, if I could just hang in there, the tide might change for me. And as the theme of momentum was playing out at a company level, and on a personal level, it was playing out on-screen, too.

The 1-2-3 Kid—a young, six-foot, two-hundred-pound high-flyer—had been beating a line of established names, against all odds, week after week, earning his way to a world title shot against "The Excellence of Execution," Bret "Hitman" Hart.

And on my first *Raw* back in the saddle, I got to call it.

"Without a doubt, ladies and gentlemen, this is one of the most anticipated matches in Monday Night Raw *history."*

I couldn't have picked a better night to return. Kid was in the ring as the pink lights shone from the rafters, signaling the entrance of the World Wrestling Federation Champion, and I was reminded once again just how much I loved this job.

"A thunderous ovation for the WWF Champion. One of the most honored athletes in the history of the World Wrestling Federation. A two-time WWF tag champion, two-time Intercontinental Champion, two-time WWF Champion. He's the King of the Ring, and last year was the WWF Superstar of the Year."

Raw at this stage of its life was a one-hour taped show that primarily featured squash matches where established talent would easily defeat enhancement talent. But this match was different. This felt big time. The stage was set. The veteran against the rookie. The master against the student. The technical champion against the speedy challenger.

And halfway in, I knew it was shaping up to be one of the greatest matches in *Raw* history. I felt alive calling it. I forgot that I was ill; I forgot that I was temporary.

"The Kid's going for it! Kid's going to take a chance. High-risk offense. Cross body off the top. 1 . . . 2 . . . and a half! A long half!"

Kid hit Hitman with a powerbomb and then began climbing the ropes once more. He knew he had to throw everything he had at the world champion, and take every risk, if he had any chance of becoming champion that night.

> *"Ladies and gentlemen, we may be seeing the crowning of the WWF Champion right here. Leg drop off the top! This should be all! 1 . . . 2 . . . he got a shoulder up! I mean, barely!"*

Bret gave and gave and gave to make his smaller, younger opponent look like a million bucks, and Kid made the most out of every single opportunity. He kicked, he jumped, he fought, and he flew.

> *"The Kid now is gonna take another chance! Can you believe this kid?!"*

As the 1-2-3 Kid launched, once more, from the top rope with everything he had, the wily champion moved just in time to let his challenger crash to the mat. Hitman then saw his opportunity to turn the momentum back in his favor.

> *"Oh, he missed the moonsault there . . . Well, they say that excellence can be attained if you risk more than others . . . The Kid looks to be in never-never land."*

As Bret hammered The Kid with punishing move after punishing move, the crowd grew more and more invested. And Bret kept giving them reasons to stay invested, as he allowed The Kid to almost pin him again and again, moving and shifting that momentum to maximum effect.

> *"On three occasions this kid has been within a one count or less of beating Bret 'The Hitman' Hart right here on* Monday Night Raw.*"*

Hart went from being in full control to being caught on the top rope, just as he'd caught The Kid in the same predicament earlier in the match. And that's why Bret is considered a master storyteller in between those ropes. The plant and payoff of the champion getting a taste of his own medicine, while the younger babyface was seen learning on the job, boosted Kid's stock with the audience immensely.

> *"Bret Hart is going to take a chance! The Hitman going up top. And The Kid's up quick. Sends Bret Hart right off the top. I can't believe it! Hart is out of it, seemingly . . . 1-2-3 Kid on top—oh, Bret Hart stands back up! He blocked the dropkick! He's going for the Sharpshooter. He's got it! He's got the Sharpshooter! And the referee is calling for the bell!"*

We all knew we'd seen something really special. Even my broadcast colleague that night, Macho Man Randy Savage, called it one of the greatest matches ever as he stood up at the announce table and gave it a standing ovation.

The people in the stands were already on their feet and roaring their approval, as Bret raised The Kid's hand and paraded him around the ring to soak up the reaction. I could only echo Macho's sentiment when it came time to wrap up what we'd just seen.

> *"One of the greatest matches I have ever seen in my entire career."*

Illnesses or misfortune visits us all, sometimes when we feel at our least able to fight it, but I truly believe that none of us can lose hope most of all, or we have nothing. And on *Raw* that day in 1994, I felt hopeful and happy to be back in the broadcast booth where I felt I belonged.

Even if I wasn't certain how long I'd be there, I felt the tide move a little bit in my favor.

"Horowitz Wins! Horowitz Wins!"

July 9, 1995
Barry Horowitz vs. Bodydonna Skip, WWF Wrestling Challenge
Wilkes University Marts Center
Wilkes-Barre, Pennsylvania

Everyone in wrestling should mean something.

Everyone.

I guess I always knew that, but I got to put it into practice in 1995 during a simple, yet effective storyline that people still remember today. In was in that same year that Brad Pitt beat me out to become the Sexiest Man Alive, and I'm still a little sore about it. (I heard it was a close call, but old Bradley Tight Britches got the cover based on his handsome features or whatever. Who'd he ever put over?) Over on TV, *Seinfeld* was king, and *Braveheart* was the winner of Best Picture at the Oscars. The news was flooded with O. J. Simpson's trial, as it captivated a whole country—while a tiny company called Amazon sold its first book. (Let me get a Mick Foley–like plug in by saying I hear you can buy my first two books, *Slobberknocker* and *Under the Black Hat,* on that very same site right now! I've also got some tasty BBQ sauce and mustar—sorry, got carried away there for a second.)

I was brought back to WWF in early 1995, but not as an announcer. I was newly married and had responsibilities I needed to look after, so I took a role backstage that involved various administrative and booking duties, which also meant I was working closer with Vince on a day-to-day basis for the first time. I didn't mind being the utility player one bit, as that was how I broke in. But with the business being as changeable as ever, I soon found myself in the shuffle of the broadcast teams again, this time calling the action on WWE's B-shows like *Wrestling Challenge* and *Action Zone*, which sometimes involved calling the same match with different partners for different markets. What I wanted to be doing was doing play-by-play on *Raw*, and I really felt my work merited it. But it just so happened that the guy sitting in the seat I wanted on *Raw* owned the company. And Vince McMahon wasn't moving from that seat anytime soon, it felt like.

Now, even though I wasn't working the main shows, I was doing other cool things while I was waiting for my shot—most notably teaming with the legendary "Gorilla" Monsoon on *Wrestling Challenge* commentary from time to time. And it was on those "lesser" shows where Gorilla and I bonded over a wrestling lesson that "Cowboy" Bill Watts had taught me in Mid-South.

And it was about the "jobbers."

Gorilla, as his name may suggest, was a huge man who had a helluva career as a wrestler, but truly became a household name as a commentator alongside the then-future governor of Minnesota, Jesse "The Body" Ventura. Gorilla was truly respected across the board, and was held in the highest esteem across the company, but in '95 he was battling some health issues that were putting him closer and closer to retirement. That meant he was coming back down the ladder, while I was trying to make my way up. Somewhere in the middle we met at a commentary booth, where I had the privilege of working with the man and got to know him as a human being.

And it was over many Bob Evans peanut butter pies during those nights on the road that Gorilla reinforced my belief in the importance of maintaining the wrestling business's integrity at all times. As a general employee, he wanted everyone in our industry to stay true to the genre, give it respect. But as a broadcaster, he made sure that he never dismissed the commitment of the men and women who entertain the fans.

And that meant *all* the workers in that ring. Not just the stars.

At that time, Gorilla and I worked on the more kid-friendly shows, fast-paced hours that mixed matches with promos and usually featured bouts that had a star facing off against an enhancement talent (or "jobbers," as they were known back then, as their job was to, uh, lose).

It was those wrestlers Gorilla particularly wanted to protect.

That was common ground for Monsoon and me, because years before I came to WWF, Bill Watts once took me to the woodshed for dismissing an enhancement talent on-air. Well, it's not that I even dismissed him; it was that I was so totally focused on getting the star over that I didn't get the enhancement talent over, too. In my young mind, the sensible thing was to relay to the viewer that our star was so good he was going to have an easy night against a much lesser man, but Watts wasn't having it. He said that everyone in his company needed to mean something, or why would Bill hire them? "You want them to think I'm an idiot for hiring a nobody? And if our star beats a 'nobody' then he's achieved nothing. If he beats a 'somebody,' then our star really is just that much better than everyone else," Cowboy said. Well, shouted, but I guess shouting is the same as "said."

And that's how both Gorilla and I came to have the same philosophy on jobbers when we worked together. After all, we all know about the headliners, the main-eventers, the history makers, and the icons. But the engine of what we do is built as much on what happens at the bottom of the card as what happens on top.

There's a whole roster of talented, hardworking, selfless men and women who travel the same miles, take sometimes worse punishment, get paid less, and never get their recognition. These people being called "jobbers" down through the years didn't do them justice, and I'm glad we've pivoted to calling them "enhancement talent" more recently, because these are the people who help hold up the whole apparatus of professional wrestling.

Mike Jackson (who is still performing this role in his seventies), The Italian Stallion, S. D. Jones, Pat Rose, The Brooklyn Brawler, and "Iron" Mike Sharpe were just some of the names that mastered the art of "dropping their gloves" so the shinier prospect is made to look their best. These wrestlers went into the ring and took all their opponents' moves, sold their offense, looked credible in brief spots, and then lay down at the end to take the pinfall.

When I worked in WCW, the stars of that company used to look at the run sheet for the night, and when they saw that Mike Jackson was working, they would ask to work with him. They knew a pro like Mike wouldn't hurt them by being reckless, and would get them over by being a professional at his job. People like Mike didn't have any ego, understood their role perfectly, and went about their duties with care and skill.

Many times these guys who weren't the featured talent were more talented than those who were—they were just cast in a different role. Like the supporting players awarded every year at the Oscars, our supporting players were there to make the leading men look great.

One such man was Barry Horowitz.

Barry was used in WWF as a "journeyman jobber," which meant he'd come in to lose, and then move down the road to his next paying gig. But in 1995, that same guy "shocked the world" when he scored his first victory on WWF TV against a main roster talent in Bodydonna Skip, the late—and brilliant—Chris Candido. When the cocky and stocky Skip decided to do push-ups mid-match to show how confident he was, Horowitz seized on the opportunity and rolled the Bodydonna into a pinning situation to win the match.

And the crowd jumped to their feet in celebration.

It was a simple piece of business on a lesser-watched show, which I got to call twice in different markets: first with Todd Pettengill on *Action Zone* (where I said, "Horowitz wins!"), and then again beside the legend Gorilla Monsoon on *Wrestling Challenge*, while doing exactly what he and Bill Watts had instilled in me all those years ago.

> *"Horowitz beat 'im! Can you believe it? Barry Horowitz has beaten Skip! Barry Horowitz has just won his first match! . . . This crowd is shocked, looking at the people standing—they can't believe it!"*

Two calls on two shows about one man's first victory in WWF. And it's one people still remember today. After all, everyone in the wrestling business must matter, or nobody does. And when egos are put aside, and people (like The Rock said) "know their role," everyone gets jelly on their bread.

Or peanut butter pie, if you're Gino "Gorilla Monsoon" Marella.

"Some folks will do a lot of things with their fifteen minutes of fame!"

September 26, 1996
ECW Invasion, In Your House 10: Mind Games
CoreStates Center
Philadelphia, Pennsylvania

Wrestling, like all entertainment, is cyclical. What's hot in one generation is rejected by the next. The wheel of taste spins until what's old is new, and what's new isn't so much new at all, just a different twist on the old.

In WWF back in the mid-nineties, we could feel that need for change again. Norms were shifting, and not just in wrestling, but in culture in general.

A huge benefit of working in the live event space for five decades is getting to watch trends change over time, and seeing the difference in the makeup of your audience down through the years. When I started it wasn't unusual to see grandmothers in the stands, then it morphed into dads and their young sons, on to rebellious college students, to nowadays the encouraging sign of more young women at our events, too.

But whatever the era, those faces in those buildings were, and are, our nightly focus groups.

So, by 1996, we knew by the empty stands, and the shrinking till receipts, that what might have worked before wasn't working now. The audience was rejecting the cartoon characters, the kids-first approach that led to WWF success in the late 1980s. The product was uncool, out of the mainstream conversation, and for the first time in Vince's reign, his stars were leaving to join WCW instead of the other way around. And to add insult to injury, their leaving had sparked a huge turnaround for WCW.

Eric Bischoff had a red hot angle involving the formation of the New World Order—a faction of ex-WWF main-eventers Hulk Hogan, Kevin Nash, and Scott Hall—that blurred the line between story and real life, as they played up the notion that they were actually WWF invaders, promising to take over WCW by any means necessary.

And while Eric was cooking with Vince's former guys, McMahon was struggling just to keep his circus financially on the road. Things were dire on the surface. Underneath, though, we had Steve Austin toiling in the mid-card, had just signed Mick "Mankind" Foley, and I'd also just closed the deal for a rookie named Dwayne "The Rock" Johnson. We didn't know it at that time, but a serious boom was bubbling right underneath our noses.

The two biggest wrestling companies in the world were hard at work trying to figure out their next steps. But it was the birth of a much smaller outfit that would tap in to that era's gritty zeitgeist the shrewdest.

When self-described "pain-in-the-ass" Paul Heyman got fired from WCW for being, well, a pain in the ass, he ended up the booker of a small NWA-affiliated territory in Philadelphia called Eastern Championship Wrestling. Finally, Paul, who'd spent his career thus far perpetually frustrated and constantly annoyed at having to listen to others, had his own little kingdom to make in his image.

It wasn't long before he was raising hell again, by throwing the NWA heavyweight title in the trash and proclaiming the "E" in ECW now stood for "Extreme." It was clear that Heyman's intention was to separate ECW from the old ties that bound it to the past, and to make this newly rebranded company immediately stand out from the pack.

And, boy, did it work.

ECW quickly built up a cultlike fan base who packed into the tiny "ECW Arena" (which Jerry "The King" Lawler routinely called "a bingo hall" on-air) to watch a wild-west wrestling show that was a mix of *Jerry Springer* and a human destruction derby. It was gritty and visceral and profane and defiant and it quickly bullied its way into the broader conversation about '90s professional wrestling.

And it was that very buzz they were creating that convinced McMahon to bring them to our PPV, "In Your House, Mind Games." The boss knew he needed to change the menu, and putting a dressing around the old classics wasn't going to do it anymore.

When Tommy Dreamer and Sandman appeared at ringside that night, they might not have brought much national name value at that time, but they sure brought a shot of energy and chaos to a WWF show that needed something to jolt it back to life creatively. And with them came *their* head of their creative, Paul Heyman.

I think Vince saw a lot of himself in Paul, and it started a relationship between the two men that's still going to this day. But back then, Paul was there to promote his tiny ragtag outfit, which he described as "*The Howard Stern Show* of professional wrestling." So right there in their home state of Philadelphia, they disrupted proceedings as planned, and Dreamer led the WWF audience in an "ECW" chant.

As I sat at the commentary table, the fan in me couldn't help but notice just how much like Mid-South ECW was. And that made the fan in me happy, to think that kind of hard-hitting, reality-based wrestling was not only still alive, but thriving in its own way, in a whole new era. The broadcaster in me knew I was there to soft sell the whole thing, to make it look as real as possible.

> *"They have a small, vocal contingent, and this is their home base, and we're just glad they bought tickets!"*

In the ring we had a Caribbean Strap Match between Justin "Hawk" Bradshaw and Savio Vega, which in no time at all spilled to the outside—right in front of our Extreme guests.

Sandman took the close-up opportunity to spit his beer at Vega, before proceeding to bust his own head open by smashing himself repeatedly in the forehead with his beer can.

Well, that was something I'd never seen before.

We were a long way away from the "take your vitamins and say your prayers" era of the Hulkster, and in the mid-nineties that wasn't a bad thing. Hell, Hulk Hogan *himself* was a long way away from the Hulkster at that point, having turned heel to huge effect on WCW.

Change was coming and Vince was beginning to move with it.

As the scene played out, McMahon chimed in over commentary and told the crew not to film "the ugly incident," while WWF officials hurried to ringside to kick out the Extreme interlopers.

It was a modest national introduction to a company whose "extreme" DNA is still found all over our business today, many years since it shut its doors. I have always saluted Heyman's creation, and his ability to motivate his team with an "us versus the world" mentality that worked and kept the ship afloat even when they were plagued by financial woes. Many viable stars were created in that company, and Heyman had the gift that many decision-makers before him possessed in the territory days: thoroughly understanding his wrestlers, and hiding their weaknesses from the TV viewer while exploiting those individuals' strengths. ECW made unique and significant contributions to the pro wrestling world before eventually being bought by Vince in 2003, and their alumni should feel a source of pride for their accumulative accomplishments.

The big talking point that night for me wasn't the attitude of ECW, though. It was the attitude of Vince McMahon. The chairman of WWF wanted something more gritty and visceral on his show after years of shine and gloss. ECW showing up at a WWF event wasn't just someone freshening their menu; it was someone who'd begun to see he needed to burn it all down and build anew.

In 1996, WCW may have struck gold, and ECW might have struck a vein, but WWF was very much the sleeping giant about to wake.

"Now, there's going to be The Man right there."

November 17, 1996
Dwayne Johnson's Debut, Royal Rumble
Madison Square Garden
New York City

I guess I always wondered what it would be like to be a head coach in the NFL. I've been around the game my whole life and made some very good friends who coached at the highest levels there, so the itch always felt strong in me.

Over the years, when I thought about what it was *specifically* that I liked about coaching, it was never the bright lights or the glitz of the position—it was always the rush of finding talented athletes, guiding their careers, and helping them become, hopefully, better people along the way.

All the great coaches I admired did a wonderful job of making those rookie breakouts their players for life, no matter what happened over the course of their careers. The best leaders invested in the people as well as their talent, and that was the part that most appealed to me.

Well, I never did get the reins of an NFL team, but I *was* hired into a position where I could discover and influence hungry new talent. The global franchise I worked for mightn't have said "football" on their business card, but my approach to finding new talent was certainly inspired by that world.

Which is why, when Dwayne Johnson hit our radar, my coach's sensibilities were at an all-time high.

DJ had just been cut from the Canadian Football League, and word was the 6'4", 275-pound defensive tackle wanted to get into the "family business," wrestling. Now, dynasties and bloodlines run strong through our genre of entertainment. The McMahon family has been in the business of promotion across several generations. Not to mention the Hart, Guerrero, Von Erich, Rhodes, Flair, and Anoa'i families, to name but a few who have bettered our business with their multigenerational offerings down through the years.

But at that time, Dwayne coming in made him the first third-generation wrestler in WWF history. His father, Rocky Johnson, became one half of the first Black WWF tag team champions of all time, and his grandfather was the legendary Samoan wrestler and promoter High Chief Peter Maivia. Not to mention, his grandmother, Lia Maivia, was one of wrestling's first-ever female promoters.

So Rock came to us with the perfect mix of business mind, wrestling blood, and football heart. And after spending time with him, I really began to understand how I'd mold the developmental process for new wrestlers if I were in charge of that area—which I wasn't, just yet—to make it more like other franchises' sports pipelines.

With Dwayne, we knew we didn't want to rush him to the main show too soon, or let him languish on the smaller shows too long. But even a blue chipper like "Dewey" needed what anyone who achieves greatness needs: reps away from the bright lights. WWF needed somewhere out of the way to let the next generation of wrestlers work on their act the way new stand-up comics hit the small clubs to work on their material. No matter the pedigree, everyone needs a quiet corner to swing and miss before the eyes of the world are on them, and it was this reoccurring reality that brought up a big flaw in the ongoing development of WWF: we were a talent-driven juggernaut that didn't have our own pipeline for developing talent.

At the beginning of Vince McMahon's run in the '80s, he used the territories to find himself the best talent. It was a practice some would say collapsed the system altogether, because Vince harvested other companies until there was no talent left. But as we rolled through the '90s, and many of the other companies went out of business or began to wind down, a great big warning light appeared on WWF's dashboard—we had no feeder system to keep the talent shelves stocked. After all, the wrestling business, just like the music business, the movie business, the theater world, the fashion world, and everything in between, thrives on new. And relying on smaller, more independent wrestling companies to incubate your top prospects—all we had at the time—was a risky proposition.

One company we liked doing business with was with the United States Wrestling Association. In 1992, their co-owner Jerry "The King" Lawler first came to wrestle for WWF, before hitting the commentary booth later, as part of a deal that allowed us to send guys who needed reps down to Memphis to work in USWA. It was the perfect place to send Dwayne, so he could figure out his persona and timing in the ring "off Broadway," so to speak, even though he didn't need as much time as most.

The thing about expectation is that it brings with it a ton of pressure. After only a few months in Memphis, word came from Vince that not only did he want Dwayne to debut on the main WWF roster, but he wanted him to do it live on PPV—and at Madison Square Garden. Pressure like that can make or fold a career, I feel. But when Dwayne came through the curtain as the newly named "Rocky Maivia"—wearing the smile that the world would come to know on the big screen—I knew he was flourishing, and not wilting, under the big bright lights of New York City.

He slapped the fans' hands while everyone on commentary, myself included, told the viewers at home exactly what we thought of the new guy.

| *"Now, there's going to be The Man right there."* |

My first public thoughts on DJ were direct and honest. Before he debuted, I got to know Dwayne as a human being behind the scenes and felt he had the immeasurable qualities that all the greats had—plus the more measurable qualities of passion, reliability, intelligence, and a steely drive to be the top guy in the business.

So when he got in the ring in Madison Square Garden that night, I really did feel like we were seeing the birth of something, and someone, that was going to rise to the top of our business. By that time, I'd seen *a lot* of talented people come and go for various reasons, but even a blind man could see that this kid was going to be something special.

With the match underway, his developmental training down in Memphis helped him to hold his own in there with seasoned heavyweights and legends like Jake "The Snake" Roberts, Crush, "Goldust" Dustin Rhodes, Barry Windham, and King.

Rock ended up in a two-on-one situation after all his teammates were eliminated—leaving room for the rookie to shine alone on his big debut. And then boom! Rocky hit a crossbody on Crush—eliminating the big Hawaiian—that left the debutant alone in there with the provocative Goldust to see who would become the sole survivor.

> *"Now it's one-on-one. Can the kid do it? Can he do it against a two-time Intercontinental Champion? . . . Put him away, Rock!"*

Dwyane wasn't the only one feeling a little bit of pressure that night, as I felt a little something myself as the guy who'd signed him. With J. J. Dillon now gone from WWF, I'd been promoted to VP of Talent Relations. The role came with a contract bump, a nice office, and a whole lot of expectation.

I knew that with anyone I wanted the company to invest in, Vince needed to see a return on his money. And that night, in the building Vince's father and grandfather promoted in, McMahon got to see DJ begin his journey in the building where Rock's father and grandfather worked, too. And he did it with a win—to become the last man standing.

"What a way to make your debut, with a big show,
in the Big Apple, at the Survivor Series!"

With Dwayne standing tall in the middle of the ring, my mind was already thinking of how we could improve the system that helped make his first splash on our TV screens so successful.

I wasn't dumb enough to think that everyone we put through a developmental process was going to end up becoming the mega-star The Rock did, but we'd gotten word that USWA was closing their doors, so I knew we needed some kind of plan for the future. And I was excited to finally try to expand our developmental program in a more pro-sports kind of way. I wanted to build something from scratch, in-house, that would power the company for decades to come.

So, instead of trying to pitch wholesale changes to Vince right out of the gate, I approached it slow, with hardly any budget at first. I was a long way off of a developmental program that looked like a sports franchise's, and I knew it would take time and success for WWF to shed its own outdated systems. But along the way it was small steps that led to major developments. We kept a blended approach, which sometimes meant classes where a seasoned veteran would come in and work with a select group of new talents, and other times meant asking new talent to work in small, regional companies for experience.

And over time we assembled an amazing team, with Dory Funk Jr., Al Snow, Tom Prichard, Rip Rogers, Danny Davis, Jim Cornette, and many others, as we selected and trained the prospects of the future. Over the years we went from one class in a warehouse to the NXT developmental brand that now airs for WWE every week on USA Network.

From the first class that brought us Edge and Christian, through our partnerships with Ohio Valley Wrestling that trained John Cena, Dave Bautista, Randy Orton, Shelton Benjamin, and Brock Lesnar, and Florida Championship Wrestling that cultivated Roman Reigns, all the way up to NXT, which produced Charlotte Flair—the new pipeline worked.

And the better success we had funneling new talent to the main roster, the more money was made available within the company to expand our system. Vince was getting exactly what he'd hoped from the new budget line in my department, and that was talent that would enhance his roster from the opening bell to the main event for years to come.

As we produced more stars, we got more budget, and that budget built a team that built a system that built more and more stars.

Watching kids we found developing into superstars, breaking PPV records, or main-eventing WrestleMania never got old. Hell, some of that talent has even done so well for themselves that I get to see them topping the bill at my local cinema several times a year, now.

I had a feeling young Rock was going to be The Man, but my feeling didn't headline PPVs; his talent did.

As I get older, I know more and more what's important in life. And giving all those talented men and women a chance to live their dreams, and make a great life for themselves and their families while doing it, will always make me as proud as anything else I've ever done in the wrestling business.

"He's on one leg, he's lost all kinds of blood, but he's refusing any kind of help. He's going to walk out of here on his own."

March 23, 1997
Bret Hart vs. Steve Austin, WrestleMania 13
Rosemont Horizon
Rosemont, Illinois

You can have everything else in wrestling—great matches, wonderful venues, top-notch production values—but if you don't have story, then it's all for nothing. The true greats can bring an arena to its feet by simply moving their head a certain way, or raising an eyebrow, or stomping a mudhole in someone and walking it dry. But the reason those actions elicit a massive response is because of the years' worth of character development and story those stars and their companies have invested in their personas.

Wrestling without storytelling is an empty pursuit.

The best stories in our genre are begun, then heightened, in buildup, and finished in the match. I know from all the years I've put in that talent going in there and trading holds isn't going to capture the audience's attention for very long, because as a species, humans need to know *why*. Even when we hear that someone in our own circle has thrown a punch somewhere, we immediately want to know what happened.

This need to know is a core tenet of professional wrestling.

The best in our business rely on the story behind their conflicts to get people invested in what they do. And they're not alone. Everywhere from boxing to politics to reality TV to MMA now uses the ingredients that professional wrestling has cooked with from the start.

When people think of storytelling in our business, they think of the great talkers on the microphone, using their charisma and catchphrases to talk the fans into needing to see them fight. But the real greats don't stop the story when the bell rings—they continue it, embellish it, and finish it. Even if the reason they're fighting is as fundamental as one needing to win more than the other.

Now, when you have two of the best ever telling that story, well, I believe in Hollywood they call that "elevating the material." And man oh man could Bret Hart and Steve Austin elevate just about any material they were given. In 1997, one wrestler was at their absolute peak, and the other was beginning a meteoric rise so huge that it broke all the box-office records, and clocked up numbers that nobody has been able to match since.

We all knew that Bret against Steve could be special, but I don't think anyone expected to witness one of the best—if not the best—WrestleMania matches of all time.

Let me just say that I was, and still am, a huge Bret Hart fan. I've always respected how The Hitman handled himself, and how he represented our business all around the world. In 2021, Bret was one of the first people to text me after my skin cancer diagnosis, and it made my day that Bret reached out to encourage me to keep fighting.

And I think by now everyone knows the deep friendship I've had with "Stone Cold" Steve Austin, reaching all the way back to our WCW days. Steve credits me with a lot over the course of his career, but he's given me so much more than I have ever given him. In 2007, he told the world that he loved me as he inducted me into the WWE Hall of Fame. Well, Steve, I love you, too. And that's why it might be a little weird for "civilians" to hear me say that in 1997, at WrestleMania 13, I was ecstatic to be telling our audience that Austin was "on one leg, he's lost all kinds of blood, but he's refusing any kind of help." It created a visual, an image in time, that will last forever in the minds of all of us who saw it. And it will endure because of the work both men put into the storytelling building up to it.

In the run-up to the match, the usually valiant Hart was whining about how he was constantly being screwed by the WWF higher-ups, and how he was getting no respect from anybody. He bemoaned the fact that the audience was changing, cheering for a vulgar, anti-authority rattlesnake like Austin instead of a heroic, straitlaced champion like him. Bret's perfect response to Austin's popularity only served to increase his already growing negative reaction from the audience, just like Bret wanted. As society was changing, so was what was generally considered a babyface in wrestling. It was no longer cool to be the straitlaced, principled, moral defender of the business, like Bret. People wanted shades of gray, and defiance, and an anti-hero to cheer on, like Steve. And this storyline put that change front and center. Now all the two men needed was time and space on the biggest stage of them all to work out the final chapter, live, in the middle of the ring.

The match itself was a submission match, so we added MMA legend Kenny Shamrock as a special guest referee, and he did the right thing and just stayed the hell out of everyone's way until he was called on after the match.

And then came the familiar glass shattering that signaled Austin was on his way to the ring.

> *"Steve Austin is six-two, two-fifty-two. Said there's not a human being walking the face of the earth that can make him say, 'I quit.' And I think I believe him."*

When Bret's music played, pyrotechnics clapped into the rafters, and The Hitman stomped down to the ring—directly into a double leg take-down from Austin. I could tell that this one was going to be a fight, and I think our audience began to notice that something different was happening, too, when the two men fought around the ring, over the barricade, and into the crowd.

> *"This resembles more of a bar fight than a wrestling match . . .*
> *Bret Hart is venting months and months of frustration . . .*
> *These two men are beating and battering each other."*

They tore it up in the stands, and back down to ringside. It was one of the rare matches where I knew the finish—Bret was going over—but I had no idea how or when. And lucky me, because I began to get as excited as our audience when it became clear what both men were serving up in the story of the match. As they got it back in the ring, Bret began to work over Stone Cold's heavily braced knee and leg.

> *"A methodical, physical dissection of the lower anatomy*
> *by doctor Bret Hart on the patient, Steve Austin."*

But the defiant Austin wouldn't give up, and the story they were telling began its final act twist.

The submission stipulation favored Bret, the master tactician, but even though the Stone Cold brawler was outmatched in this situation, he defiantly gave it everything he had anyway. And with that the theme of the bout became apparent to the audience and the people back home: in this war, Bret had the bigger arsenal, but Steve had the bigger heart.

I hooked on to their passionate performances as best I could. This was art, and I didn't want to become unhitched from it. If they were upping their game minute on minute, I knew that I needed to try to do the same.

> *"It's not about talking about it. It's not talking about the*
> *past. It's not posing, or covering a bald spot. This is about*
> *athleticism, a helluva fight, between two great athletes!"*

The money for a broadcaster is figuring out how to follow the monitor—how to see what your audience at home is seeing. Even though the action is live right in front of you, you gotta keep your head in the monitor so you can experience exactly what your viewers are experiencing. And not just to see what they're seeing, but to *feel* what they're seeing. Which isn't hard when you're sitting in front of the greatest WrestleMania match in history. The roar of the live crowd, the passion of the wrestlers in front of you—the adrenaline begins to build.

> *"Austin's face smacked the steel, and now Austin is a bloody mess!"*

Rock versus Hogan at WrestleMania 18 was an amazing attraction match. But the crowd wrote the story of that match, and Rock and Hogan were smart enough to accept their new script and act accordingly. And if Rock versus Hogan was a masterclass in creating on the fly, Hart versus Austin was a masterclass in executing on months of buildup in the most perfect way possible.

And even with the story as tight as it was, they were still building to a final twist in the tale.

> *"I guarantee you if Ken Shamrock stops this match without a submission, Stone Cold Steve Austin will attempt to kill him."*

Austin was busted open (Bret had sliced him open with a perfect sleight of hand) and he was getting beaten badly in a pool of his own blood in the middle of the ring. And then Bret grabbed a chair and went to work on The Rattlesnake's bad wheels.

> *"Right on the leg, right on the knee brace, right on the injured knee. Bret Hart now is like an animal out of control and is trying to break Austin's leg!!"*

Stone Cold fought back with everything he had, until finally Hart got him locked in his finishing move: the Sharpshooter. With the blue ring canvas already painted with Steve's dry blood, Austin made sure to lift his head to give the perfect shot of how badly he was bleeding. Blood down his face, streaming between his teeth, The Texas Rattlesnake clawed and screamed in pain as Hart sat farther down on his spine.

> "Bret Hart has beaten every Superstar with this move. How in the hell Austin has not given up I cannot understand."

And then, after fighting as long and as hard as he possibly could, Stone Cold went limp. But he did so without uttering any words of surrender.

> "Austin passed out! Austin is unconscious! Austin never gave up, but he passed out from the pain!!"

Even though he'd technically "lost," Steve knew by the reaction of the crowd that Bret, a maestro who had given the match everything he had, had gotten Steve over even more.

And Bret still had one more trick up his sleeve to turn the audience even more toward the newly crowned babyface in Stone Cold, and away from himself as a newly minted heel.

The Hitman attacked the knee of the lifeless Austin once again as the audience booed him in unison, until Shamrock intervened. Only then did The Hitman back away from the fight.

Each little beat of the story played out perfectly within the building, and at home. All the while, Steve lay there knowing he was like a boxing prospect going fifteen rounds versus Mike Tyson in Iron Mike's prime. And Austin's later performance in majestical Madison Square Garden put Steve on the pro wrestling lexicon as the next main event star in our business.

What Bret and Steve did together was truly magical.

And it helped make Stone Cold a made man.

"They're cuffing Austin. He has let the police put the handcuffs on him. Austin is going directly to jail!"

September 22, 1997
Steve Austin Stuns Vince McMahon, Monday Night Raw
Madison Square Garden
New York City

WWE's marketing will tell you that the Attitude Era started in November of 1997. A lot of fans say it began in 1996, when "Stone Cold" Steve Austin grabbed the microphone at the King of the Ring PPV and said in reference to his born-again opponent, Jake The Snake Roberts, "You talk Psalms, talk about John 3:16. AUSTIN 3:16 said I just kicked your ass." Other fans will tell you it started in Montreal, discussed in our next chapter, and some others will tell you it kicked off with Austin versus Hart from our last one.

And the reason nobody, including myself, can tell you exactly when it started is because, like most great things in life, it wasn't planned. It wasn't conceived in a boardroom or a writer's meeting. It came about organically because of the nature of the players involved: Vince McMahon and Steve Austin.

In the era of *South Park, Jerry Springer,* and *Howard Stern,* the advertiser-preferred eighteen-to-thirty-four demographic wasn't watching WWF's more cartoonish product anymore. But that demo *was* beginning to watch WWF's rival company, WCW, led by their groundbreaking faction New World Order. Vince's biggest-ever draw up that point, Hulk Hogan, was the top draw in the business again—only this time for the competition—and the former kids' hero was now dressed all in black, jumping people from behind, and spray-painting "NWO" on his victims.

McMahon's business had been sinking for years, but by the late nineties it had become so weak that Vince had to tell his world champion, Bret "The Hitman" Hart, that he couldn't honor their previously agreed contract, and that Bret should seek out the WCW offer Bret had previously turned down.

So that will tell you just how badly WWF needed something to hit. And just when it looked like we had someone getting super over in Steve Austin, he was put on the long-term injured list after being accidentally dropped on his head in a match by Owen Hart a few months prior.

Austin didn't want to sit at home with his broken neck while he was getting hotter than hell, though. And we knew our audience just wanted to see him doing something, anything, every week. So he remained a TV character even though he couldn't work an actual match. And because Austin was injured and couldn't go, we needed a foil for him that would keep him out of the ring and give him someone to feud with at the same time.

Austin knew he needed to remain defiant—that's what got him over in the first place—and who better to rage against than the man who owns the whole machine?

That's when the pieces began to fall into place for something truly special to happen. And it was perfect. Austin's real-life inability to wrestle forced the company to add more and more soap opera–like episodic storytelling that certainly wouldn't have been such a focus if the company could have relied on matches alone.

Steve's blue-collar character wanted to fight again, but his corporate boss was stopping him from doing just that. Vince McMahon would become Mr. McMahon and Steve Austin would become white hot—but not before we built the story to get them there. And it would all kick off on our first-ever *Monday Night Raw* from Madison Square Garden.

Defying his boss's orders, and a restraining order taken out by Owen Hart, Stone Cold ran into the ring, unannounced, to attack the man who broke his neck. Immediately, some New York cops rushed the ring ready to arrest Austin, but the incensed Texas Rattlesnake stood his ground and dared the baton-wielding policemen to come arrest him.

And that was McMahon's cue.

He shot up from his announce position beside me and marched into the ring, mic in hand, ready to play peacemaker. This was a role that the audience wasn't used to seeing all that often, because for years Vince hid the fact that he was the owner of WWF. He was "just" the lead announcer in the fans' eyes. So Vince breaking character added a realism to what was about to come. We never explicitly said who Vince was, but implied it heavily enough that we knew fans would take to the then-new invention called the internet to research and discuss. McMahon hurried between the ropes and implored Steve not to cause any more trouble. He reminded Stone Cold that he was physically unable to wrestle, as doing so could cause paralysis. And for a couple of rare minutes it looked like Austin and McMahon might actually have found some common ground.

Steve even backed down a little and began to listen to reason.

| *"He's telling the truth; it makes all the sense in the world."* |

And then Vince laid out the theme of their whole storied saga right there in one sentence, by telling Steve that he's got to "work within the system— that's all you got to do." Well, The Rattlesnake didn't like the thought of that and told his employer to kiss his ass, before—out of nowhere—hitting McMahon with a Stone Cold Stunner right in the middle of the ring.

| *"Oh God! Oh my God!!"* |

Vince might have taken the move unconventionally, but his sell afterward was priceless—his eyes glazed, body convulsing in shock. The New York faithful ate it up, as Steve got down low and personal into his boss's face and talked all kinds of shit as the cameras closed in for the perfect framing. Austin knew his action would mean jail, but it was too sweet an opportunity to pass up. He rose up, turned his back, and let the cops cuff him. All while never shutting off his machine-gun mouth for one second.

> *"They're cuffing Austin! He has let the police put the handcuffs on him! Austin is going directly to jail! And Vince McMahon is out!!"*

Now, the Garden is special for anyone who's worked there, but for the McMahon family, it was the Cathedral, because Vince was the third generation of his family to promote there. What better place to up the ante of his biggest star than right there?

> *"I'll tell you what. How do you keep your job now!? Austin doesn't give a damn if he's employed or not!"*

But Austin wasn't finished just yet; there were a few more precious seconds to maximize as the cops marched him up the ramp. Steve made sure to give the cameramen some more gold as he flipped off McMahon while his hands were still cuffed—and Madison Square Garden showered the scene with "AUSTIN! AUSTIN!" chants.

> *"You got to believe Austin is fired, and he's on his way to jail!!"*

It was the most significant angle that we'd ever attempted on *Raw* up to that point. It was the boss of the company getting physically assaulted; it was the star of the company arrested. It was gasoline and matches. The perfect ingredients for something new and special. And boy did those two have chemistry.

We'd hoped it would be magic, but I think anyone who says they knew then that it would become the most iconic feud in WWE history is not telling the truth.

Whatever was supposed to be, or not supposed to be, once Vince heard the pop from him getting the Stunner, plans began to develop very quickly indeed. He knew they had something. Now it became about how to create what the people wanted in a way that could raise the ratings, and make Austin into the top-drawing superstar of all time.

And Steve, broken neck or not, was ready to deliver.

"You talk about controversy. This crowd is livid."

November 9, 1997
The Montreal Screwjob, Survivor Series
Molson Centre
Montreal, Quebec

The WWF "Winged Eagle" world title belt is the one many people grew up with. It was the one Hogan wore, Macho Man, Warrior—Shawn Michaels and Bret Hart, too. Just like "Big Gold," the iconic world title that NWA/WCW fans had grown up with, the WWF title was imprinted on millions of brains around the world. The lineage of those titles has been passed down for over half a century, so they're a weird mix of prop and very real at the same time. And that mix means they can elicit very different kinds of personal reactions from the people who wear them. Some take the role of champion too seriously, and some not seriously enough. It just depends whether they see it as prop or championship.

What's universal in wrestling's own unique language, though, is that those belts of leather and gold have usually translated into big money for the person picked to wear them. Wrestlers know that if they become the champion, it's a cash and cachet type of situation, where you usually become the face of the company—and level up not just in position, but in all manner of payments. And that's why those titles can be so political, and the planning around them so fraught.

But no matter how you slice it, the significance of the world championships has endured because an unbroken line of legendary names carried them when they were chosen—and passed them on when they were told their time was over. And it was that proud tradition, held dear and true by second-generation traditionalist Bret Hart, that led to a decision that changed the course of wrestling forever. And that's no hyperbole, either.

In 1997, Bret was the world champion who was soon leaving WWF because they could no longer afford his contract. WWF wanted Bret to drop the title on his way out, and The Hitman seemingly had no problem doing so—he just didn't want to drop it to a guy he felt wasn't worthy—and unfortunately, the company booked him to lose against Shawn Michaels, a guy who told Bret that if the roles were reversed, he wouldn't drop the belt to him.

This led to a standoff, with only a few dates left for Bret to drop the title before his contract's end.

Bret and Shawn weren't just chalk and cheese on-screen together; they were like that backstage, too. Bret was raised by his legendary wrestling father, Stu Hart, to have respect for the business, and particularly for the world title. Shawn was an amazing talent, but reveled in any opportunity to rub people the wrong way.

So with the two men butting heads, Vince McMahon agreed that their upcoming PPV match would end in a draw, to give Bret, his loyal and long-serving champion, an opportunity to pass the belt to someone other than Shawn before Bret left.

In Montreal, as both men headed toward their agreed-upon finish, in the middle of the ring, the obnoxious challenger put the national hero in the hero's own move. The script read that Bret fights out of it, but this was a night when wrestling's script went out the window, right in front of everyone's eyes.

Michaels grabbed a downed Hart, and turned him. He sat back on The Hitman's spine, wrapping his legs in Bret's own submission hold—and waited for a new, secretly written storyline to play out.

> *"Aw, you're kidding me! Michaels, is he going to try to beat Bret Hart with a Sharpshooter? Yes, he is!"*

And just like that, before Bret could even attempt to counter his own hold, the referee called for the bell as if Hart had surrendered. The look on Bret's face told me that he didn't, in fact, give up. And not only that he didn't give up, but that he was being relieved of the world title in a way he had not agreed to.

> *"Michaels with the Sharpshooter has become WWF Champion! And Bret Hart is standing in disbelief!"*

Hitman was not the only one in disbelief. Jerry and I, and all the thousands of fans around us, knew something was not right in what had just gone down—*especially* when Vince McMahon showed up at ringside, a rarity in those days. And as the camera truck moved from shot to shot of the building confusion and anger, Vince's former world champion, now livid and aware of what just happened, spat in McMahon's face just before we went off air.

As Shawn got out of there, there was bedlam on both sides of the curtain. This was the kind of decision they used to make in the territories when the owner felt a wrestler who was leaving "wouldn't do business"—he'd send in a legit tough guy "shooter" to beat the departing champion, to insure his title stayed in his territory. But here Hart and McMahon had agreed that Bret would lose it before he left—just in a different place to a different guy. There was never any suggestion that Bret wouldn't do business, but the boss decided to "screw" him, as McMahon later put it, anyway. This was a decision so very rare that it reverberated around the business.

Shawn wasn't a legit tough guy, so a "setup" was devised instead, the fallout of which led to Bret legitimately knocking out Vince McMahon backstage for double-crossing him.

And this is where the very real nature of professional wrestling intersected perfectly with its storytelling alter ego. On its face, this was a storyline being played out, but in reality that "storyline" had very real effects on the whole business. It was that moment that gave rise to the Mr. McMahon character, a character that would help usher in the greatest era (in my humble opinion) that the company had ever seen: the Attitude Era.

After Vince screwed Bret live on PPV, he went on *Raw* and blamed Bret for it, with the now-iconic phrase, "I didn't screw Bret; Bret screwed Bret." Fans hated Vince's attitude toward their beloved Hitman. But that negative reaction to McMahon's callous approach just made the path to him stepping in front of the cameras full-time easier. After all, the promoter in Vince felt that if the fans, who loved Bret all around the world, might boo him for this anyway, going forward, then why not turn that reaction into box office receipts?

At the time, Montreal felt monumental in terms of the day-to-day approach to my job as head of talent relations. I had to first convince the roster that I didn't know that a man as respected as I'd ever encountered in our business was going to be screwed. And then I had to convince them to do business the right way, even though they'd just seen their boss do it "the wrong way," and that he wasn't going to do it to them in the future.

Trust was rocked in a business that was powered on it. You can love or hate the person across from you, but when it comes down to it, you have to trust them with your body or the business doesn't work.

It was also that moment that had very real effects on Bret's life, Shawn's life, and, I'm sure, Vince's life, too. Bret found himself in a dark place after this, even more so when his beloved brother Owen died shortly afterward in a WWF ring after falling, during an entrance, from the rafters of the Kemper Arena. Shawn tried for years to tell people he didn't know the referee was going to call the match, but he was booed mercilessly in arenas all over Canada for most of his career, before admitting later on, after he became a born-again Christian, that he'd been in on it.

Each of these men, plus referee Earl Hebner, would be defined by that moment where the script was thrown out the window for the rest of their careers. And it was all because of a prop. A prop that was very real for the boss who owned it, and the wrestler who proudly wore it.

"All hell has broken loose!"

January 19, 1998
Steve Austin Shoves Mike Tyson, Monday Night Raw
Pyramid Arena
Memphis, Tennessee

After the Montreal Screwjob, as it came to be known, Vince decided to lean fully into his character on TV. Fans had already made up their minds that McMahon was an asshole for what happened to Bret, so the gasoline was right there to fuel the flames of heat around the owner of the company.

And this was all happening at a time when Vince was lucky enough to find his next Main Guy, Steve Austin, and he knew if he wanted to "strap a rocket" to him and make him the face of his whole company, then that "rocket" needed fuel. Well, in 1998, Vince McMahon was sure he'd found the perfect rocket fuel to launch that bald-headed, foul-mouthed Texan from stardom into mega-stardom. So that's why, one Monday night in January '98, *Mr.* McMahon had horror on his face, but *Vince* McMahon had dollar signs in his eyes. And those dollars appearing came not a moment too soon.

The Monday Night War, as it became known, was a TV ratings battle between the WCW and WWF. WCW's *Monday Nitro* was playing on TNT the same night and time as *Raw* was on the USA Network, and both were aiming for, more or less, the same fan base every week. For some, the battle became personal. I know it did for Vince, as he felt Ted Turner was using his real-life billions to lure away Vince's top talent in an effort to put McMahon out of business. Maybe it was a little revenge for Vince's Black Saturday dalliance on Turner's network in 1988, or maybe it was just straight up business. Either way, the net effect of dwindling ratings for any TV show is cancellation, and at that point, the TV shows were the pipeline that led to the PPV and live event sales. The loss of any of those things, but especially TV, meant financial ruin for the then-family-owned WWF.

At this point, WCW was still kicking our asses in those coveted ratings, with their NWO storytelling and their endless supply of surprise debuts of former WWF names, but we felt we now had the better roster, a shifting momentum, and the better top guy in Steve.

And it was time to go all-in, to make sure lapsed fans and new fans alike were aware that this wasn't kids' programming anymore. This was worth another look.

To do that, Vince knew that he needed something that would bring us back into the mainstream conversation, and carry the name of his new number-one draw with it. What he needed was to find someone on the mainstream audience's mind, someone whose mere name got headlines. And in 1998, there was nothing and no one bigger in sports *or* entertainment than Holyfield ear-biter Mike Tyson.

That's why, from the center of the *Monday Night Raw* ring, Mr. McMahon bounced with joy as he announced that he had made a deal with the man the whole world was talking about, and that "Iron" Mike Tyson would be involved in WrestleMania just a few months later.

For Mr. McMahon, that night was a celebration, a reintroduction to the mainstream, a night for the WWF to put its best foot forward and show the world once again that they were the show to watch. He was jubilant making his announcement.

But, just as *Vince* McMahon planned, the night would go horribly for Mr. McMahon, and in doing so, would get the world talking about his company, and its top star—*our* resident badass, Stone Cold Steve Austin— once again.

Over the years, at various times across different companies, our world has been visited by Muhammad Ali, Shaquille O'Neal, Dennis Rodman, and Mr. T. We even had Arnold Schwarzenegger punch Triple H in the face one *SmackDown* because "The Game" ran his mouth a little too close to "The Terminator."

All these cameos—and many hundreds more—happened mostly to expose our audience to the celeb's product, or to expose the celeb's audience to our product. That's why Vince knew his Tyson plan going well could turn WWF's momentum around ratings-wise—but if it sucked, it could hurt the biggest prospect he'd had in years. McMahon had to be careful to get the right mix of the reality of boxing and fiction of wrestling—and simply put, he needed something that would go viral, before going viral was even a thing.

With the newly arrived Tyson and exultant Mr. McMahon now getting pally in the *Raw* ring, and with a celebratory feeling in the air, the mood turned quickly when the glass shattered, signaling the uninvited Austin was on his way. And as The Texas Rattlesnake stomped down the aisle, Mr. McMahon looked suddenly despondent, as if seeing his perfect coming-out party suddenly go up in flames. The boss knew the resident pain in his corporate ass wasn't here to celebrate; he was here to do what Austin did best—raise hell.

> *"Yes indeed, Mike Tyson is standing in Stone Cold's ring, and business is damn sure about to pick up!"*

I wanted the first thing new ears heard to be that this was Austin's world, and the former World Heavyweight Boxing Champion was standing in it. As Austin marched toward Tyson in the middle of the ring, the boxer's massive entourage tightened around him, leaving Stone Cold and Iron Mike Tyson eye to eye in a sea of humanity.

As the crowd went bananas, Mr. McMahon looked on like his biggest birthday had just been ruined—even though nothing could have been further from the truth.

Stone Cold got right in Mike's face, proceeding to talk smack to "The Baddest Man on the Planet," until Tyson, having heard enough, shoved the defiant Austin, igniting a melee inside the ring.

> *"Tyson wants Austin! Austin wants Tyson!*
> *It is pandemonium in WWF!"*

The whole interaction had an edge to it. The shove Tyson gave Austin looked like an offensive lineman on a pass block. It was very snug, and it ignited the audience even more, as thousands of dollars exploded from Mike's pockets in the ensuing brawl.

The melee made all the headlines, and put Austin in the spot he needed to be in, as the anti-corporate protagonist.

Now, wrestling is such a nonstop grind from town to town, TV taping to TV taping, that it was sometimes hard to get moments to stand out in my mind. But it hit me immediately, as Tyson's entourage ran around the ring picking up his stacks of hundred-dollar bills, that this was indeed awesome.

> *"Steve Austin is being restrained from attacking Mike*
> *Tyson. Austin takes pride in being the toughest SOB in*
> *the WWF . . . Vince McMahon said, 'You've ruined it.*
> *You've ruined it.' Maybe the big deal has been blown with*
> *Mike Tyson thanks to Steve Austin? This is chaotic . . .*
> *Austin nailed one of Tyson's people! We'll be right back!"*

And with that piece of business, the transfer of heat between Austin and Tyson was in motion, as we began a story that would peak in the main event of WrestleMania. Austin was scheduled to take on the charismatic outgoing WWF champion, Shawn Michaels—and now Iron Mike would be the special referee.

This put Austin in a position to win his first-ever WWF world title, in a match where Tyson would bring extra eyeballs and intrigue.

While Mr. McMahon would continue his hatred of Steve, Vince loved the numbers he was bringing to the company. Austin and McMahon, with a Tyson chaser, began the uptick in ratings, ticket sales, and PPV numbers that helped set the stage for WWF's comeback.

Mission accomplished.

"Well, look who's back . . . A new day is dawning."

March 30, 1998
Sean Waltman's Debut, Monday Night Raw
Pepsi Arena
Albany, New York

Like most things in business, any new approach comes down to money. No matter how we feel about it, money usually dictates the pace of change in business and society in general. If it's flowing, then everything stays as it is; if it's not, then things begin to change.

So when Sean Waltman, far removed from his previous WWF persona of The 1-2-3 Kid, strode down the *Raw* ramp on his way to the ring for the first time in 1998, it represented a shift in the way money worked at WWF and in the business in general—and how that shift was effecting change on-screen.

Waltman was joining real-life friend Triple H in the WWF, having said goodbye to his other real-life friends Kevin Nash and Scott Hall in WCW. When Waltman, Triple H, Hall, Nash, and Shawn Michaels were all working together in WWF in the early nineties, they were so tight behind the scenes that they were simply known as The Kliq. And during the Monday

Night Wars, even though The Kliq was broken across two companies—Hall, Nash, and Sean in WCW's New World Order, and Triple H and Shawn in WWF's D-Generation X—that bond never fractured. So it only made sense, when Michaels had to retire because of injury, that the new DX leader, Triple H, would call upon a friend to come fight by his side.

And it marked a reversal in the nonstop flow of talent from WWF to WCW—now that the money to do it was more readily available, with the success of Austin on top.

In the early to mid-nineties, WCW started offering guaranteed contracts to tempt top talent away from WWF. It was a business move that helped them become the highest-rated wrestling show on TV. Fans wondering who might show up next on *Nitro* gave WCW programming that intrigue that we lacked. And what started as a trickle of talent leaving ended up being a river.

Hulk Hogan, Scott Hall, Kevin Nash, Roddy Piper, and "Macho Man" Randy Savage were just some of the names that left for greener pastures—and the *green* in that particular pasture was that guaranteed money.

And I can't say I blame them one bit.

As much as the wrestling business has evolved over the years, the *money* in the wrestling business has been slow to evolve with it. Back when I started in '74, talent didn't know what they'd be paid, or *if* they'd be paid. Not for sure. Wrestlers would hope they'd get booked on a card, because the only way they got paid is if they got to the ring—and even then, it was the bookers' discretion as to how much went from the box office to the wrestlers. If you got injured, or weren't booked, you didn't make any money.

In the territories, the rough formula used was the main event draw would get 3 percent of the net after tax. That meant that if there was a $100,000 house, the guy on top got $3,000 and every payment after that down the card was stair-stepped, all the way down to the referees. You'd have to take what was left over after the top talents were paid and use it to make sure your payments at the very bottom of the card didn't starve anyone out of the territory. Every night was different pay, and nothing was guaranteed to anyone.

That's why there was so much resistance to women wrestlers coming into the territories, because on a twelve-man card, it was usually a tag team match that was cut to make room, meaning four guys who needed to feed their families were sitting at home while the promoter saved money by underpaying two women instead. Both the men and the women in that scenario were being treated poorly, as the money "saved" didn't go to either of them.

But as unforgiving as the territories' payment system was, it carried itself all the way to the '90s without being changed all that much. WWE Hall of Famer Mick Foley has shared in interviews that, in his first deal with WWF, he was only guaranteed for five matches a year at $150 for five years. Another HOFer, Scott Hall, has said publicly that he was in a similar situation, where his original WWF deal was for ten matches a year at $150 a pop.

As tough as those contracts sound—and they were both tough and not uncommon—Mick and Scott took those deals as a bet on themselves. They bet that WWF would see their worth and book them far beyond the few matches a year they were guaranteed, and put them on live events and PPV where they could get a share of the revenue generated—and that's where the bigger money was earned.

But it would be that same Scott Hall jumping to WCW in 1993 with his best friend, Kevin Nash, that would spark the next phase in talent pay in our business. Both Hall and Nash moved from WWF to WCW for contracts that gave them far more money guaranteed for far fewer dates than they'd work in WWF. For the first time in their careers, they knew exactly how much they'd be making, and for how many appearances. And that number was guaranteed no matter what.

While Hall and Nash weren't the first to get guaranteed contracts in WCW, their contracts were the most generous in WCW history. WCW had in Senior Vice President Eric Bischoff someone who was spending a corporation's money and not his own like Vince was. Eric was keeping WCW hot as hell by going live every week, taking creative risks, signing big names, and giving his show that "anything can happen" feel that fans love to see.

Word of the favorable WCW contracts traveled fast. More big stars were looking to jump from WWF, and they wanted contracts that looked like Hall's and Nash's. So, what was once a contractual outlier became more and more prevalent down in Atlanta—and that meant Vince's WWF had to pay attention if they wanted to compete.

Wrestling is a talent-led business, and it's almost impossible to compete if all the name-brand talent was exiting for your competitor. McMahon knew that WWF's payment model needed to modernize while still keeping the incentive-based system he preferred. He and I both agreed that paying on incentives generated more wealth for those who were earning it, while not letting anyone rest on their laurels. And while Vince had also made guaranteed deals before, it was around the time that Waltman showed up that the dam burst, and a new approach began to roll out across the roster in general.

While WCW was offering guaranteed contracts, WWF began offering *downside* guaranteed contracts. While WCW was offering *the most* you could expect to earn, WWF was offering *the least* you could expect to earn. That meant WCW had a ceiling on what talent could earn, where WWF did not.

If you got hot in WCW, you still only got your contract number. But if you got hot in WWF, you could make far more than your contract number, because you shared in the profits.

That's the deal we went to prospective talent with, including Sean Waltman. And for the first time in the Monday Night Wars, someone from WCW's hottest act, the NWO, jumped ship and came to WWF.

Waltman was the turning of the tide. We were building momentum, building our audience, building buzz, and we were building a roster that many consider the greatest of all time.

Our talent now knew that they'd receive a check every week that they could take as earned, and use that number to create family budgets and plan what their financial year would look like. But if they worked hard and got over with our audience, they could expect significant "bonus" payments on top of that guaranteed money, too.

After all, the "professional" part of "professional wrestling" is the money part. It's the *How much for how many dates?* The money and the miles are what most performers ask about when it comes time to sign a contract—and rightfully so. If you're going to be away from your family, putting your body on the line, you want to know it's going to be worth it.

And that kind of payment system lasted all the way up to around 2022, when things shifted again. AEW and WWE now pay their talent on a salary, where they get paid one large number, and that's that. With the decline in PPV and the rise in rights fees, both companies now know the number *they* can expect over the life of their contract with the networks, which means they know the kinds of deals they can comfortably offer talent. And the numbers are bigger than ever, because the profits in wrestling are bigger than ever.

In a cyclical business that revolves around momentum and buzz, we seem to be on the upswing again as I write this. In June 2023, AEW both launched another two-hour live show on TNT called *Collision* and sold tens of thousands of tickets to an event in Wembley without announcing a single match. And WWE is on the verge of a huge merger on the back of their biggest earnings ever.

All the metrics are up, and both WWE and AEW are making more money than they have at any time in their long and short history, respectively. And what that means for talent, I'm thrilled to say, is that there are more millionaires in our locker rooms than at any time before.

As a guy who started on $120 a week, and moved to being the guy who negotiated deals with talent in the Attitude Era, seeing the wealth this business is creating makes me very happy. Sometimes it takes a long time for change to happen. But when it does, it's usually because of money and how well it's moving.

Turns out that, right now, it's moving well.

"As God is my witness, he's broken in half!"

June 28, 1998
Hell in a Cell, King of the Ring
Civic Arena
Pittsburgh, Pennsylvania

I've found in life that, when we talk about toughness, there's a couple of different kinds. There's people who are considered tough because of the kind of punishment they can dish out, and then there's the flip side of that coin, those who are considered tough because of the kind of punishment they can take. It's usually the person who can dish it that gets the most column inches or statues made in their honor. There aren't many Hollywood epics about people who got their ass beaten so spectacularly that it went down in history.

I guess humans tend to celebrate the hammer, not the nail. But in our world, that's what made Mick Foley so unique, and so beloved—he made us root for the nail.

It didn't matter if he wrestled as Cactus Jack, Dude Love, or Mankind, Mick made us rally behind him because of his heart, because of his testicular fortitude, as he likes to call it, and because of his toughness. Because in a business that has a long history of truly tough men and women, Mick

Foley was something else. The pain that big, lovable frame endured on a nightly basis, for years and years, was hard for us to wrap our heads around in real time—and it doesn't get any easier to understand looking back on it now, either.

How could he keep walking after that?

How could he make the next town after that?

And why would he continue to do that?

I hear some old-school guys say that today's wrestlers aren't tough like their generation was, but I don't necessarily agree. There're people in the locker room now who could win a bar fight against three locals at two in the morning, just like in the '70s—if maybe not as many.

But I think we sometimes fall into the trap of comparing toughness against progress. "In my day we had to walk backward in the snow, uphill both ways, just to get to school" isn't a mentality you want to find yourself in. I mean, I think anyone who makes a living beating their body up for art and entertainment is tough. I think anyone who can go through the mental grind that this business puts on people is tough, too. I think anyone who is smart, and thoughtful, and understanding of the risks—and still decides to do it—is tougher than a two-dollar steak.

That's our people.

And I'm proud of that.

But some of the hardships that guys had to face in the '70s aren't around now, and we should be celebrating that as an industry. The schedule when I started was brutal on the human body. Wrestling six to ten times a week, then bundling yourself into a cramped car full of beer and weed, probably wouldn't make it onto many health gurus' lists of how to maintain optimal performance these days. But I bet there are plenty today who would be up for that life, if they had to be.

The point is, they don't.

I remember those guys in the car giving out about the new generation in the '80s who flew into towns, and that generation giving out about the next generation who flew first class, and that generation giving out about the next buying their own tour buses, and so on and so on.

Each new generation of talent found a way to lessen the toll travel takes on their body. And that's as it should be.

A lot of the worst bumps Mick Foley took were in small venues, for even smaller crowds, as he earned his way to the top in the late '80s and early '90s. Just one of the bumps he would take was falling backward off the apron to the concrete floor and landing on the back of his head. He did that particular move so much around the loop in Memphis that his back was purple with bruising and he couldn't bump for a month. And then he'd cram himself into a small rental and drive hundreds of miles to the next gig, either sleeping in the back of the car or finding a chair in the hotel lobby.

And I kinda get why he did that. Foley felt like to get to the big time, he needed to bring something to the table that nobody else could. Or would. He needed to go a little bit further than the last guy, and a little bit further than the next guy. And he needed to do that over and over again until someone noticed.

Well, I noticed. And I know many of you did, too.

I worked with Mick in WCW, and when I got some power to hire people in WWF, he was one of the guys I was passionate about hiring. Mick tried out for Vince three times unsuccessfully, until I finally convinced the boss to let me bring him in.

> "He was born Mick Foley on Long Island, New York. His manifestations as Dude Love and Cactus Jack are infamous. But none are more deranged than Mankind. His scarred body—he's missing half an ear. He says when he gets inside the steel, he will feel at home . . . Can you imagine what this human being will do to himself? . . . He's not very logical. He needs therapy. Who knows what he's thinking?"

Mick's opponent that night in Hell in a Cell was the conscience of the WWF, The Undertaker. 'Taker said no several times to what Mick wanted to do in this match, until Foley finally ground The Deadman down enough to where he gave in.

That's why, when Mick made his entrance, 'Taker was already on top of the sixteen-foot steel cage waiting for Foley to join him. This wasn't normal. He was too big to be so high, and who knew what he had in mind?

King and I were sandwiched into the narrow space between the giant structure of the Cell and the barriers around the audience, and had no idea what was about to happen next.

> *"There's two three-hundred-pounders up there . . . My God, don't get them over here where we are . . . They're right above us, folks, and I don't like it a damn bit."*

Mick drove down to my house to visit recently, and I'm sorry to say that he's physically paying a price for that kind of career now. And that night, I genuinely thought that his own toughness had led him to kill himself. I thought he had convinced himself that he could withstand anything—that he wasn't enough for the audience without giving them something crazy in return.

How did he know he was going to be okay plummeting off the top of the Cell, live, for the first time ever, where the margin for error was zero? And if he didn't know he'd be okay—because he couldn't know—just how badly would he be hurt?

And then we all found out together.

Undertaker brought Foley to the edge of the Cell, where seconds later Mick Foley plummeted from the top of the Cell all the way down, through the Spanish announce table inches from where King and I were sitting, his twisted, lifeless body landing half in the crowd and half under the feet of the stunned Spanish announce team.

> *"My God almighty! Good God almighty! That killed him! As God is my witness, he's broken in half!!"*

I didn't know he was going to do it, and King didn't know he was going to do it. Nobody out there did. But we all damn sure knew, about two seconds after he did it, that there was a good chance he wasn't getting back up.

We'd all just witnessed a six-foot, three-hundred-pound human be launched from the top of the sixteen-foot Hell in a Cell structure—and now we were trying to assess just how badly injured that same man was.

> *"Someone get out here, really. I mean it! I cannot believe . . . that cage is sixteen feet high."*

I'd talked to Mick many times about his need to take big chances, and how someday one of them was going to get his ass blown up. Well, watching him bomb down from the top of the cage, through the Spanish announce table—then looking at him, motionless, buried underneath that now-exploded Spanish announce table—well, I thought that was where it all had caught up to him.

> *"Our Spanish announce team are down. We need doctors out here if someone can get off their butts in the back and get some people out here!"*

I wanted Mick to at least limit the amount of opportunities to put himself in the hospital. And I don't want to say he didn't listen, because I know Mick appreciated the concern that we all had for him—especially me, because I put my reputation on the line to get him hired.

But I guess he didn't listen.

That night Vince himself broke character to come down to ringside and join Mick's mentor and great friend, Terry Funk, in checking on Foley. EMTs and a stretcher soon appeared, too. Finally, Mick was being wheeled backstage to get the medical attention he so clearly needed.

But the stretcher only got halfway down the aisle before Mick began to stir, before he was standing again with a wicked twinkle in his eye.

> *"How in the hell is he standing?! And he's got a smile on his face, for God's sakes! Are you kidding me?! He wants to go back up! Mankind is going back up and so is The Undertaker!!"*

Foley, that tough son of a bitch, proceeded to not only miraculously get up from that first fall, but drag his broken body up the side of the Cell again and make his way to the top once more—all for something much, much worse to happen.

| *"This is absolutely amazing!"* |

The toughness, folks. I had never seen anything like it. I don't know if any of us had. But as Mick and 'Taker went back to work up there, the wire mesh in the structure was clearly sagging under their weight.

'Taker grabbed Mick by the throat, and lifted him into The Deadman's signature choke-slam—only for the flimsy cable ties that held the structure together to break as Mick came down on his back and "Mrs. Foley's Baby Boy" disappeared through the Cell, hurtling back-first all the way down to the rock-hard ring below.

If the first fall was sickening, and it was, this one was absolutely terrifying. Mick bounced high on the back of his head off the canvas, the impact of which contorted his unconscious body and left it unmoving on the ground.

| *"Good God! Good God! Will somebody stop* *the damn match?! Enough's enough!"* |

At that point, I later came to learn, The Undertaker—or more specifically, the man who played The Undertaker, Mark Calaway—genuinely thought he'd just seen a man die.

I was pretty sure we had, too.

After the fact, Mick told me that because he was so beaten up by the first fall, and tired from climbing the Cell again, he didn't have the energy to jump as high as he normally would when taking the choke-slam. That one detail, more than anything else, saved Mick's life. Because if he'd gone up as high as he usually did, then he would have over-rotated on his way down and landed directly on top of his head in the ring.

The thing with Mick was, you couldn't convince him to take fewer risks. He was a wild horse, and wild horses are going to run.

Mick Foley, now concussed, with a dislocated shoulder, bruised ribs, and a tooth hanging from his nose, and dealing with internal bleeding, got up once more and finished the match that still had some horrific bumps left for him.

> *"That ring is like concrete . . . He's either crazy as hell, or he's the toughest SOB I've ever seen, in this environment!"*

I paused a little in delivering that call, because I had always reserved the "toughest SOB" moniker for Stone Cold. But I had no idea how else to describe what I was seeing, or how else to describe the man doing it.

Mick wasn't just great at getting "beat up." He was great at getting beaten down, and then standing back up after. Foley was the guy who took the punishment and kept moving forward. And even though we needed no further evidence of that Foley toughness, Hell in a Cell etched it in stone forever. Mick was the living embodiment of the human spirit in there, and we all saw it live.

> *"If there is a more courageous individual in this sort of environment, I would like, folks, for you to introduce them to us."*

"The truth is, when I reached the top, I was thinking, 'You've got to be kidding me.' Certainly there was no way I could be thrown off that structure and survive. And yet I was, and I did. Today—and wisely so—they'd stop it," Mick said years later on the *Two Man Power Trip* podcast.

And he's right—it would be stopped or not allowed in the first place. Because, sometimes, the toughest people in the world just have to be saved from themselves.

"Aw, sonofabitch . . ."

June 7, 1999
The Higher Power, Monday Night Raw
The FleetCenter
Boston, Massachusetts

1999. Britney Spears blew up (not literally). *The Matrix* changed action sequences and sci-fi forever; fingerboards were small skateboards for your, uh, your fingers; and WWF went from family business to a publicly traded company.

WWF's meteoric rise in popularity led Vince to launch an IPO on the New York Stock Exchange that year, which yielded a $170 million infusion of capital right out of the gate. For a man who bought the company from his father (and other minority owners) for one million dollars, paid in monthly installments, this was a huge day in the McMahon family history, and the history of professional wrestling.

When Vince got control of WWF in 1982, and aggressively went into expansion mode across the US, he hadn't cared whose toes he stepped on, or what traditional agreements the promoters back then had with each other—Vince wasn't his father, and he didn't see the future of professional wrestling like these guys saw the future of professional wrestling. And watching Vince ring that opening bell on the NYSE, how can anyone say he wasn't right all along? I'd personally watched him navigate the possibility of bankruptcy several times, just a few years before, and here he was doing what no other wrestling promoter in history had been able to do: begin to legitimize our industry in the mainstream business world.

Vince stood before the money minds of the world, representing a business that had clocked up some serious numbers, and he did it on his terms. It was a move that put him and his company on a different level, when his competitors were wavering.

At a time when we were all "Livin' la Vida Loca," it was truly remarkable to watch the ratings pendulum swing from WCW to WWF. We had Austin versus McMahon, the lightning bolt run of The Rock, the birth of DX, the Three Faces of Foley, Head Cheese, and so much more, while WCW was struggling with the NWO's collapse, a generally stale product, and a lack of new faces in their main event scene.

With the threat of losing the Monday Night War in his rearview, Vince began to insulate WWF (or as he would later call it, the "WWE Universe") from the rest of the business and build his own fiefdom.

As the company grew, and McMahon's power rose with it, more and more people on the creative side strived to tailor the show to Vince instead of the audience. Now, a lot of time what they thought Vince wanted and what the audience wanted were the same thing. But sometimes they weren't. And the duality of Vince was he could be a shark in the boardroom and a teenage boy in the writers' room.

So, for me, 1999 was the start of some really nonsensical storylines that made me think for the first time that we might be on the wrong path creatively as a company.

To be fair, I guess over the course of programming fifty-two weeks a year of nonstop live shows, sometimes you get magic like The Undertaker and Kane saga, but other times, you get, how do I say, shit. But in the year we witnessed the rise of peak storytelling from *The Sopranos,* the contribution to the form we offered up was "the Higher Power" arc.

I came back to work in 1999 after another bout of Bell's palsy that had left me on the sidelines for four months, and on my return, it was clear to me that the company was going through massive changes again behind the scenes. As everything began to move in WWF's favor on the corporate level, creatively we were chasing shock over substance and quick hits over longer-term arcs. While WCW was putting out content that suffered from a lack of direction, we were beginning to put out content that suffered from catering to only one man's direction.

WWE had always been Vince's vision, of course, but he always tried to give the people what they wanted, whether it was to his personal taste or not. But now Vince's own tastes were showing up more and more on-air, unchallenged.

Would you forgive me if I was to remind you (do you need reminding?) of a certain angle in 2002 that involved a car crash, a secret, a funeral home, and sex in a coffin?

Now, for those who don't know the Katie Vick storyline, I believe it involved one wrestler having sex with the corpse of another wrestler's girlfriend to get him angry. I can't be sure, because there's no way I'm going back to watch that, but it was something along those lines. I just remember the story was so bad that I instinctively tried to turn off the channel when I saw it, even though I was live on-air at the time. I was shocked, at both the subject matter and the fact that so many grown people planned it, shot it, edited it, without any of them saying, "Mmm, this is offensively dumb." Or maybe they did, but they just didn't say it to Vince.

Well, 1999 was a banner year for that kind of approach. That's also the year we produced the Kennel from Hell match. Listen, the only thing I can say about the Kennel from Hell match is that we never tried to repeat it. Who knew that surrounding a cage with dogs, while placing a cell over the cage, as one wrestler hung another from that cell with a noose, would have been a truly awful idea?

But whereas the Kennel from Hell was a one-and-done concept gone wrong, the Higher Power happened week after week, and after we had been on such a creative roll. Not everyone would agree with the gritty and in-your-face path the company had taken (me included, sometimes), but there was no denying it was working. All the numbers that mattered were spiking, with ratings and revenue peaking at new record levels, and all that came from us being able to execute episodic, long-term storylines with engaging, fleshed-out characters on our flagship show.

But something was starting to not work. Just small stuff. Subtle things. Lack of vision. Lack of planning. We were taking our eye off the ball, and moving more and more toward a week-by-week approach in the storytelling instead of the long-term booking that had served us so well.

And that's what the Higher Power angle signaled to me more than anything.

OK, I can't type around it anymore, so let's take a look at that angle, shall we?

(Forgive me if I go from Good 'Ol JR here into Red Ass JR as I relive this.)

Like all good stories, it started with The Undertaker sacrificing people. Then Undertaker put together a faction of guys called The Ministry of Darkness, who began a feud with Vince's own faction called The Corporation. Somehow Undertaker ended up facing his brother Kane in an inferno match, which is a normal match but with flames. Anyway, midway through this match, The Undertaker and Kane's father, Paul Bearer, came to ringside with a teddy bear, which Undertaker proceeded to burn on the flames at ringside. This, naturally, made Mr. McMahon cry, because that teddy belonged to his daughter, Stephanie (who is now a grown woman), and everyone was sad. So we were fighting over a teddy bear at this point. After that, there was really only one way to go, and that's have The Undertaker kidnap Stephanie and try to sacrifice her. Huh? Anyway, then The Undertaker told McMahon that he, Undertaker, answered to a Higher Power.

You know what—in going back for this book, I'm reminded of how Mark Calaway has made so much challenging material work over the years. No matter what was asked of him as The Undertaker, I have never seen him complain, never seen him not give it his all. But even he had to read this manure and shake his head every Monday before he went through the curtains. Thing is, if he did, the professional in him would never let anyone know.

So, where were we? Right. Burned teddy, kidnapping, and more than a subtle nod to witchcraft and satanic rituals.

I should mention, this was the same year we had a storyline where The Big Boss Man pulled Big Show's newly dead father through a graveyard after attaching his car to the freshly dead gentleman's coffin. That's the same Big Boss Man who also served Al Snow a nice meal that turned out to be Al's beloved dog (yes, that was in 1999, too). Which I bring up here to say: this wasn't one bad, disjointed storyline; this was a run of them, all in the same vein, all around the same time.

Anyway, so Undertaker kidnaps Stephanie to sacrifice her on a cross in the middle of the ring to marry her. Because that's how sacrifices work. Then Mr. McMahon's team and The Undertaker's team join forces, and reveal they're going to bring "the Higher Power" to WWF.

And would you believe it, that last bit actually created some heavy buzz.

All we needed to do was plan it out and deliver, so that the end of this story was worth the journey to get there. For weeks fans were speculating all over the still-kinda-new thing called the internet about who would be revealed as the new big star in WWF. Everyone from Raven to Jake "The Snake" Roberts were rumored to be the Higher Power. And then, one fine Monday night in June, it was time to find out.

Out came Undertaker flanked by his boys. And then came showtime. Months of build. The lights went out and everyone, except Undertaker, knelt in the ring as the cloaked and hooded "Higher Power" walked to ringside, while monks chanted over the loudspeakers. I had no idea who it was, and didn't want to know. I wanted to find out with the fans, and react accordingly.

And then the lights came up and "the Higher Power" pulled back his hood to reveal . . . that it was Vince under there. And it sucked all the oxygen out of the building.

| *"Aw, sonofabitch . . ."* |

I said it on-air because I meant it.

I knew we couldn't hit them all out of the park, but with our competition fading, were we even trying to anymore?

"Chyna has made history! Chyna, the first woman to become the Intercontinental Champion!"

October 17, 1999
Chyna vs. Jeff Jarrett, No Mercy
Gund Arena
Cleveland, Ohio

In 1999, it honestly felt like everything was up for grabs. It was a wild time, mostly because WWF had now hit the mainstream. Our superstars were appearing on every TV show from *Nash Bridges* to *Deep Space Nine*, and featuring on the cover of every magazine from *TV Guide* to *Playboy*.

Wrestling was hot as hell, with ECW finding a home for their weekly show on TNN, to WWF adding another live two-hour show on UPN called *SmackDown*. And in a sign of the times, our flagship show, *Raw*, hit its highest rating ever (a record that still stands) when a Rock and Mick Foley segment delivered a monster 8.1 rating. We were a long way from the 1.6 we'd gotten just a few years before.

We were now a couple of years into our Attitude Era—with a couple more years still left in the tank—and our outrageous storylines and larger-than-life characters were keeping us ahead of WCW in the ratings in a meaningful way. This led to a change of leadership in World Champion-ship Wrestling, as Eric Bischoff was ousted and our former head writers at WWF, Vince Russo and Ed Ferrera, headed to Atlanta to fill that void.

While others were focused on the numbers and the backroom reshuf-fles, I kept my eye firmly on the roster, signing WCW standout Chris Jericho to our already stacked ranks. My pitch to Chris was simple: our downside guaranteed contracts were making more millionaires than I'd ever seen in wrestling, and after Jericho signed, he saw firsthand how accu-rate my pitch to him was.

With all the opportunities out there to make money, our wrestlers wanted to make that hay while that sun shone bright. It was a time of rapid growth, home runs, mistakes, and experimentation throughout the company—and that left a lot of opportunity for new approaches to be taken, new alliances to be formed, and old boundaries to be challenged.

Massive growth led the business to, once again, go through rapid change, as everyone in the office chased a bigger Nielsen number and everyone in the locker room chased a bigger bonus number. But with a show that featured "Stone Cold" Steve Austin, The Rock, Mick Foley, The Undertaker, HHH, the McMahons, and so many more, just how do you stand out?

Well, I guess if you're standing in a field of "athletic tens"—a phrase Vince used for women who looked like supermodels but could move in the ring—you stand out by being 5'10" and two hundred pounds of muscle who answers to the nickname "The Ninth Wonder of the World."

And if she didn't stand out enough already, Joanie "Chyna" Laurer had another way she wanted to carve her own path in the company: she didn't want to wrestle women anymore.

Now, here's the thing. I'm not a huge fan of inter-gender wrestling. I just don't like to watch men being aggressive toward women on our shows. I do understand that there are people out there who feel differently, and I understand their positions, too. It's a taste thing—a preference, if you will. But in 1999, I was head of talent relations, and having the biggest in-ring star in her division telling you that she no longer wanted to work with any of the other talent in that division wasn't a clash of tastes; it was a huge blow for the already struggling-for-parity women's division. But Chyna was in a relationship with Triple H, a man who had the ear of Vince McMahon— which wasn't a bad thing, because Hunter had great instincts—so she had political cover.

Against my wishes, Chyna got her way, and was featured in the men's division whenever possible. I could see Joanie's side of it, as it would mean more spotlight for her, but the women's division losing its biggest star meant less focus for the women in general.

And in this weird time, the only woman who was "allowed" to wrestle with the men was about to do so in a "Good Housekeeping" match. That's right—Chyna's opponent, Jeff Jarrett, wanted her to "understand the role of a woman" and challenged her to a gimmick match that revolved around housecleaning.

So what's that, one step forward, one step back?

In the buildup, Jarrett had been physically attacking all the women on the roster, proclaiming, "I'll put you all back in your place."

I guess the only good thing you could say about this was that Jarrett was clearly written to be the ignorant jackass who was going to be defeated by the strong crusading woman in the end. Lines like "women are weak and men are the dominant species" were designed to enrage the audience *and* to set the stage for us to crown a new champion. And at the No Mercy PPV, that's exactly what we set out to do.

> *"Chyna has one thing on her mind: revenge for herself. And to walk out of here as the first woman in WWF history to be the Intercontinental Champion. That is Chyna's goal . . ."*

Chyna was changing how women were seen in wrestling, the audience was cheering her on, and the company was actively steering it. But I couldn't help but think there had to be a better way to elevate a truly unique and powerful woman than hitting her over the head with an ironing board.

"Chyna, the first woman to enter the Royal Rumble, the first woman to qualify in the King of the Ring tournament. But will she be the first woman to wear intercontinental gold? We're going to find out right here, right now, tonight!"

And with the Good Housekeeping match underway, Jeff and Chyna proceeded to beat the living hell out of each other with household implements like mops, garbage cans, a frying pan, a toilet seat, a stick of salami, a flounder fish, and the dreaded whipped cream.

As we hit the middle of the match, Chyna used kitchen tongs to grab Jarrett by his little Jeffs, and proceeded to *literally* pie face him.

"I've never seen anything like this in my life. I'll never forget this night. And they just wasted two good pies!"

It was goofy, it was silly—if you wanted to know just how subtle wrestling can be, Chyna hit Jarrett with an actual kitchen sink for a close two count—but the audience seemed into most of it, and the end would justify the means.

Backward and forward they went with every trick in the book, and adding some new ones, like incorporating cake mix, a banana, and a pot. They even went with a finish where Chyna lost initially, but they restarted the match because Jarrett won the fall with the title belt, which was deemed not a "household item" and therefore illegal.

After the restart, Chyna quickly blasted Jeff over the head with his own guitar (which was deemed a household item, I guess?) and scored the pinfall.

"Chyna has made history! Chyna, the first woman to become the Intercontinental Champion!!"

Chyna was the first woman to ever win that title, and so far the only woman, too, in the forty-plus years the title's been in existence.

A couple of years later, Joanie left WWF when she sought the same money in her contract renewal as Steve Austin. The Ninth Wonder of the World wouldn't waver on her terms, and in the end it broke my heart to be unable to renew her deal.

Unfortunately, Joanie never found the same happiness in her life that she did during her run in WWF. She'd had a chaotic childhood and carried a lot of trauma with her—which she talked about a lot with me in our quieter moments together. In WWF, she found a place where she was happy, famous, and earning big money.

But then in 2016, tragically, her substance misuse issues got the best of her.

I mightn't like inter-gender wrestling, but I do like what it brought us: Chyna's name sitting alongside such Intercontinental Champions as Pat Patterson, The Rock, Steve Austin, Shawn Michaels, Bret "Hitman" Hart, and so many more. She earned her reputation as the biggest female star in the Attitude Era and was truly a trendsetter, a trailblazer, and a pioneer that will be remembered for many years to come.

"How do you learn to fall off a damn ladder?"

August 27, 2000
Tables, Ladders, and Chairs, SummerSlam
PNC Arena
Raleigh, North Carolina

2000 was a risk and reward year. The turn of the millennium brought the chameleon, multi-hyphenate of wrestling Chris Jericho to WWF, after having inked the deal a few months before. Jericho had no idea what leaving WCW was going to bring, but considering that over twenty years later he's still a main event player, commentator, sounding board, tutor, and many other things in AEW, I'd say his risk paid off.

The year 2000 was also when Mick Foley ended his amazing run of matches with Triple H in a retirement match that didn't go his way. Mick, like most in our business, would come back a short time later and continue to wrestle on and off for WWE, and others, for many more years. But in 2000 his body had earned the break, and nobody could begrudge any Face of Foley—whether that was Dude Love, Cactus Jack, or Mankind—seeing out the rest of his career any way he wanted to.

WCW was crumbling under the weight of political maneuvering behind the scenes, and a destabilizing merry-go-round of leadership at the top led them further into a creative and financial spiral.

And while the guaranteed contract main-eventers in WCW were beginning to age out of their roles, the top of our roster was stacked with talent eager to work hard and earn big, led by the likes of The Rock, Triple H, Undertaker, Jericho, Kurt Angle, Eddie Guerrero, Kane, Big Show, and Steve Austin. But as hungry as our top talent was, it was in our tag division where the biggest risks led to the biggest rewards of the year.

Betting on yourself is something you have to embrace in wrestling, and in life in general, I feel. You try to make your gamble as calculated and controlled as possible, but nothing in life is a guarantee; that's why, when you get your chance, you'd better "maximize your minutes" and make sure you leave your mark.

Sometimes in wrestling those chances were taken on the business side of the curtain, and sometimes, like during SummerSlam 2000, they were very much taken on the ring side of that curtain.

And as the head of talent relations, I winced at those risks the most. Getting to know our guys on a personal level really left me with a strong desire to see them be safe, be smart, and remain healthy. After all, the "professional" part of professional wrestling is the bit where you get paid. And your options are quickly and drastically cut in that regard if you can't make it to the next show, or the next town.

But pro wrestlers have pushed the boundaries of what was thought to be possible since the beginning. Year after year, talent after talent, new and jaw-dropping ways to entertain have been introduced all around the world.

A lot of it was dangerous. And that's why I had mixed feelings when I heard there was going to be the first-ever Tables, Ladders, and Chairs match at SummerSlam. Especially when I heard who was going to be in that match: Edge and Christian versus The Hardy Boyz (Matt and Jeff) versus The Dudley Boyz (Bubba Ray and D-Von).

I mean, I was worried about all the men, but particularly The Hardy Boyz, because I knew the match was in their home state of North Carolina and they would do everything and anything to make it spectacular.

You add to that the desire all six men had to move up the card and make bigger names for themselves, and let's just say I walked into the building with a little trepidation.

I saw a lot of our guys do risky stuff, and do it amazingly well, but most of the time they had a blueprint of how to pull it off because someone else had already done something similar that they could learn from. If it's never been done before, that ups the chances of something going wrong, because nobody knows how it's going to play out.

Even though we imagined these six hungry, creative guys might innovate in this unique environment, nobody really had any idea just how amazing it would be. I mean, I guess the breadcrumbs were there, because these guys had a fantastic build where they blended tables, then ladders, then chairs into their matches in the weeks leading to the event. The story being told was each team had a "speciality" weapon, with the Dudleys smashing their opponents through tables, the Hardys assaulting the other teams with ladders, and Edge and Christian terrorizing everyone with chair shots.

And so a new match was born.

The stage was set on one of the biggest nights of the year, and all three teams were finally standing in the ring, ready to make a name for themselves and burn the memory of their match into the minds of wrestling fans around the world.

Me being one of them.

> *"The goal here is to incapacitate your opponent to the degree that a ladder can be set up . . . and climbed . . . and those tag team belts can be pulled down."*

It was like the Joie Chitwood Thrill Show from the first second the bell rang. Chairs were flung in the opening seconds into people's faces. But the real carnage began with Bubba Ray catching Christian high on the ladder and taking him for a long drop back to the canvas in the most unconventional way.

> *"For the love of God, did you see that!? Good God almighty. Bubba Dudley used that Full Nelson into a . . . almost an Atomic Drop. That was unreal. That just jammed Christian's spine!"*

And before anyone could take another breath, Jeff Hardy fell backward off one ladder, onto another, which in turn seesawed upward, smacking his brother in the face.

> *"How do you learn to fall off a damn ladder? You don't! It looks like a car wreck!"*

There's no test-runs in a match like that. You can't go out in the afternoon before the crowd comes in to see how it all might feel. In a match like this, you do it live for the first time, every time. And that's what they did.

Bodies, ladders, and chairs were all twisted into one messy scene in the ring, and we were only about three minutes into the match. For all we knew, that could have been all this match had to offer, as nobody had competed in a TLC match before, much less perfected one. We hadn't seen too many of the three-team match concept without the TLC, never mind with. And those Damn Dudleys signaled for the introduction of tables!

> *"I feel some wood coming on . . . Here comes D-Von with one of those Dudleyville tables . . . Eliminating everyone who's living and breathing!"*

And with the stack of tables set up at ringside, and more slid into the ring, we had all our ingredients in the stew: six talented, hungry wrestlers; unlimited chairs; several tables; and rows of ladders, each one bigger than the next.

With innovative move after innovated move, all six men began to put it all on the line in bolder and more creative ways.

Jeff launched himself off the ladder on the outside, crashing through the tables. And then the biggest man in the match, Bubba Ray Dudley, climbed to the top of the ladder—only for it to be tipped over, spilling Bubba over the top rope and through the stack of tables left ringside.

> *"GOOD GOD! A human body from twenty feet in the air, through four tables!! I have never seen carnage like this!"*

Then Matt suffered a similar fate when he was thrown backward from the ladder to the outside, too. And this left a pathway for Edge and Christian to climb the ladder and retain their titles.

> *"Edge and Christian have done it! . . . I don't think I've ever seen anything quite like what we've just witnessed. These six young studs put their careers on the line for everybody watching around the world here tonight."*

I can honestly say that there's only three matches I didn't see coming. One was Hulk Hogan versus The Rock at WrestleMania 18—which I write about in *Under the Black Hat*—when the audience led the match, and both wrestlers, in a direction completely opposite the one that was planned. Another was Steve Austin versus Bret Hart, where they managed to pull off the perfect double turn, which I write about in this book. And the last one was this match.

I'd like to think King and I called the hell out of it because, sitting there, I was a fan with the greatest seat in the house. Edge and Christian, the Hardys, and the Dudleys overachieved to a staggering degree. They weren't main event guys, but they went into a tag team situation on a stacked SummerSlam card and stole the show with a match that was so innovative and violent, so fresh and thrilling, that it spawned not only rematches, but a whole brand, too, with WWE naming a yearly PPV TLC many years later.

As head of talent relations, I was worried they were willing to take on too much risk, but sitting back now, with the luxury of time, I'm not only proud of what those men achieved then. I'm also proud of what they've gone on to achieve in their careers since.

This time, the risk was worth it.

And I've never been happier that it was.

"Damn Triple H! Damn his soul!!"

January 8, 2001
Steve Austin vs. Kurt Angle, Monday Night Raw
San Jose Arena
San Jose, California

The best gift a broadcaster can give the number-one bad guy in wrestling is their full, unadulterated boiling venom and disgust. Now, Jim Ross likes Paul Levesque, but Good Ol' JR had a special kind of hatred for that vile and despicable human being, Triple H. Even though it was over twenty years ago, the fans remind me all the time of just how many times I called that man a son of a bitch over the course of Triple H's great run as the lead villain on WWE programming. And, boy oh boy, did that son of a bitch deserve it.

On WWE screens he broke my arm, he retired Mick Foley, he slept with Kane's girlfriend, who just happened to be . . . you know, let's forget that one. But there's a long list of despicable acts and reasons why "The Game" triggered such bile in yours truly. And that's the biggest compliment I can give him.

For our heroes to remain heroes, they need bad guys to beat. They need dragons to slay, and from about 1999 to 2006, there was no bigger dragon than Hunter Hearst Helmsley. And that's because, at that time, nobody in the wrestling business put more effort into being despised, and Hunter being a son of a bitch, and me calling him out on it, seemed to go hand in hand for a good chunk of his run at the top of the card. Still to this day, people won't believe me when I tell them that I like Hunter, and I think he's been a huge positive for the business inside and outside the ring.

Hunter was so meticulously sound in the ring that it's no surprise that he's brought that same level of detail to his leadership role in WWE. Triple H knew how to make the belts mean something when he was a wrestler, and he knows how to make them mean something now that he's head of creative in WWE.

When he was active in-ring, he focused on the story and the build, and now that he's booking, I can see that same approach running through WWE's whole programming.

But I guess, in 2001, my opinion of the man came from a very different place. His success as lead heel came from his commitment to making people believe, and I went along for the ride with him in that regard. When you see someone putting out that kind of performance, as a broadcaster you want to keep up. You want to be able to carry your load in terms of telling the story. And you want to make the audience at home feel what our audience in the arena is feeling—and that was pure hatred for "The King of Kings."

Triple H wanted nothing more than for the audience to hate his guts. And I wanted nothing more than to do my part to make that happen. Especially after one of his dastardly acts was to orchestrate Steve Austin being run over by a vehicle backstage—putting my friend out of action for months.

Originally it was revealed to be the dyed-blond, thicc Samoan Rikishi who took Austin out, but when that storyline went nowhere, it was decided to have Triple H reveal himself as the mastermind, who was pulling the strings all along.

This revelation, of course, led to a bitter rivalry between Austin and Hunter, which led to Steve getting revenge by lifting Hunter's car, with Triple H still in it, high into the air with a forklift and dumping it all the way down onto the concrete below.

With regard to trying to kill each other, they seemed kind of even up to that point.

This led to the main event of *Raw* in 2001, when Stone Cold Steve Austin went up against former Olympic gold medalist and all-around ass-kicker Kurt Angle in a WWF title match. In the midst of a hellacious match, Angle and Austin were fighting toward the finish, and the audience seemed ready for Stone Cold to once again become the WWF Champion. The Texas Rattlesnake struck with a Stone Cold Stunner, and the audience popped in joyous acknowledgment. It was now just the formality of the referee's three count to crown Steve the new champion.

1 . . . 2 . . .

But the WWF official suddenly disappeared from the frame, having been yanked swiftly and suddenly from the ring before he could complete his count—by none other than a returning Triple H.

Time to go to work.

> *"Wait a minute, that's Triple H! That son of a bitch!*
> *Austin had that match won. Triple H assaulted*
> *the referee but Austin had the title won!"*

Hunter then completed his mission of making sure Steve didn't win the title that night by eliminating the referee completely with a solid right hand to the face.

> *"Austin had the title won, and there goes the referee.*
> *Triple H just assaulted the referee . . . Damn Triple*
> *H. Damn his soul! . . . This is not right!"*

Triple H backed up the ramp, still running his mouth, and with the referee down and no chance of winning anyway, Austin threw Angle out of the ring and summoned "The Game" to come back. Stone Cold wanted to settle their business right there and then in the middle of the ring.

"Austin telling 'The Game' to get his ass into the ring!
Austin wants Helmsley. 'The Game' has screwed Stone
Cold out of the WWE, by God, title . . . Well, let's get
it on here. You cost Austin the title, you bastard!!"

Hunter was seething, too. He walked back to the ring and climbed the steps slowly as he and Austin stared each other down. Both men expertly listened to the audience, letting the anticipation of a fight build and build, as I threw some gasoline on an already-white-hot situation.

"Get in there and fight him. You screwed him out of the title.
There ain't no anchor tied to his ass. Get in there and fight him,
'Game'!! . . . You can feel it! You can see it! You can taste it!!"

And then the biggest heel and the biggest babyface in the entire business ran toward each other like Kong and Godzilla, greeting each other with punches in a sudden act of violence, one man trying to lay dominance over the other.

"And, by God, there they go! Rights and lefts, no
referee! Austin just got screwed out of the title,
and now he's whipping 'The Game's' ass! Austin
kicking 'The Game's' ass right out of the ring!"

I might have called Triple H "The Cerebral Assassin," but nobody beat "The Toughest SOB in WWE," Steve Austin, in a fistfight. The Rattlesnake unloaded some furious right hands until outside the ring the brawl went, Austin in full control. That is, until Hunter found the steel pipe he'd planted at ringside—and proceeded to crack The Rattlesnake right in the head with it.

Austin's limp body slid over our announce table as King and I stood as far back from the fight as our headset cables would allow.

> *"'The Game' just hit Austin right in the head with a steel pipe. The son of a bitch has hit him in the head with a steel pipe! What the hell is this?! Austin got hit right between the eyes with that lead pipe!! For God's sakes. Austin is busted wide open. Austin is bleeding like an animal."*

And Hunter wasn't finished yet. He proceeded to assault Austin with the pipe a couple more times, until Steve lay prone on our announce table and Triple H stood over his limp body in celebration.

> *"Good God almighty, Austin hit the face twice, three, times with that pipe. For the love of God, somebody stop this! 'The Game' has busted Austin open. 'The Game' has cost Austin the WWE title."*

I had no idea at the time, but in framing Austin and Hunter, the TV camera also caught me looking up at "The Game" with venom in my eyes and bile in my voice. In that moment it wasn't an act for me. I was living it, feeling it, as I described it to the people at home.

> *"Damn you, Helmsley! Damn you! Damn you! Damn you all to hell, Triple H, you son of a bitch! Austin just got cost his dream. Austin's dream is over. Triple H, you son of a bitch!!"*

Hunter was so good at being bad that I guess he made me believe, too.

"The Million Dollar Princess has become a Dairy Queen!"

August 20, 2001
Milk-O-Mania, Monday Night Raw
Arco Arena
Sacramento, California

The longer I live, the more I realize just how important family is. In my younger years, when I was trying to make a name for myself, I spent a lot of time away from my kids in the pursuit of earning extra money on the road, and that's time I know I'll never get back. And even though my kids and I have a great relationship now, it's become so clear to me that everything else—money, power, fame—pales in comparison to family. I consider myself one of the lucky ones who saw that before it was too late. I've seen time and again how this business can come between families if you let it.

And nobody is immune, not even the family at the top of it all.

In 2001, the first iPod and Xbox were released, everyone was watching *Friends* or *SpongeBob SquarePants*, and *Gladiator* won the Best Picture Oscar.

It was also the year that WCW went out of business.

Many reasons come to mind as to why, but it was clear to me as someone who ran talent relations that they should have been creating new stars back when they had the chance. They depended too heavily on bringing in ex-WWF talent—including our ex-creative talent—and never looked to the future. As the main event scene grew stale, the fans demanded something new, and WCW had nothing lined up to give them.

In the end, they sank under the weight of their guaranteed contracts, which had to be paid no matter how much the box office was dwindling. Top talent and executives turned on each other, and political lines were drawn in the dressing room and the boardroom, until eventually there was nothing left for them to fight over.

It was done.

The Monday Night War was over.

Wrestling's hot streak was now all WWF's hot streak, as that year ECW, too, went bankrupt and closed its doors. The little engine that could ran out of money as they tried to scale to keep up, and it eventually broke them.

After WCW and ECW both folded, Vince bought all their intellectual property and tape libraries, and began to run an ill-fated Invasion angle on his TV shows where "ECW" and "WCW" tried to take over WWE.

For the first time in wrestling's history, there was no competition. But on WWE TV, we could pretend there was. We could write a story that kept both defunct companies alive on our show.

It was a storyline that also offered Vince a chance to keep his two kids, Shane and Stephanie, front and center with him, as storyline owners of WCW and ECW, coming to remove their father from atop the wrestling business.

Vince loved nothing more than mixing his family into the soap opera–style stories, particularly if it pitted the actually close-knit McMahon family against each other on TV. But it's not like the kids were given special treatment, or couldn't hold up their end of the deal when it came to showtime.

Through the Attitude Era, Stephanie was second only to her father, Vince, when it came to being the best heel in the business. Considering she'd only been on-screen for two years at that point, that's a big claim to make, but she was a natural like Vince when it came time to turn on that performance. Father and daughter both had that tone, body English, and command that made them easy to dislike in their roles.

It helps that both also relished the opportunity to get the audience to hate them. They were a little different there, because I think Vince would tell you that he has a "screw you" attitude baked into his DNA, whereas Stephanie has a kinder, more sensitive demeanor when the cameras are off. But whenever we went live, she excelled in what was a new role in wrestling—one that hadn't been played out, or even seen before—that of the boss's daughter.

Vince McMahon asked a lot of his performers, but he was notorious for never asking for something he wouldn't do himself. Whether it be dangerous, humiliating, or downright stupid, the McMahons in general were never afraid to "show their ass" on TV. (I got a real up-close look at Vince's ass once in front of thousands in attendance and millions watching at home, but more on that special memory for me in *Under the Black Hat*.) And as hard as Vince was on his staff, he was even more so toward his family.

The Old Man made sure both Stephanie and her brother, Shane, started low down in WWE and worked whatever jobs needed to be done as they went through school. If an employee made a mistake somewhere, Vince could be tough, but not as tough as he was on his kids in terms of them delivering on his expectations.

Whether or not I would have personally done it that way, the end result was that when Shane and Stephanie first appeared on TV, they already had great minds for the business and were eager to prove themselves.

Shane was willing to do anything, and I do mean anything. He'd climb the stages and jump off, take the worst beatings, and put himself in all kinds of legitimate danger to get that crowd pop. Or maybe it was to get a hug from his father. I'm not sure what motivated some of the crazy stuff he did, but if it was for love and affection, then, coming from someone who had a hard-ass father myself, I can understand it.

Whereas Shane was on the outside trying to fight his way into his father's good graces, Stephanie was the Golden Child. Vince saw her as the future of the business, and she was groomed for that position from the first moment she appeared backstage.

Both kids felt pressure in different ways. Shane was all about the stunts, but his sister was all about the performance, and at the beginning of her journey, she'd never let her clout backstage take the sting out of any medicine her character had to take. Whether it was being verbally humiliated, or having her clothes torn off—as, unfortunately, was a staple for women in wrestling at that time—Stephanie never said no to getting what she "deserved" in the end. As a matter of fact, the only time I've ever heard of her saying no to a "creative" idea is when she became pregnant in real life and her father proposed that he be revealed on TV as the father of her baby.

So, Stephanie was ready, during the Invasion angle, alongside her heel Alliance (the combined WCW and ECW rosters), to take her medicine in a most unusual way.

One night in California, during an over-the-top appreciation (ass-kissing) night for the now corporate suck-up "Stone Cold" Steve Austin (that's right, it still breaks my heart: The Texas Rattlesnake made a deal with the devil himself and went from being a thorn in WWF corporate's side to a jewel in their crown), the straitlaced American Hero Kurt Angle drove up to the ring in a milk wagon.

The Alliance were halfway through a rendition of "Wind Beneath My Wings" for Stone Cold when Angle, thankfully, proceeded to take the hose attached to the wagon and drench the ring with a hydrant-like blast of fresh milk.

> "Milk-o-mania is running wild! It's milkman madness, by God! . . . The Million Dollar Princess has become the Dairy Queen!"

Inside the ring, Stephanie and all her "employees" overdramatically flopped and slid around like they were being hit with rubber bullets in a ring made of banana peels. Then Kurt climbed to the top of the truck to rip open a couple of cold cartons of milk and chugged them down, in a wholesome reenactment of Austin's usual post-match beer bash celebrations, as the crowd went wild.

> *"Look at Kurt Angle standing on top of the milk wagon. And now he's pulling out the heavy stuff. It's HOMOGENIZED."*

The Invasion angle was a flop, but this particular chapter of it tends to stand out in the fans' minds as an all-time classic moment. When I think of this night, though, I think of the atmosphere afterward with Stephanie and Vince laughing about it backstage. I remember it being a close moment between family members, in the middle of a corporate empire.

No matter the money, no matter the "prize," there's nothing more precious in life than your bond with your family.

Stephanie went on from getting hosed down by Kurt in the Attitude Era to, in 2022, becoming co-CEO of WWE when Vince retired, after allegedly engaging in repeated unprofessional behavior as WWE's CEO. Then, in early 2023, when Vince returned as chairman of the board, Stephanie resigned as co-CEO, leaving WWE completely.

Vince made a deal with Endeavor to merge WWE and UFC into one publicly traded company worth twenty-one billion dollars shortly thereafter.

Hearing what's going on from the outside, after years of observing them from the inside, it seems the McMahon family is more divided than ever. And I honestly have no idea what Vince's motivation was in coming back and flaming up all the embarrassment and scrutiny again for his family. WWE was doing well in his absence. Stock was up, ratings and revenue were up, and a sales deal was looking likely in his absence.

But maybe that's why he returned.

I just have no idea what dollar amount or percentage of an ego boost is worth seemingly dividing a family. How much money is enough? How much control does one person need in life?

I dunno, I guess sometimes money and success and power just makes relationships—and the people in them—less happy?

I have no idea what will become of the McMahon family. Maybe this is all just business around the dinner table. But I suspect not.

Putting milk trucks and memories aside for a minute, my hope for the McMahon family at the end of this so called "civil war" is that business matters will take the appropriate place in their lives.

The grandchildren deserve better.

I hope the McMahons are some of the lucky ones, who see what's important before it's too late.

"Oh, he's talkin', he's walkin'!"

July 16, 2001
Steve Austin vs. The Alliance, Monday Night Raw
Providence Civic Center
Providence, Rhode Island

At its core, wrestling is a marketing business, and like all marketing businesses, its effectiveness is judged solely on the buy-in of its customer base. Everyone backstage knows this—we live and die on the reaction of the crowd. Their response is the greatest market research we have, and if we're smart as a business, we listen to it more than anything else that might guide us. Red hot financials are nice, but they usually tell you that you've done something that worked in the past. A red hot crowd tells you you're doing something that's working right now.

Anything that grows week to week and year to year needs constant calibration and reinvention; that's the push and pull of the relationship between company and fan. Down through the years, I've seen bookers and owners push all their chips in on someone who looks great on a poster, but then the audience rejects them as soon as they get in the ring. Conversely, I've seen crowds pick a talent that a company isn't featuring prominently enough for their liking—and the people take it upon themselves to elevate that wrestler with their voice and merch muscle.

This push and pull between fan and company can lead to some over-thinking, to say the least. And that was encapsulated perfectly for me in the Invasion angle, where WWF's two rival companies began to "invade" our show.

It was a perfect case study in how overthinking and underthinking can affect a character, an angle, and a couple of different companies along the way.

When Crockett bought Mid-South, the idea was to keep his own company and the new company he was buying totally separate. He wanted to do so because owning both, and all the talent that entailed, would give him a unique position in the wrestling business. He could have both companies feud against each other, and have a PPV blow-off once a year where the wrestlers from both would finally fight each other. After all, it was one thing to have creative control over two guys in one match; to have total control over two companies elevated the sense of rivalry to a degree you usually only saw in sporting events.

In entertainment terms, it was like owning both Marvel and DC Comics. If you have one fan base who supports one brand, and another base that supports the other, the chance to pay to see who would "win" might be a proposition too tempting for both those fan bases to turn down.

Vince McMahon in 2001, just like Crockett in 1987, had the opportunity to make "dream matches" and cash in on the immense interest that such a position could bring. But unlike Crockett, Vince didn't only purchase one "rival" company—he purchased two, WCW and ECW. He now owned three rosters. Three world titles. And three distinct brands.

Yet it all culminated in one giant fart because creative began by telling the story of WWF being invaded by having the WWF guys defeat the invading forces—which, remember, Vince owned now, too—at every turn.

Maybe Vince was out to prove how much better WWF was than the companies he had already outlasted, outdrew in the ratings, and ultimately bought and owned in real life. But when it came to storytelling, it made no sense. If your hero—be it a person or, as in this scenario, a company—is never in any real jeopardy, then it's impossible to generate any emotion from your fans. No real stakes means no real investment in the outcome. And the fans were telling us online and in the arenas that they wanted something completely different than the one-sided affair we were giving them.

Now, there were external issues, like the WCW brand being badly damaged and a lot of their top stars deciding not to come to WWF right away because they were on guaranteed contracts after the buyout and didn't want to stop cashing their million-dollar checks from home to come work on the road for WWF for three hundred dates a year.

But still, even with all those hurdles in place, we could have done better to deliver the dream matches and scenarios that the fans expected now that one brand of characters had all of a sudden teleported to the same universe as their long-term rivals.

Simply put, even though we now owned WCW and the smaller, but rabidly popular, Extreme Championship Wrestling (now known collectively as The Alliance), we continued to see them as the brands we needed to dominate to prove we were the number-one company. And we did it over and over again, despite audience reaction.

As the Invasion angle was coming to a close, we did take the time to recalibrate the perception of our top star, "Stone Cold" Steve Austin, who had been suffering from overthinking at the other end of the scale. Just before the Invasion began, Steve—the biggest draw in the world, a pure box-office machine—was worried about becoming stale or complacent, so, at WrestleMania 17, he turned heel. It was a move neither Vince nor I agreed with him on, but with everything Steve brought to the company, McMahon felt he owed it to his biggest draw to at least try.

The turn produced some great TV, where Austin went from beating his best friend, poor Ol' JR, into a bloody mess, to forming a comic duo with Kurt Angle where they competed for Vince's attention. However, overall, the people just didn't want to boo Steve, no matter what he did. And as the Invasion angle began to fizzle and come to an end, a chance to course correct Austin's character arc raised its head.

When it came down to the final battle between WWF and The Alliance, Steve decided to rejoin team WWF just in time to help us fight off the (flaccid) threat of the invaders winning the war (or something) and reestablish our dominance (that we never once relinquished).

After some will-he-won't-he setup over the course of the show, WWF's biggest star showed up to join the fight against the outsiders that he had previously aligned himself with, lighting those sons of bitches up with a pool cue and a Stone Cold Stunner for everyone who got in his way.

And boy were the fans hot for this one.

The "AUSTIN" chants rang loud and long through the arena before Stone Cold even appeared. Then the glass broke, and he stomped his way to the ring striking anything that moved—and the people were coming unglued in the stands. It was genuinely one of the biggest pops I'd ever heard in my career.

> *"Oh, he's talkin', he's walkin'! The BMF walk!*
> *The Rattlesnake is back! Stone Cold Steve Austin*
> *is striking anything that by God moves!"*

It did this old Okie good amidst the bad storytelling to see Stone Cold Steve Austin coming back from the dead. Now, that might seem a little dramatic, as Austin never left our screens, but as anyone who saw that walk to the ring might tell you—it was pure excitement and mayhem as The Texas Rattlesnake came back to where he belonged, as the attitudinal babyface who kicked ass. Steve was a John Wayne–like character, and I thought making major TV persona changes would harm Steve's audience perception. Can you imagine Stone Cold as a hated TV villain? Me, neither. Guess our audience felt the same. Because that night, when he stormed into the ring, the reaction was up there with the most passionate I've ever heard.

> *"Austin has parted the Red Sea . . . STUNNER!*
> *ANOTHER STUNNER . . . THE WHOLE GAME*
> *CHANGED WHEN AUSTIN CAME OUT HERE.*
> *THE TEXAS RATTLESNAKE IS ON FIRE!!!"*

And after the ring was cleared of twenty or so Alliance members, and Austin's iconic music hit, the crowd got even louder.

I was hoping that hitting the reset button on Austin's babyface reputation would work.

Sometimes it doesn't work.

But the fans wanted the established Rattlesnake, and gave him one of the loudest ovations I've heard to this day.

They were ready for his attitudinal homecoming.

And, by God, so was I.

"AUSTIN HAS INVIGORATED THE WWF.
THE RATTLESNAKE IS BACK."

"God, what impact! What impact!"

April 21, 2002
Eddie Guerrero vs. Rob Van Dam, Backlash
Hy-Vee Arena
Kansas City, Missouri

Wrestling can be a story of triumph or a story of heartbreak. A lot of times, if you're around long enough, it can be both.

But to get a shot at any kind of triumph at all, you first have to get in the door, and breaking through in wrestling is a hard puzzle to crack sometimes. I see young wrestlers all the time wondering how to get noticed, how to stand out in a business full of people trying to stand out. Sometimes they go for some hair dye. Other times it's a new tattoo. They convince themselves that to be memorable they should be easily, physically identifiable.

And that approach can definitely work for people. Bam Bam Bigelow was a four-hundred-pound high-flyer with flames tattooed on his skull. Sheamus was an Irish ass-kicker with pale white skin and a ten-inch ginger mohawk. And Gangrel was a vampire character who superglued press-on nails onto his real teeth before later getting actual fangs made and bonded into his mouth.

These men knew they needed to stand out because there's always been a kind of litmus test in WWE. It was something I knew well, too, as head of talent relations: it was always easier for me to sell Vince McMahon on a wrestler if that same wrestler could "turn heads in an airport." Was there something about that person that just stood out in the crowd and made other people take notice? Usually that thing would be height. There was nothing McMahon loved more than a guy over six feet. Better still if the height came with a shredded upper body to match. No two ways about it, Vince loved guys that would cause people to stare whenever they walked into a terminal.

And because of that airport litmus test, I had a real hard time filling the WWE roster with people who could actually get it done in the ring, sometimes. We've had some amazing talents who just happened to be physical specimens. Brock Lesnar, Dave Bautista, John Cena, Hulk Hogan, Bill Goldberg, Scott Steiner, Triple H, and many, many more all knew how to command an audience and give them a helluva show while also being head turners in public. But not every big guy is as coordinated or charismatic or explosive as the men above.

Then, through a perfect storm of Vince buying up a lot of smaller wrestler contracts in the WCW and ECW deals, and a lot of WWE's biggest draws retiring or aging out of the live event grind, 2002 was the year we found our list of smaller guys on the roster just grew organically.

Not that I was consumed by anyone's size either way when it came to hiring. I was more interested in potential, reliability, and having good people in our locker room. But Vince's preferences meant I had a hard time, sometimes, getting him to take a look at wrestlers who didn't fit his mold. But the one guy in particular that Vince went out of his way to tell me how "tiny" he was in real life ended up being the biggest undersized star in the business: Eddie Guerrero.

A man who I knew could triumph if given the opportunity.

Now, I brought a few guys to Vince's house over the years, because I knew the boss would be resistant to signing them based on their stats alone. Eddie came with me to the McMansion in Connecticut in 2000, in an effort to get Vince to see past the tape measure and connect with the man instead. Eddie didn't have tattoos or a red mohawk, but he had a natural charisma that I hoped would grab Vince. Because I knew it sure as hell would grab an audience.

After our meeting, the boss said that if I believed in him, then I should think about hiring him. What was there to think about? "Latino Heat" was five-eight and 210 pounds of Mexican magic that I couldn't wait to get started on our roster. He might not have been the tallest or heaviest, but he came with everything that made wrestlers great: charisma for days, timing, a keen ear for the audience, and a fundamental understanding of how to get the biggest response—and when to seek it.

And he learned it all as a child, growing up as part of the trailblazing Guerrero family from El Paso, Texas.

Eddie was the youngest son of Lucha pioneer Gory Guerrero, and became a wrestler just like his brothers Chavo, Mando, and Hector. Eddie's mother had three brothers who were also wrestlers, and his uncle, Chavo Junior, was also a prominent name.

But while all the Guerreros were talented, Eddie was the most talented of them all.

While Eddie came with an abundance of skill, he came with some challenges, too, especially issues with alcohol and painkillers. And it was for those very same issues that I had to let Eddie go, one year after hiring him and watching him triumph within WWE, when he was arrested for drunk driving in 2001. We tried to help him get the help he needed, but Eddie was adamant he wanted to do the work by himself.

And that's why it was all the sweeter when "Latino Heat" came back clean and sober, in 2002, to attack former ECW standout and Intercontinental Champion Rob Van Dam from behind.

Eddie was back after the heartbreak, clearheaded and full of fire.

And his attack earned him a PPV title match with Rob.

> *"Guerrero just planted Van Dam with a neck breaker right on the Intercontinental Title . . . Guerrero with a look of confidence on his face . . . Guerrero on top— look at Van Dam's positioning. Can Eddie Guerrero*

even reach him? . . . God, what impact! What impact!
And Eddie Guerrero has just defeated RVD!"

The triumph returned, and the whole business was cheering for Eddie to succeed—not just in wrestling, but in life. That charisma I told Vince about, that ability to connect with people, it brought Guerrero an army of fans and colleagues who rooted for him on his journey.

After he won the Intercontinental Championship, Eddie moved to *SmackDown*, a show I wasn't calling at that time. Even though my voice wasn't accompanying Eddie's journey in WWE anymore, I was with him every step of the way behind the scenes.

And Vince became a huge fan of Eddie's along the way, too. He loved that Eddie could work with anybody and make it real. When all the top talents went to Vince and asked to work with Guerrero, it made McMahon see him in a different light.

Eddie might not have been a giant, but he didn't want to be known or labeled as a cruiserweight, because of the hard ceiling that kind of label can put on a person's upward mobility. He was a main-event star who just happened to be smaller than everyone else in that bracket—and he worked in such a way that his size never became part of the story he was telling.

Seriously, go find the Lesnar match with Eddie from the Cow Palace, and you'll see exactly what I'm talking about. He beat the Viking destroyer, Brock Lesnar, to become WWE Champion in that match, and a lot of grizzled veterans cried, me being one of them, at the sight of Eddie fulfilling his lifelong dream of becoming the top star in the world's biggest company.

An absolute triumph, after a lot of heartbreak.

It was a shift in attitude, a shift in focus, and a shift in what makes a wrestler a "WWE Superstar." Eddie was being given the most prized possession that Vince McMahon had. To me, it was the most impressive redemption story in WWE history, on both sides of the curtain.

Even though I wasn't commentating on the *SmackDown* brand, and I didn't get the pleasure of calling Eddie's rise to world champion, I felt a personal pride in what I was seeing. And it continued to feel personal when

Eddie's demons caught back up with him again near the end of his young life. He and I would sit in a closed dressing room while Eddie read me his favorite bible passages to try to give himself some perspective, some relief from the torrent in his head at that time.

And there was more heartbreak yet to come. Eddie died at just thirty-eight years old from underlying atherosclerotic cardiovascular disease.

I will remember Eddie as a top ten talent of all time. A man who walked the path of giants so many others his size could follow. When we look at AEW and WWE right now, both locker rooms are full of men and women who have charisma, athleticism, and passion. Size might add to presentation, but it certainly isn't the top priority like it once was. And that's because of talents like Eddie who smashed the mold in our business for good.

I'm glad that, before he passed, Eddie got to experience all those moments on top. He got to feel what it was like to defy the odds and not only arrive, but arrive in a way that vastly overdelivered.

I was there when Eddie was on top; I know what an impact he had at that time, in our company. And now, when I see the younger wrestlers like Sammy Guevara or Sasha Banks mimic his moves in the ring, I also know what impact he's still having, on this generation, in all companies—and in every division, too.

Triumph after the heartbreak.

"Climb the ladder, kid! Make yourself famous!"

July 1, 2002

The Undertaker vs. Jeff Hardy, Monday Night Raw

Verizon Wireless Arena

Manchester, New Hampshire

If you get stuck in your comfort zone, you begin to die. It's true of life, and it's also true of wrestling. I've seen it so many times, it's become one of the main things I task new wrestlers to be aware of as they move through their careers. The best talents are always pushing themselves out of their comfort zone, to stay as far ahead of the game as they possibly can, for as long as they can.

And in 2002, a great example of that philosophy led to one of the most unexpectedly memorable *Raw* title matches in history.

It was a year where everything was still kinda Linkin Park-y and Nickleback-y. It was also the year of the sequel, with Harry Potter and Lord of the Rings giving us the second installments of their huge franchises, and the year *American Idol* popped up and never went away again (although I will admit to loving certain talent shows, and maybe even having a little cry whenever someone gets the Golden Buzzer on *America's Got Talent*).

In wrestling, Shawn Michaels returned to the ring after a four-year absence, and Brock Lesnar, Randy Orton, Dave Bautista, and John Cena, men who would go on to become the backbone of the company for decades to come, debuted out of our developmental system.

As a company, we were now out of the Attitude Era and into the Ruthless Aggression Era. We were gradually moving away from the more hot-button parts of our shows, highlighting the in-ring action a little more and the controversial topics a little less. This rebranding came after a lawsuit from the World Wildlife Fund forced WWF to become WWE, and the company used the opportunity to rethink its next moves.

Those next moves also involved a "brand extension," where separate rosters were drawn up for *Raw* and *SmackDown* as a way of giving more names more time over the four hours (it's five now) of main roster live TV WWE was producing per week.

2002 was also the year that The Undertaker got one of his rare runs as WWE Champion, after defeating Hulk Hogan for the title in a match that wasn't all that well received at the time. Both men tried, but Hogan's back and age were really starting to limit what he could do in there, which was never more evident than when 'Taker tried to get Hulk up in the air for his choke-slam—and Hogan's boots barely left the mat.

It was a slow, uncoordinated bout that couldn't end too soon.

Still, the match seemed to light a fire under 'Taker, who wanted to show the world just how good he was by toning down the more outlandish parts of the character and upping the more realistic side of his personality. This decision would allow 'Taker to go on to produce some of the greatest matches in wrestling history, on some of the biggest stages ever. But in 2002, he was a bully champion, ready to ground and pound anyone who stepped in his path.

And at the beginning of July that year, the person in front of him was the tag-team specialist, fan favorite, and charismatic enigma Jeff Hardy.

Jeff was a handsome risk-taker who had a connection with the crowd even though he never spoke that much. He made his debut at sixteen, but first began to feature prominently, with his brother, Matt, as part of The Hardy Boyz in 1998. In 2002 The Hardy Boyz broke up on-screen, and WWE was interested in seeing if Jeff could become a star in the singles division—but had no idea how to get him there.

So up stepped The Undertaker to help Jeff move outside his comfort zone as a tag team wrestler, while 'Taker moved outside his comfort zone by agreeing to Jeff's specialty at that time—a ladder match. Now, I don't know how many six-ten, three-hundred-pound men like to climb, wrestle on, and fall off a sixteen-foot ladder, but Undertaker was not one of those men. He hated doing this match so much that it was his only ladder match in a thirty-five-year career. But he knew it was the optimal setting to highlight Jeff's more flashy, daredevil style, so a ladder match it was.

Now, in pro wrestling, there's usually a winner and a loser, but when you control the outcome for both guys, you can have the loser leave more elevated in the fans' eyes than when he walked in. And for me, this match not only showcased how great both Undertaker and Jeff were between the ropes, but also let the world see just how amazing Undertaker was at telling the stories that complement his matches. And the premise of this match was one as old as the business itself: one takes the victory, and one takes victory in defeat.

Or, one goes over, one gets over.

Now, that has been a saying in our business for as long as I can remember. And it signifies the best outcome, the one you get when all the pieces of what we do click together—but it's hard as all hell to pull off unless you're an egoless veteran who can pull all the levers that are necessary in a skillful and timely manner.

Now, you've probably read some other chapter before this one where 'Taker showed up, and he was probably sacrificing people. However, by 2002, with the tone of the WWE as a company changing, The Undertaker, as was his tendency, changed right along with it. And it was no surprise to anyone who knew him what he could bring to the ring when he was positioned to do so. This is why Mark had such an amazing career with just one character in WWE. He was able to adjust and overcome all the fads, changes, and eras to keep his work fresh, varied—and always at the top of the card.

In my view, he's WWE's greatest character ever.

And despite Undertaker being the champion, he understood that this was a decision to put the shine on Jeff and his daredevil skill set, to give him hope against the much bigger, much stronger champion.

> *"This will be the biggest train wreck in history, or the biggest upset in history . . . There you see the title, hanging high above the ring, King . . . In this matchup there are no pitfalls, no submissions, there are no disqualifications, nor count-outs. There's one way to win, that's by climbing the ladder and securing the undisputed championship belt that hangs high above the center of the ring."*

I like to know as little as possible before a show so my reactions out there are real and unrehearsed, but when that bell rang, I could tell immediately that Undertaker had a hand in laying out the match itself. He was always fully engaged in what he did, and who he did it with, but I could tell he was involved mostly because of the story they were telling. It was deliberate, building, and paced in a way that made the audience wait as long as possible—without ever losing them—before hitting the higher gears.

I could also tell that, under the beating he was receiving, Jeff Hardy was excited to have been given the opportunity to wrestle The Undertaker in a one-on-one match on *Raw*, live.

All signs pointed to this one being a classic.

Through hellacious bumps and stiff chair shots, Hardy and 'Taker made the audience believe. They made me believe, too. Deep into the match, the towering champion had the opportunity to win but instead chose to inflict some more punishment on the now-defenseless challenger.

And he did it by press slamming him right on the announce table in front of us.

"What are you doing? You're breaking this kid in half . . .
I'm not trying to provoke him [The Undertaker], but
there's another human being being destroyed in front
of our very eyes, and some of us give a damn!"

The bully champion didn't care. As a matter of fact, I think he liked dismantling his opponent piece by piece. And as he upped his punishment of Hardy, the crowd grew more and more sympathetic toward the handsome, young challenger.

Then Hardy landed a desperate hit in 'Taker's big Texan balls.

And with that the audience roared in hope.

Hardy grabbed a ladder, dragged his broken body up every rung.

"Jeff Hardy can live his dream. Jeff Hardy can make
history. This could be the biggest upset ever . . . his body
wracked with pain, trying to climb the ladder."

But the dastardly Undertaker cut him off, and lifted Hardy's wilting body high in the air—only for Jeff to turn Undertaker's move against him and flip the champion out of the ring, far away from being able to stop him this time.

The crowd stomped to their collective feet and filled the arena with their pleas for Hardy to climb again.

"Go for it! Go for it! Climb your ass off! . . . Jeff
Hardy is a step or two away from history."

But no. Here comes the double-tough champion again to cut the challenger's journey off with a stair chair to his back.

"Jeff Hardy is close. He's—what a vile shot to the spine by The
Undertaker . . . Undertaker said Jeff Hardy wasn't going to
walk out of here. He may be right, but again he may be wrong."

And just as I said it, Hardy cracked Undertaker across the head with the chair 'Taker had introduced to the no-disqualification match.

> *"He hit The Undertaker in the head! It may be the night! It may be the biggest night! . . . Oh, God almighty! A knockout shot . . . Climb the ladder, kid; make yourself famous! Jeff Hardy is in pain from head to toe. He's inches away from immortality!!"*

I felt every second of that match, because I got lost in it. The passion of it, the will to win. Undertaker beat that kid in the ring and around the ring with everything he had. And still, there was Jeff, pulling himself up the ladder in the closing moments. But alas, it wasn't to be.

> *"And The Undertaker with a choke-slam off the ladder has won one helluva fight. This match took a tremendous amount out of The Undertaker, and poor Jeff Hardy gave us everything he had."*

Outweighed, outmatched, outgunned from the beginning, the much smaller challenger showed the world that he's as tough as they come and possessed the heart of a fighter. And they loved him for it.

But the last act happened after the match. Jeff stood, defeated but defiant, only for 'Taker to put him down again and take the ramp out of there. But before Undertaker could leave, Hardy, unable to stand, called him back once again, telling The Deadman that he hadn't broken him. 'Taker returned as the audience pleaded with the champion not to inflict any more pain on the barely conscious challenger.

Undertaker pulled him to his feet, balled his fist—but instead of punching Hardy in the face, raised Jeff's hand in a sign of respect.

And with that little piece of business, the story was told.

And the challenger, now broken out of his tag-team-only mold, was suddenly seen as a main-event player.

Jeff went on over the course of his career to become a six-time world champion across a few different companies. But it was that magical night on *Raw* where the battered challenger's heart won everyone over—even the bully champion.

This was two men, at completely different stages in their careers, moving past their comfort zones on live TV—and it created a match, a career, and a call that fans never forgot.

"The pride of Edna, raised a country boy down in Texas, grew up wanting to be here, wanting to do this. This is his life; this is his destiny."

March 30, 2003
Steve Austin vs. The Rock, WrestleMania 19
Safeco Field
Seattle, Washington

For wrestling history, WrestleMania 19 was monumental. As "Stone Cold" Steve Austin walked down the aisle to the ring that night, surrounded by 54,000 people, there were only a few in the whole place that knew the match was his last.

Vince, who was producing him, knew.

The Rock, who he was wrestling, knew.

And I, who was praising him, knew.

"He has earned the reputation as the toughest son of a bitch in WWE!"

The biggest draw in professional wrestling history was stomping down to the ring one last time, after leading the hottest streak in WWE's existence. But the road to get there was the most bizarre road to WrestleMania I'd ever seen.

WWE was, and is still, a pressure cooker. It's truly live, without a net, both a live event experience and a TV show at the same time. On any given week, in any given town, the pressure to nail many live broadcasts, over and over again, can be overwhelming. But when you're talking about delivering the biggest PPV of the year in WrestleMania, that pressure cooker can suddenly blow.

We call WrestleMania many things, but "Showcase of the Immortals" is probably the one that the talent can relate to most, because, as they're keenly aware, if you're lucky enough to be booked at WrestleMania, then whatever you do is likely to live in wrestling history forever.

That thought motivates some people, but it can overwhelm others.

Now, I'm not sure why there was more pressure in the air in the run-up to WrestleMania 19 than ever before, but it sure made for a stressful time to be heading talent relations.

Injuries ran rampant through our roster, with Edge out for a year with a broken neck, and Randy Orton and Dave Bautista both injured in the same match, where Randy broke his ankle and Dave tore his triceps. We brought in a huge WCW veteran in Scott Steiner to work with Triple H, but it fell apart because of a myriad of injuries Scott was carrying, which ultimately limited his ability to work like we'd hoped. And Kurt Angle, who won an Olympic gold medal with a freaking broken neck, was banged up so badly that he couldn't be involved in any physicality in the lead-up to his WrestleMania match with Brock Lesnar. All of these serious injuries plus the usual knocks and nagging war wounds led to reshuffling, rethinking, and replanning aplenty.

And it wasn't just in-ring where things were getting a little weird and hairy. Behind the scenes, two of our top writers, Brian Gewirtz and Paul Heyman, were suspended after a scuffle backstage over the creative direction of our shows.

Add to that Ric Flair throwing punches at Eric Bischoff because of how Ric felt Eric treated him years before in WCW, and I began to wonder if there was something weird in the WWE water.

All of this was happening during a time when ratings were dropping, and mainstream attention for our brand was lessening at the point in the year when it usually began to peak. And as a touring troupe, we were hurting, tired, injured, and stressed. The Ruthless Aggression era was beginning to sputter, and we could all feel it.

But the guy who felt the pressure the most, and was limping along the worst, was the guy who had been pulling the wagon the hardest: "Stone Cold" Steve Austin.

Steve's body was giving out on him after years of working all the main events, doing all the promotion, and carrying all the stress that being the top name on the billing of a touring company brings. Never off the road, never allowing himself an off night, he was always the last one out of the building, and always the first name PR people requested when promotion was needed. It was nonstop: never home, no time to recover, just hit the next town, days blurring together. On to the next *Raw*, build to the next PPV. Ice things that needed more attention. Always on. Always on call.

And it burned him out, both mentally and physically.

Being the headline attraction of WWE's busiest, craziest, most profitable, and most expansive time ever eventually ran Steve right into the wall.

He'd reached his limit.

If anyone had earned the right to sail off into the sunset, it was him. But that's not what he wanted. Austin wanted to retire with only three people knowing about it in advance. He didn't want any fuss, or any celebration of his career and achievements, because he felt he was letting people down by having to step away.

As WrestleMania drew closer, Austin pushed himself too hard, dehydrated his body too much, and was struck with panic attacks so severe, he ended up in the ER the night before his final match.

But he did what he always did—he got up and walked through whatever issue was in his way to make the booking.

So WrestleMania 19 was going to be historic, but the audience didn't know it at the time. They were just there to see two of the biggest draws in the history of the business, Rock and Austin, finishing out their Wrestle-Mania trilogy.

And despite the stress and the uncertainty, and Steve's ER visit and impending retirement, both men gave it everything they had. Austin left the newly Hollywood-minted Rock with a victory to end their Wrestle-Mania trilogy. And when the match was over, the 1A and 1B of the Attitude Era lay side by side, covered in sweat, and took a moment with each other.

Rock leaned down into Austin's ear, and whispered so the cameras couldn't hear, "I can't thank you enough for everything you've done. I love you."

"I love you, too," Austin replied.

> *"It took three Rock Bottoms, but The Rock has finally broken the jinx . . . You are looking, ladies and gentlemen, at perhaps two of the greatest, when all is said and done, that this business will have ever offered you."*

And with that, Steve pulled himself from the mat and began his walk back up the ramp, toward a retirement that his worn body and spent mind put in motion.

One that he didn't want to have to take.

When I saw Austin leaving, I had to fight back tears more than at any other time in my career. I was emotionally spent. Not just because of the drama of the match, as it ebbed and flowed, twisted and turned—but because it was the end of The Rattlesnake. The end of the monster pops, the *visceral* audience reactions, the mayhem, the beer drinking. The end of the ass-kicking, foul-mouthed, tough-as-nails Texan son of a bitch.

Wherever the giant circus was heading to next, it was going to do its thing without its highest drawing act of all time. But more importantly than that to me, I'd have to do my thing without my friend Steve coming with me.

99.9999 percent of wrestling retirements don't last, unless you get to the age where the good Lord is thinking about tapping you on the shoulder. But I knew Austin was gone forever as a full-time guy. His word was always solid, and when he said it, I knew it was going to stick. And believe me, WWE tried to get him to come back many times, with many Brinks trucks full of money, but it wasn't until almost twenty years later, at WrestleMania 38, that he decided to come back for a one-off singles match.

Steve Austin was thirty-eight years old when he bowed out after his match with The Rock. And he left in time for his body to bounce back to normal, and his previously broken neck to heal to the point where it doesn't bother him on a day-to-day basis. Steve leaving then made sure he ended up in a position few wrestlers from previous generations did, which was healthy and wealthy in his life after wrestling.

In 2003, Austin literally pulled himself from a hospital bed that morning to walk into Safeco Field that night, because he wanted to leave in the same way he'd led: with determination, passion, and two middle fingers on show.

> *"There's only one Texas Rattlesnake, and there'll never be another like him."*

"I'd like to see Bischoff get every bone in his body broken and then be left in a bloody heap. Then I'd like to see Kane walk outside the building and get his seven-foot ass run over by a damn truck."

August 11, 2003
Eric Bischoff vs. Kane, Monday Night Raw
The Mark of the Quad Cities
Moline, Illinois

I was never really comfortable playing a character on TV. I just wanted to do my job as a broadcaster as well as I possibly could, but it's always been that the wants of the company come before what Good Ol' JR wants. And as uncomfortable as that made me sometimes, I tried to make whatever creative came my way in that regard the best I possibly could.

I think we all knew some kind of changes were coming when Vince McMahon hugged his old WCW rival Eric Bischoff on the set of *Raw*, as the crowd rained heavy boos down on both men. During the Monday

Night Wars, Eric vowed to put Vince out of business, and even challenged McMahon to fight him on PPV. And yet, here, in 2003, both men shook on a deal for Eric to come work for Vince as the on-screen general manager of the show that beat him.

> *"They're probably picking each other's pockets. I got years in the business and it comes down to Eric Bischoff is my new boss. By God, am I a lucky, fat Oklahoman."*

The Monday Night War was already dead, but this was a visual a lot of people needed to truly believe that a new era of professional wrestling had begun. McMahon was without competition, and he owned everything—including, now, the contract of the man he was hugging, the man who once swore to put Vince out of business.

I guess you've seen me calling what we do a "business" quite a lot in this book. But for all the money, corporate structure, board seats, and balance sheets, boy, it sure does feel personal sometimes. I think it might be because of the weird space we occupy in the general entertainment field. In wrestling, most are "cast" in a role, and then that's not what they do, it's who they are.

If you said Tyson Smith was making an appearance or doing an interview, you might not get much traction. But if you used his "stage name," Kenny Omega, then the fan buy-in would be quite different. It's certainly expected less so these days, but even now a lot of our performers move through the world as the persona you see on TV.

Steve Austin doesn't promote his reality TV shows as Steve Williams, Undertaker isn't on the poster of his speaking tours as Mark Calaway, and even though my black cowboy hat was given to me as on-air costuming (which I originally hated), I've since become so attached to and intertwined with it that I'm not sure where "Good Ol' JR" ends and Jim Ross begins.

In wrestling, a lot of times you aren't given a character to go act, you're given a starting point to inhabit. Omega, Austin, and 'Taker on-screen are more or less who they are backstage (apart from Undertaker shooting lightning bolts from his hands), so, somewhere over the course of their careers, they mixed the "character" they were given into their own DNA.

Or vice versa. If you're around long enough and you inhabit a character every day, year on year, it becomes you, and you become it. And that makes it hard to detach sometimes. Actors play their most famous characters; wrestlers *are* their most famous characters.

How could it not feel personal sometimes?

I've had the company I work for mock my weight, my accent, my looks, my Bell's palsy, and a life-threatening surgery. All of it was done on national TV, and mostly done with the owner "playing" me or laughing along when someone else was sticking the knife in.

And all of it felt damn sure personal.

Other times, the deaths of wrestlers' loved ones were used in storylines to get a bad guy booed. Or someone's real-life struggles with sobriety were put center-stage to add some "realism" to a feud. And it's not just the company coming up with this stuff; sometimes it's talent, too. As I'm writing this, current AEW champion Maxwell Jacob Friedman has stirred up fan reaction online by cutting a promo about his fiancée leaving him, and many can't tell if it's real or not. He's always blended his real life with the story he's telling, and it's been the driving factor behind his whole presentation for a long time. And that's all Max who's doing that.

"Loose Canon" Brian Pillman, back in the day, loved to "method act" his character, too. He once did it so successfully that he swerved Bischoff into agreeing to genuinely fire him to add extra realism to their storyline, only for Pillman to sign with WWE in the meantime.

Wrestling is a weird deal, in that sometimes we all bring our personal lives into the mix "to entertain the people," because the machine needs to be constantly fed.

Over the years, everything was slowly put up for grabs—and it mostly came from the McMahon family themselves, who would do just about anything to get attention for their flagship TV show. Never has one family mined so much of their "personal" lives for ratings in the history of wrestling. And like with anything that's live and fluid, we never really know where the line is until it's crossed. That's a nice way of saying that wrestling, and WWE, has definitely crossed the line in using talent's personal headlines, struggles, love lives, and, sometimes, trauma as part of the show.

Now, sometimes those real elements have added to the overall product, but other times their use has been cheap, tacky, and deplorable—not just in WWE, but in the business in general. I think it's the complex the business has about the "f word" (I mean "fake") that makes it try to overcompensate by loading its programming up with "real" comments and scenarios that add "legitimacy" to the presentation.

And then, sometimes, it's a storyline that you should be sensitive about that comes calling—but in reality, you couldn't care less about. Like when former WCW head honcho Eric Bischoff came to work in WWE as storyline general manager of the brand I was working on.

As a smiling Bischoff walked down the ramp in 2002, I was asked to mine my history again to get heat on Eric for being an asshole. The thinking behind it was if "Good Ol' JR" hated this man, then our audience would hate him that much more. But where I had to completely pull my distain for Triple H out of nowhere, I guess Eric and I actually had some history.

| *"He's ruthless, folks. Very ruthless . . . Jerry, this is surreal."* |

In real life, a decade before, Eric hadn't seen a role for me in WCW, as he'd replaced my old mentor Bill Watts in the top job and felt I wouldn't be loyal. He wanted his own guys in key positions.

I guess I didn't leave with the fondest of memories of Eric, but I'm glad I ended up coming to WWE instead of staying in WCW. At the time my ego felt badly bruised at being taken off the air in WCW—I took it personally. But in the interim, Eric and I closed all our old open wounds over a call, and it was easy to bury the hatchet.

Then, about a decade after I left WCW, that same Eric Bischoff followed me through the looking glass and ended up working for Vince, too. And by the time he landed there, the fans knew our real-life story, but more pointedly, the head honchos knew our real-life story, too. And that's why

I was asked to play Eric's mere existence as something that was personally offensive to me. In reality I had no animosity toward him whatsoever, but if the show needed me to show disgust toward "Easy E," well, let's just say I didn't have to dig too deep in that well.

> *"Well, I tell you what. I've seen a lot of things in this company transpire. I can't tell you what this means to me, personally."*

It was one of those "hell froze over" moments when the man who tried to put the WWE out of business showed up on Vince's TV to hug McMahon and begin his storyline. And I was right there to add my vocal to the music Vince and Eric were playing.

That storyline peaked for me about a year later on August 11, 2003, when it looked like Bischoff might finally get his comeuppance at the hands of the madman Kane, who had set me on fire a few weeks before. (Yes, you read that right.) And like all things in wrestling, it was headed to the ring.

> *"Bischoff is finally, finally going to get what's coming to him. All the people he's screwed over in his life is going to come full circle . . . at the hands of this damn monster."*

And just like that, the floors exploded with fire, and the chained monster, Kane, was brought down the aisle, flanked by police officers, as Eric panicked in the ring. I watched from the announce booth, selling my injuries after being BBQed by "The Big Red Machine," as King asked me what I'd like to see happen from the two guys I "personally" hated getting in the ring.

> *"I'd like to see Bischoff get every bone in his body broken and then be left in a bloody heap. Then I'd like to see Kane walk outside the building and get his seven-foot ass run over by a damn truck."*

As Kane was being unshackled, Eric prayed to the heavens in fear.

> *"I gotta think the good Lord's line is busy where*
> *Bischoff is concerned. But here comes hell."*

Kane got into the ring. And Eric, like the coward he was, lay down, looking for his giant opponent to just pin him and move on. But Kane wasn't having it. He locked his huge hand around Eric's throat, lifted him into the air, and held him high above his head.

> *"Choke-slam him to hell, you freak, you monster!*
> *Choke-slam that son of a bitch all the way to hell!!*
> *CHOKE-SLAM HIM. CHOKE-SLAM HIM!!!"*

I've never had as much fun as I did hating on someone who I didn't hate, but maybe people thought I should have hated, in a storyline where I was set on fire by the person doing my bidding.

Wrestling is strangely personal sometimes.

And then other times it couldn't be further from the truth.

"Two miles of steel chain, and Triple H's blood is a part of it."

August 24, 2003
Elimination Chamber, SummerSlam
America West Arena
Phoenix, Arizona

WWE is a leading man company. It's been in their DNA since day one, and it will probably be their model forever. But what happens when you have a brand split, where you have two shows to serve on two different networks, and you're struggling to find one leading man, much less two?

In 2003, iTunes opened for business, *Friends* announced it was ending its run on TV, Ruben Studdard won the second season of *American Idol*, and WWE was struggling through another transitional period, as the Attitude Era's baby brother, the Ruthless Aggression Era, wasn't shaping up to be nearly as successful.

There was a whole host of talent gone, retired, or put on the shelf— including me, as I suddenly found myself in a long, and sometimes humiliating, period where I was being replaced and fired pretty regularly. The storyline stemmed from Vince's real search to replace me as lead announcer, which, like most things in WWE, began to trickle into the broadcasts.

On the roster side of things, Rock was off to Hollywood and Austin had retired at WrestleMania; the two most popular faces of a generation were gone as full-time talents. The search was on to replace the irreplaceable. As head of talent relations I knew I had some talent on the way up who could be WrestleMania main-event players if given the right creative and the right amount of time, but Rock and Austin were two once-in-a-generation wrestlers who just happened to come along at the same time.

So, while Vince figured out who to throw the weight of the company behind, the likes of Hulk Hogan, Roddy Piper, Scott Steiner, Kevin Nash, and Sable were brought back to the company to bring some name value and maybe some lapsed fans, too. All these names had made tons of money working on top, but they weren't going to be working the live events every week and didn't have the kinds of years left in them to build a company around. So, as we looked for who was going to lead the company into the future, everything was in a state of flux. And while we had Randy Orton, Bautista, Brock Lesnar, and John Cena all at various stages of readiness, we also had a talent in Bill Goldberg who was on a big one-year deal and ready for those open main event slots immediately.

The timing finally looked right for Bill to make a splash in WWE after world champion Triple H picked up a groin tear that made handing the title over make all the more sense. At least in theory.

Goldberg was a fascinating prospect for anyone in wrestling. Bill came to WWE first, fresh off his days as an Atlanta Falcon defensive tackle and ready to make the jump from football to wrestling, but back then we didn't have the system to train someone like him, and Vince didn't have the appetite to pay the big guy the kind of money he was looking for right out of the gate. So Goldberg wound up in WCW, where he became a huge star, because he was "kept clean," booked as an unstoppable monster in the ring who never lost. He definitely began to feel like the one who got away.

But a couple of years after WCW's closing—and after Bill's guaranteed contract with Turner ran out—Goldberg wanted back in the business, and

WWE was the only game in town who could afford his contract. But for a talent to go from being a top guy to the top guy, he needed one special ingredient: commitment from Vince McMahon.

Rock and Austin burned up all the metrics we had; they did numbers Vince and WWE had never seen before. But they'd also put in the time to build that important relationship with Vince that made him comfortable putting all the company's chips on them.

Vince always liked to pick his leading man, then cast the production around him. With Hulk Hogan it was red, white, and blue, Americana, Rock 'n' Wrestle, brother. When Steve Austin came along, it was Attitude Era and all the chaos and anti-authority mayhem it brought with it. The Reality Era that would come next perfectly cast John Cena to lead the company into its publicly traded, more PG phase. And today, through the COVID empty arenas and the streaming age, it's Roman Reigns who toplines the company.

But Vince didn't know Goldberg that way. And he knew he wouldn't get the chance to really build that relationship, as Bill was on a one-year deal.

The thing was, in 2003, we knew how to book a guy like Goldberg. We knew how to get an ass-kicking, bald, no-nonsense guy over. But Bill wasn't a Vince creation like Austin was, so even though he was under contract and officially a WWE Superstar, there was a little hesitation to pull the trigger on him. It didn't seem to matter that the audience clearly wanted that crowning moment for Goldberg in the main event of SummerSlam that year, when he motored through the participants in the Elimination Chamber match to leave just him and Hunter at the end.

The unique nature of the match meant two men started the match while four others waited in plexiglass pods to be introduced into the match "randomly," one at a time. However, with just Bill left in the center of the ring, "The Game" wouldn't leave his plexiglass pod to face the snarling challenger who stood in wait—so Goldberg smashed the pod in a memorable, star-defining moment that left no barrier between the champion and challenger.

> *"Oh my God! Feet and fists. The unbreakable*
> *plexiglass wasn't!. . .Triple H is like a trapped*
> *rat in the corner with nowhere to go."*

Like Jack Nicholson in *The Shining*, Goldberg chopped his way in, before grabbing the stunned champion and beginning to beat his ass in the small pod.

> *"Piston-like right hands by this wrecking machine,*
> *Goldberg! Listen to the crowd chanting for Goldberg!"*

Oh man, I don't know if Bill had the years left in him to be The Guy across an entire era, but that night in Arizona it was clear that the WWE fans wanted him to become champion, to become the badass spearing machine that he once was in WCW.

And they could feel it happening right before their very eyes.

Goldberg pulled Triple H from the destroyed pod and bounced "The Game" around the steel structure of the Elimination Chamber with ease.

> *"Triple H, he's wounded. Two miles of steel chain, and Triple*
> *H's blood is a part of it. God almighty, this is getting ugly . . .*
> *Everything high impact from Goldberg. But remember,*
> *that world title means more to Triple H than life itself."*

The place was electric. Triple H sold for Goldberg as best he could to help erase Bill's dubious creative up to that point. In his early WCW run, Goldberg was a wrecking ball phenomenon, but in his start with WWE he was booked a little more tame, a little more cautiously. There was no run of destruction, no list of notable WWE names he'd destroyed. Goldberg wasn't booked the way fans wanted him to be, which was as the spear-tackling, two-minute match demolisher. But here, "The Game" was selling like the Goldberg of old had finally arrived. And the people loved it.

Then came the moment where the Goldberg character got caught in the tumult of a company in transition. Now, I'm not saying it was right or wrong, just that in booking the finish of the match, it was clear McMahon was reluctant to push his chips all-in on a character he didn't create.

So, just as Goldberg got into his destructive groove, Ric Flair, who was there as Hunter's backup, covertly slid Triple H's trusty sledgehammer into the ring, and as Bill soared through the air to hit his finishing Spear, "The Game" sidestepped and caught Goldberg with a sledgehammer to the head, just as scripted.

> "Wait a minute, that's a sledgehammer! Flair must have handed Triple H that sledgehammer, and he hit Goldberg in the head with it. I don't believe it. Just when it looked like Goldberg had the World's Heavyweight Championship in his grasp, apparently Ric Flair gave 'The Game' that sledgehammer and 'The Game' turned off the lights of Bill Goldberg."

Vince saw enough in Goldberg to make him look strong against his world champion, but hadn't seen enough yet to allow him to beat his world champion. And I guess if you're going to get screwed over by a pair of dastardly heels, then there's no shame at all in losing to a hammer to the head.

Vince didn't yet know who was going to be his leading man going forward—but he did know who wasn't. And this kind of booking just showed that the boss wanted to reserve the right to change his mind, and that meant beating Goldberg, but not cleanly. It was a foot-in, foot-out kind of decision that left WWE's options open going forward. But the momentum and excitement for Goldberg were hard to re-create again during that run.

Bill did win the title from Triple H a short time later, but it was in a match that didn't click, and through no fault of Bill's, his run was kind of short-lived and not all that memorable.

Of course, Vince and Goldberg have done business together several times since 2003, with Bill being perfectly used as an attraction, coming in for one-off matches and special appearances.

And while McMahon never did put all in on the former WCW Heavyweight Champion, Bill made more money in his fifties in WWE than he did at his peak in WCW. So even with initial less than stellar creative, some missed opportunities, and reluctant pushes, I'm guessing there's no hard feelings on either side at the end of the day.

"Lita might have a broken neck, but she's by-God still competing! She's still in the hunt here. That's how bad she wants to win it!"

December 6, 2004
Lita vs. Trish Stratus, Monday Night Raw
Cricket Arena
Charlotte, North Carolina

Like we've seen in this book already, the wrestling business doesn't have the best history when it comes to our women's division. In the early days of the 1930s and '40s, the amazing Mildred Burke could, and would, headline shows and draw numbers. She made her way from the carnivals, where she wrestled men from the crowd for money, to the main event in the 1950s. But when Mildred split from her booker, manager, and husband, Billy Wolfe, in the mid-'50s, she was blacklisted by the NWA in a meeting that Wolfe attended, but Mildred wasn't permitted to because of her sex.

After that era, the most significant woman in wrestling was the new protégé of Burke's ex-husband, The Fabulous Moolah. Moolah was a double-tough world champion who reigned for decades over a division she also booked and managed. Most women who worked in the business in the '60s, '70s, and '80s came through Moolah, and as some who went that route have said, not in a good way. But if you were a female wrestler, and you wanted to get booked, then Moolah was the best conduit, because most of the bookers didn't care how the women were treated; they just brought in "Moolah and her girls" to fill the women's slot on their cards.

As we moved away from "lady wrestlers," as they were called, in the 1990s, the WWF chairman and CEO, Vince McMahon, wanted "athletic tens" on his television show instead. This was a phrase he used for women who looked like supermodels but could move in the ring—with the former being most important and the latter being negotiable. Vince wasn't too worried about the caliber of wrestling those women could bring to the table; he was just focused on the look. If he wanted guys to pass the airport test because of their size, he wanted women to pass that test because of their beauty. All in all, Vince wanted the image of his company to be tall, ripped, sexy, and young.

But even within those tight parameters, we sought to find actual talent.

Sunny, in my opinion, bridged the gap between what wrestling was and what it would come to be for the women's division. She wasn't the most athletic in the ring, but she was smart as just about anyone, having learned the business from the polarizing encyclopedia of professional wrestling, Jim Cornette, in Smoky Mountain. Sunny specialized in getting tag teams who lacked natural charisma to the next level, using her natural appeal to put the focus on whatever team needed attention at that time.

She was unique in that she was a heel manager whose job it was to stand at ringside and advise and cheerlead through the match, then usually help her team cheat at the end—but didn't really take bumps. And that was kind of a time-honored tradition in our business: if you were the bad guy manager running your mouth on the outside, sooner or later you got a punch in the face from the hero to pop the crowd. Sunny didn't do that, and yet she was a definite boon for any talents that got to work with her.

Over the course of that same period in the '90s, we brought in the enigmatic, cigar-smoking Marlena, who completed the presentation of the androgynous and mysterious Goldust character. Both Dustin and Terri, who played Goldust and Marlena, were 100 percent committed to making their duo bold, brash, and a lightning rod for attention—and sometimes controversy.

But I think the peak of Vince's "athletic ten" era was the hiring of Sable in 1997. She came into the company because her husband at the time, Marc Mero, had a meeting with Vince about joining the company. (Rena, Sable's real-life alter ego, is now married to Brock Lesnar.) When Vince saw Marc's wife, he immediately became more interested in getting her on TV than Marc. He said to me after the meeting that Sable was the bigger star, and he wanted to get her on TV as soon as possible.

And Vince was right.

Sable popped huge minute-by-minute ratings for WWF, even when she was only on-screen to sell T-shirts. In very short order we knew we had a bona fide star on our hands, even though the timeline from Sable's first WWF meeting to her TV debut was a very short runway indeed. Usually it takes time to train someone to an executable TV standard. And even after that, it can take years for some people to get over, and most never get over to the level the non-trained Sable got over to in no time at all.

But it wasn't all about the glitz and the glamour in the women's division. We also had women who could go in the ring—and none more so than Jackie Moore. Jackie mightn't have made the biggest splash of the Attitude Era, or be a first pick on people's Mount Rushmore of Women's Wrestling, but let me tell you, she was the most valuable woman I ever hired. Jackie was never late, was always a professional, and could wrestle anybody of any gender that you wanted to book her with. She looked believable in there with just about anyone because she wasn't pretending. Jackie was no-nonsense, hard-hitting, fundamentally sound, a pleasure to be around, and always made a difference.

I was thrilled she made the WWE Hall of Fame in 2016, and I despise the fact that people say she was in the Hall of Fame because they "had" to induct a woman, and a Black woman was "even better." That's bullshit. She was inducted in the Hall of Fame because of all of her years of service to the wrestling business, and how much she contributed to legitimizing the women's division. Jackie (or Jacqueline, as she was known on TV) walked so the women's rosters of today could soar.

But the two standout difference-makers of this era in the ring were Trish Stratus and Lita. Both women came in to the company having traveled wildly different paths—Trish coming straight in from fitness modeling, and Lita joining us from the Mexican wrestling scene. Like most women back then, they both ended up in supporting roles, managing separate tag teams at ringside. But over time, both broke out of those roles with surprising results.

Sometimes, in wrestling, your "look" can give you more opportunities than your talent level might warrant. But sometimes, your look can limit the roles you're considered for, too.

For Trish, it was the latter.

Her blonde fitness model good looks held her back from what she considered the more viable paths for her in WWE. Trish didn't want to just look pretty; she wanted to wrestle, and felt she had something to prove. To her credit, she busted out of the box she was put in by being consistent, patient, and, most of all, talented as all hell. At the start, she did what was asked of her, smiled and waved, but in the background, she was working her ass off to become a wrestler.

And, boy, did she succeed.

Across the locker room, Lita, a tattooed redhead, was brought in as the eye-catching valet, too. However, Lita could do flashy, high-flying Lucha moves, which meant she spent a lot more time flying off the turnbuckle than doing headlocks on the mat. But it was when she was paired with The Hardy Boyz tag team that her talent really came into focus. As hugely popular as that legendary team of brothers was, Lita managed to not only hold her own, but grow to be a fully equal drawing member of the threesome dubbed Team Xtreme.

Like all the women of that era, Lita and Trish paid their dues, earned their money, and worked as hard as anyone—male or female—in the company. And on December 6, 2004, they became the first women to main-event WWE's flagship show, *Monday Night Raw*.

That night, some of the guys in the back were uneasy. Wrestling is a male-driven world, and those at the top made the most money. Trish and Lita had pushed for their main event slot, as they felt (rightly so) that their heated, soap opera–like storyline warranted it. After months of build that involved marriages, miscarriages, backstabbing, broken noses, and Trish treating Lita to months of physical and verbal abuse, they promised to deliver in not just the quality of the match, but in the coveted ratings, too.

Their pitch didn't seem to garner much steam until Stephanie McMahon pushed hard behind the scenes, and to a lot of people's surprise, Vince okayed the first female main event in his flagship show's history.

I think Vince liked the women betting on themselves so prominently. He knew, as I knew, and as the women knew, too, that you need to be careful what you wish for sometimes in life. If Lita and Trish didn't deliver a rating in that top slot, then it would give the naysayers all the ammunition in the world to make sure women main-eventing *Raw* never happened again.

Both Trish and Lita still wanted the baton.

And when their entrance music played that night to finish off the show, it felt like we were heading reluctantly into a new era. The women were about to step into the hallowed time slot that was usually reserved for The Rock or Steve Austin—who were both very supportive—and they needed to deliver.

I know the whole women's locker room wanted to move the business past the time of The Fabulous Moolah and beyond "athletic tens" to begin the march to something better. They wanted young girls watching at home to see what they were doing. They wanted what the guys have had in this business since the beginning: the opportunity to look great, sound great—but still kick ass in the ring when the bell rang.

Which is what those two did.

They broke the mold.

They ate the pressure, and delivered.

Back then I had no idea how long the "trend" of women in WWE main events was going to last, but I knew that times were changing for the better yet again. The guys who were complaining backstage were told under no uncertain terms that they needed to work harder to catch this new crop of hungry, talented women. And to stop complaining. As with most things in life, some got it, and some didn't.

It was a slow road to change the company was on, but at least it was on it.

Since then, the WWE and wrestling in general has made strides in evolving the role of women on-screen and in the ring. It's not unusual to find women main-eventing not only our TV shows, but PPVs, too. After Trish and Lita came a slew of amazingly talented women who were judged on their skill as well as their "look." And AEW has worked hard recruiting the right talent to give that new division the best chance of shining through. From Britt Baker to Jade Cargill, Ruby Riott to Jamie Hayter, AEW's building in that division is just beginning, but the future looks stronger than it ever has.

I've seen a lot of changes with regard to women in our business over fifty years, and I couldn't be happier to say that the most unique thing about women's wrestling main-eventing and stealing the show is that it's not unique at all anymore. And in large part, it all grew from the seeds planted on this night, when risks were taken in a slot that would help move the women's division forward or backward, depending on the outcome.

They killed it.

"The three-hundred-and-seventeen pounder is hungry. He is thirsty for the World's Heavyweight Championship."

April 3, 2005
Triple H vs. Batista, WrestleMania 21
Staples Center
Los Angeles, California

Professional wrestling has been loved by presidents and movie stars, musicians and writers, from the beginning. From Abe Lincoln to Slipknot, Matthew McConaughey to Bob Dylan, George H. W. Bush to Timothée Chalamet, our corner of the entertainment world has entertained and influenced celebrity names across the spectrum. And it's not just performers who appreciate what we do. Our business model itself has been aped by reality TV, political discourse, boxing promotion, and Mixed Martial Artists.

Yet we've always been the outsiders of the entertainment business.

Maybe that's why Vince decided that WrestleMania 21 would be "Going Hollywood" in 2005 at the sold-out Staples Center—to begin a charm offensive in the entertainment capital of the world. Vince wanted to remove the stigma of what people thought we did, and bring his company from the outhouse of entertainment to the penthouse.

Now, 2004 had some bright spots for sure, but it was generally a down year for WWE in terms of their creative output. For fans of WWE's over-the-top storylines, it was a rough twelve months, but I guess for the more hard-core fan, it was a welcome change of pace, as WWE TV concentrated more on the matches than the mayhem, and more on the athleticism than the soap opera. This change in direction led to Eddie Guerrero and his friend Chris Benoit, both smaller, more technical wrestlers, winning the world titles that year. And while the matches were great, the sizzle to go with that kind of steak was missing—and Vince liked the sizzle more than the steak.

So, in 2005, Vince wanted to reset and revert back to his usual tastes. Vince's usual tastes usually meant tall, jacked, hot, and fresh.

Basically, me.

I mean, basically the *opposite* of me.

I knew my clock was ticking with WWE. About a year before, I was "promoted" out of my role as head of talent relations, and it was becoming more and more clear that my time as a full-time broadcaster in WWE was also limited. Vince wanted a younger, less southern, more photogenic face to be the lead broadcaster of his company. And because Vince's preferences involved someone without my face, my age, and accent, I was probably out of the running to replace me.

So because my boss was once again trying to hire another broadcaster to finally move me on, I felt more than lucky to still be sitting at ringside for WrestleMania, to see two of my developmental hires ascend to the top of the business in the same night I was heading down.

2005 wasn't only a wild year for me. It also saw former WCW Champion and yoga guru Diamond Dallas Page sue Jay-Z for using the Diamond Cutter hand sign that DDP had trademarked years before. I cried when I heard Destiny's Child broke up—while so did Brad and Jen. Break up, not cry. Well, I'm sure they cried, too. It was that year, too, when we collectively learned that John Cena and Dave Bautista had that star potential that was just too present to deny. And we learned it at the event titled "WrestleMania Goes Hollywood."

With WrestleMania heading to one of the world's major media markets, Vince reverted back to type and made his two world title matches at that show true heavyweight affairs. With the glare of late-night and morning shows on his company, gone were the smaller champions and underdog stories of 2004, and back were the ripped giants who turned those airport heads in 2005.

Cena and Bautista were Vince's picks to spearhead his company on its biggest night, in the bosom of its entertainment siblings. And so, with celebs, agents, producers, and a host of TV execs in the crowd, future box-office heavyweights Dave and Jon were "made" under the hot lights in LA—long before LA embraced them like the movie stars they are today.

Looking back now, their future success seems obvious, but back then, I'm sure Cena and Bautista didn't even have the movie business on their radar at the time, as tinsel town back then still saw wrestlers as coming with a ton of baggage. Even The Rock, who would go on to be the biggest movie star in the world, was struggling to ignite in 2005.

Breaking into Hollywood was tough for wrestlers, but not impossible. From Roddy Piper tearing it up in John Carpenter's *They Live*, to Jesse Ventura chasing the Predator with Arnie, wrestlers have always been a great fit for TV and movies, because many of the attributes our screen rewards, so does theirs. The need for charisma, reliability, professionalism, and the ability to emote to any country in the world is common across both forms of entertainment.

And that's why, when our guys have been given the opportunity, they always shone away from their day jobs.

People still talk about Andre The Giant over thirty years since he lit up *The Princess Bride*. Anybody want a peanut? Or think of Hulk Hogan in *Mr. Nanny*. Okay, not the same, but part of the reason Hulk became one of the most recognizable faces on planet Earth was his appearances as "Thunderlips" in *Rocky III*. And what about Hulk's old nemesis "Macho

Man" Randy Savage, jumping off the screen as "Bone Saw McGraw" in *Spider-Man*? Ohhh, yeaaaahhh. Or Kevin Nash standing out as a stripper in *Magic Mike*, or Terry Funk causing havoc as the lead henchman in *Road House*? Even Good Ol' JR here adorned the silver screen for several seconds in Jim Carrey's *Man in the Moon*.

Wrestling has always represented itself admirably in Hollywood.

And WrestleMania 21 was no different.

With Cena winning his first-ever world title for the *SmackDown* brand earlier in the night, it all came down to Dave Bautista versus Triple H in the main event for the *Raw* heavyweight title.

And despite my feeling increasingly on the outside at WWE, as the main event headed into the home stretch, my sole focus was on that final match, and making sure our viewers felt what I felt as I watched it with them.

> *"The world champion has been busted wide*
> *open at the hands of The Animal!"*

Triple H walked, stunned, around ringside after being catapulted into the ring post, his face turning into a crimson mask. He stood shook and confused at ringside until Bautista caught back up with him and slammed him headfirst into the ring steps.

> *"I have never seen such power in my life, 'The Game'*
> *catapulted . . . man, will that be the turning point in*
> *this match? 'The Game' is losing blood every time his*
> *heart beats. The three-hundred-and-seventeen pounder*
> *is hungry. He is thirsty for the World's Heavyweight*
> *Championship and it is now within his grasp!"*

John's match had been called wonderfully by Michael Cole and Taz from the *SmackDown* brand earlier in the night, so it was up to King and me to call Bautista's match from the *Raw* brand with everything we had.

> *"Triple H literally out on his feet. His equilibrium*
> *is gone to hell. His championship may be going*
> *with it and leaving. Bautista back in control.*
> *Another clubbing shot. There's nothing pretty*
> *or finessed about it. Vile, nasty shot right to the*
> *head. The animalistic instincts of Bautista . . ."*

The bloody violence of the match was a stark contrast to the storyline that built it. Bautista was the quiet enforcer of the faction Evolution, which included Randy Orton, Triple H, and Ric Flair. We didn't know it then, but Dave's performance in that group was indicative of the kinds of measured roles he would become known for in a myriad of movies.

It might seem like it'd be a challenge to stand out, being the quieter, more introspective guy in the middle of those huge personalities. I mean, Flair alone would chew up whole arenas solo. But within a small amount of time, Dave managed to stand apart from those huge personalities by not saying too much. He let his stillness do the talking—another sensibility that would become a hallmark of his acting career many years later.

Now, granted, this six-four, three-hundred-pound man beating the living shit out of Triple H didn't scream control or stillness. But in our business, there's a time to be still, and there's a time to kick ass, and Dave was working on the second of those scenarios in front of the LA crowd.

Even after "The Game" hit a low blow and tried to steal the win right at the end, Bautista was too strong to be taken down.

> *"Before over twenty thousand fans and a worldwide*
> *audience, The Beast has been unleashed. Bautista is*
> *the new heavyweight champion of the world!"*

The big man dreamed, worked, and achieved, and I know that I was cheering him every step of the way. Because of people like Dwayne, John, and Dave—three men with three different personalities, going in three different directions in the same field—the tide has finally begun to turn regarding wrestling's legitimacy in the entertainment business.

But it was bittersweet to watch two of my hires in John Cena and Dave Bautista become the champions of their respective brands, on wrestling's biggest night, in entertainment's biggest city, while I wondered what was next for me.

"I think Vince looks forward to going to hell. He can take over. Satan would be out of business."

April 30, 2006
Vince McMahon vs. God, Backlash
Rupp Arena
Lexington, Kentucky

Heat, brother.

Every wrestler in the world has thought or said it at some point in their career, when things haven't been rolling too well. That's because "heat" is the audible glue that bonds your career to bigger paychecks. "Heat" is the sound an audience makes when you're in their presence. It's the feeling you've stoked, the energy you've created—and if you're a bad guy, it's the sound and sights of your performance working.

It's what makes this whole wheel turn.

Everyone from "Rowdy" Roddy Piper to Triple H to "Superstar" Billy Graham to Paul Heyman, and many, many more, have traded on their ability to make you feel something about them. And in their line of work as heels, that "something" was an intense desire to see them get their asses kicked.

These performers, playing their roles in this marketing machine called wrestling, are the ones who keep it all going—making those who can elicit that precious heat from our audience a commodity in our business.

But like all high-wire acts, it's tough to keep it going all year round, show after show, TV taping after TV taping. How far can you push the boundaries to keep your antagonistic fire lit?

In AEW, the current top heel is an always-on dynamic personality who wants to be the headline of every event—and he recently crossed the line in looking for boos. Maxwell Jacob Friedman has so woven his real-life personality into his TV persona that I'll be damned if the fans aren't wondering which is which with this guy. He is so committed to the task of being an asshole that I'm sure there's still people who work with him who don't know the difference.

And that's what makes him stand out on our roster.

But last week (as I write this), while in pursuit of the sweet nectar that is heat, he took a glass of water and dunked it on a fan to "hydrate" him at one of our biggest PPVs of the year. Problem was, the fan was a child and the water was tequila.

Yeah, not good.

Max found himself in a situation where he was in the crowd, surrounded by people who all hate him, and in that intense environment, he reacted instinctively as a heel and took it way too far.

However, when that heat builds week on week, you can hear and see there's a rhythm to the audience's reaction that can go from apathy to annoyance to anger, if you're doing it right. You want people to pay to boo you, whether in person or on PPV, because the natural flow of money through wrestling is dependent on how badly the audience wants to see the bad guys get their asses whipped.

The best heels I've ever encountered are almost always part asshole in real life, which is why I'm sure the happiest day in Vince McMahon's life was the day he figured out he could be Mr. McMahon, and not the jovial TV announcer Vince McMahon. It was right around the time he was growing tired of being his company's on-screen broadcaster (which worked out perfectly for me, because I stepped into the role when Mr. McMahon strutted out of it) that the pieces began to fall into place to free him from the shackles of niceness and unleash his inner asshole.

Over the years, Vince had sent other men out to get the heat he wanted, and I know that inside he figured a lot of the time he could do a better job himself. And you know what? He was right, in most cases. Because when it came time for the owner to get showered in that negative reaction, he just about drowned in it, such were the tidal waves of boos that came his way.

But even the best heel in the world can get lost sometimes, looking for ways to keep their heat—especially after ten years of playing the heel in all of WWE's top programs. And in 2006, McMahon had run out of babyface heroes to "dance" with on TV. So, in lining up his next opponent, I guess he went with the only one he could think of that was on his level.

God.

Yeah, God.

At this point I had been removed from *Raw* at the end of 2005 after requesting time off for colon surgery, and Vince thought it would be funny to do a skit on *Raw* the night I was recovering from surgery where he played "Doctor Heiney" and proceeded to pull various implements from "my" ass. Which I mention not because mocking my surgery was in bad taste—which it was—but to highlight just how out there Vince's creative had gotten in his quest to keep the ratings up.

WWE's shows were now very much catered to what the boss liked, versus what the audience might like. And that's the context in which God was introduced as Vince's next opponent. With very little interest from the audience, Vince booked himself and his son, Shane, in a PPV tag match against born-again Christian Shawn Michaels and a spotlight in the ring, which represented "God."

And I was there to call it.

After Vince fired my replacement on *Raw*, then fired his replacement, I found myself temporarily back on TV, and calling PPVs, too, until Vince found a replacement for my replacements' replacement, who I was replacing.

So, while he was looking to replace me again, I had the joy of being ringside as, wearing an oily brown spray tan, and with a strut so wide he almost had a foot in neighboring states, Mr. McMahon made his way to ringside to join his son, Shane, in a tag match against Shawn Michaels and "God."

> *"There were several lightning strikes in the area today. Let's just hope they don't make their way to Rupp Arena."*

Now, McMahon had the audience in the palm of his hand, but unlike most of the great heels in history, he had very limited skill in the ring, so he needed both Shawn and a little divine intervention to pull this match off.

> *"I have a hard time understanding the doctrine of McMahonism . . . Thou shalt tan?"*

I could see just how much fun the naturally antagonistic CEO was having in there with this one. And then, with the biggest grin on his face, he introduced, and I quote, "The Holy Roller, Hipster from Heaven, the Man Upstairs. From the Kingdom of Heaven, please welcome . . . God!"

And bang on cue came angelic harp music and the spotlight at the top of the ramp as "God" made his entrance into the arena. I thought it was going pretty well until Mr. McMahon berated "God" for his boring entrance, and demanded he do it "WWE style" as more upbeat music played.

> *"McMahon wants God to 'get jiggy' with it."*

Now, the God stuff was like a few other "creative" ideas during the Attitude Era—it just wasn't for me. I'm a firm believer in keeping religion and politics out of wrestling, but what Vince was trying to do with every single minute of TV that he was involved in (which was all minutes, because he vetted every segment, word, and idea before it aired) was get a reaction. It didn't matter to him anymore what kind. Anything would do. Outrage, horror, anger, vitriol—the man loved it all equally.

> *"Can even Shawn Michaels overcome . . .*
> *two desperate individuals such as Vince*
> *McMahon and his demon seed, Shane?"*

While Shawn and Shane did most of the heavy lifting in the match, Vince showed up intermittently to get his ass kicked and to pay for all the things he was saying—including taking a blind back bump off the stage when Michaels hit him with a cross body that took them right over the edge and through a table below.

> *"My God, cross body! And Michaels took the sixty-year-*
> *old chairman of WWE from the stage to the floor!"*

Michaels stood first, and took the slow climb back to the stage, only to be met by a stiff chair shot to the head by the waiting Shane McMahon. It was a blow that busted Michaels open, and gave Shane time to go down to the floor and pull his unconscious father to his feet.

> *"And now the Boy Sperm, I mean, the Boy Wonder,*
> *going to check on his black-hearted daddy . . . How*
> *can a family be so devoid of human kindness when they*
> *have so many things to be thankful for? How can the*
> *McMahons conduct themselves like soulless heathens? . . .*
> *I mean, they're richer than eight foot up a bull's ass . . .*
> *It's the fact that Vince McMahon is losing his mind, in my*
> *opinion. And this may be my last broadcast, I guess."*

Shawn and Shane beat the living hell out of each other as Vince continued to make well-timed cameos to take big hits when they were called for.

Because that's the thing about seeking out that sweet, sweet heat as a heel. If you're gonna run your mouth, then you gotta be okay with getting punched in that same mouth when it comes time to take your medicine. And one thing nobody can say about Vince is that he was ever afraid to take an ass whooping when it came time.

> *"There's nothing wrong with talking to God, but that*
> *demented son of a bitch thought he saw him."*

And just as I spoke, Vince took a brutal chair shot to the head in a mistimed swing from his own son. Then Michaels began his comeback, as the audience vocally ushered him on. And as Shane ate a kick to the face, his father stood once more, only to get the very same right boot to his own mouth.

The Heartbreak Kid picked up both McMahons and laid them across a couple of tables as the audience chanted, "HBK! HBK!" And then out came the ladder, over twenty foot in height.

> *"This is a suicidal-like maneuver for*
> *everybody in the equation."*

But ringside was then flooded by the male cheerleading squad that Vince was palling around with. (If it sounds weird, it's because it was weird.) The Spirit Squad, as they were known (no relation to God), interfered on the chairman's behalf, throwing the match into a seven-on-one scenario against HBK. God, it seems, had left the building, which left HBK alone to be pinned by McMahon.

> *"Look at the look on the face of Mr. McMahon. His eyes*
> *look, he looks like a soulless, soulless human being. You gotta*
> *be kidding me. Oh, that's bullshit! Excuse my language.*
> *I apologize. But it's damn sure horse manure that Mr.*
> *McMahon beat Shawn Michaels . . . This just makes me ill."*

And I was hoping that it made you ill, too. Because that's the whole point. The heels winning was meant to make you hate them. It was meant to make you root for the good guys to whip their ass. Whether it's through using "God" or some other means to poke the audience, heels run the business. Without them, everything else means nothing.

So, to the generations of little assholes future, just like the generations past: seek out that heat, brother. And there will always be someone like me on commentary to tell the world just how vile you are.

Because that's how this whole wheel turns.

"My break came in 1993 when I married my wife, Jan."

March 31, 2007
Hall of Fame Induction Ceremony
Fox Theatre
Detroit, Michigan

The WWE Hall of Fame isn't a physical building, and its inductees aren't chosen based on any exact science—but it means a lot to a lot of people to celebrate your career in an auditorium full of your peers.

The first inductee was Andre The Giant, who was inducted posthumously in 1993. His year was the only year where just one person was inducted, and it was a fitting tribute to a man who stood in a class of his own his whole career.

After Andre, everyone from Vince McMahon Sr. to "Big Cat" Ernie Ladd to William "The Refrigerator" Perry to Hulk Hogan were inducted before my class in 2007. And I'm delighted to say that my great friend and longtime partner Jerry Lawler and I got inducted the same year, which meant the world me, and Jerry, too. King and I were joining other commentators like Gorilla Monsoon, Jesse Ventura, Bobby Heenan, and Gordon Solie in very select broadcasting company.

Initially, Vince planned to use my induction as a fitting way to put me out to pasture, as he'd lined up replacement number four to come in and lead the *Raw* broadcast team. However, when he saw the reaction and genuine outpouring of emotion my induction announcement got live on *Raw*, as the people in the building gave me a standing ovation, the boss had a change of heart.

For a little while, anyway.

And while the Hall of Fame itself will always be special to me, my induction year takes on an even greater level of importance in my story now—because of who I got to share it with.

I guess it's a little hard for me to talk about, but dating in your seventies is more complicated than I ever would have imagined. I guess I've tried it a few times since my wife passed away, but it's been tough to make my way through it because I was unprepared for how it would make me feel.

At the start I tried to push past the guilt of even trying to imagine being with anyone other than my wife. I beat myself up quite a bit on that one, because I felt I was betraying her in some way to look at another woman like that. Then I made the huge mistake of measuring other women against Jan, and that was a contest nobody could win. So, in the end, I guess I stopped trying to date, and just kinda moved away from that scene altogether, because true love is hard to distance yourself from.

Now that my wife is no longer with me, I get a kick out of watching different years of the WWE Hall of Fame so I can see her pop up in shots of the crowd. But when I feel I really need to see her, I close my eyes and picture her sitting there in the front row the year I got inducted. I can see her now, man, looking up at me on the stage, and her face is lit differently than everyone else's. It's not a lighting thing, and there's no TV magic— she's just beaming with pride.

Jan was so excited in the run-up to that event in 2007. She wanted to look good, and made sure I did, too. Well, as good as I could. I wasn't blessed that way, but the Good Lord sure sent me a woman who was.

The two of us looked at my induction from kinda different perspectives. From my point of view, I was standing before my peers—many of whom

I'd worked with for years and years—feeling like I might actually fit in after three decades of trying. I felt that maybe all my hard work had paid off, and I'd made some people proud, and that my work meant something to people.

From Jan's point of view, she was looking at it with pure pride. I was her husband, and she'd watched me, us, our family, go through it all over the period of time I was getting recognition for. All the nights apart, all the stress and worry, all the medical challenges and the career lows and highs. All the names we signed, and the wrestlers who preferred sleeping in our spare room to the finest hotels because of Jan's cooking and counsel. All the wives she talked to about the hard road in wrestling.

Jan used to learn what meals different Superstars grew up with and would make them from scratch when they came over to talk shop, or just get away from the road. When I was trying to sign Paul Wight from WCW, I mentioned in one of my conversations at home that he liked apple butter, like the good 'ol southern boy he is. Well, when Paul came over to talk to me about coming to work in WWE, Jan had his favorite ready, and the future Big Show scoffed it down while I laid out what we could offer him. The one-two combination worked, with Paul saying many times how impressive and thoughtful it was that Jan would open her home to him in that way.

But that's the thing: my wife played a huge role in whatever success my time in WWE yielded—and she was always her usual demure self about it.

At the peak of the Attitude Era, our washing machine cleaned some of the most iconic trunks of all time, and our spare room housed more WWE Champions than WWE's own Hall of Fame—and I can tell you, they weren't coming to our house for my magnetic personality and hospitality.

And nobody would even know how much credit she deserves if I didn't go hoarse telling them, because Jan was the kind of woman who just wanted everything good to come my way. She didn't need it if she saw I had it. But, thankfully, that's not the way our relationship worked. We were a team. And I knew I was blessed to be with her from the very first days.

Then, in 2017, my wife was killed.

She left this world a woman loved, and she left me a man who felt the same. I had comments all the time asking what a woman like Jan was doing with a man like me, and to tell you the truth, I agreed with them sometimes. But the older I get, and the more time that passes since I last held her, the more I know what she saw in me: a man who showed her sides of himself that nobody else saw. She loved me for who I was at home: vulnerable, cranky, worried, thoughtful, passionate, and, more often than not, trying to do the right thing.

When Jan looked at me on that stage that night, she didn't see "Good Ol' JR" like the fans and wrestlers did. She saw a man who doubted himself large parts of the way. A man who cried, and laughed, and planned for a future together. A man who told her he loved her, and she could see he meant it. A man who was flawed and stubborn, and did I mention, cranky sometimes?

But a man she left a better version of the one she met.

A lonelier version now, maybe.

Certainly a more heartbroken version.

But a man who has hope, and family, and a career he still loves.

When I think of Jan now, I think of her living the life she was meant to live with me. We sacrificed, and went through the grind, all to get to a place where we could retire to the beach together. And here I am, thinking about her again, in a condo she was planning on living in with me. But she's not here to enjoy it.

I'm living now from the fruits of our labor together.

The peace I find is in the fact we had twenty-six wonderful years together. But I can't help but wish I could talk to her once more. She was my morning coffee buddy, my last conversation before I headed out on the road. When she was lying in the hospital, I talked to her a lot, but she never came around to answering me back, the woman who I loved talking to the most in the world.

I was lucky to have her in my life, and I hope my angel is in heaven now thinking, "I was lucky to have you in mine, too."

Everyone deserves true love.

But I was one of the lucky ones that actually found it.

"Wait a minute. What the hell?! It's John Cena!"

January 27, 2008
John Cena Returns, Royal Rumble
Madison Square Garden
New York City

There's been many great returns in wrestling: Triple H on *Raw* in 2002 after his quad tear, Undertaker as the American Badass at Judgement Day 2000, and The Rock on *Raw* in 2011 after seven years away.

But the one that really sticks out in my mind when I think back is John Cena at the 2008 Royal Rumble. The visual of Cena coming back months before he was expected to after a torn pectoral muscle, just standing there in Madison Square Garden as the fans around him went nuts, is an easy one to remember. And I think the reason for that is because it felt like such a surprise. It felt like nobody knew. It felt . . . old school.

> *"The roof is exploding off Madison Square Garden.*
> *John Cena, the thirtieth entrant in the Royal Rumble*
> *match! Yes, indeed business just picked up!!"*

Back when I broke in, the people running the business and the wrestlers in the business had a pact not to "spoil" what was going to happen, or how it was happening. We went to great lengths to keep the backstage goings-on from the fans because that approach kept the business stronger and the product better. We only had one source of income in the early days and that was ticket sales—and if the fans knew what was going to happen, then why pay to see it? Our box office told us that the less fans knew, the better for everyone.

Even my first wife didn't know the inner workings of our business. Not that I think she wanted to know. The more I learned about the entertainment business in general, the more I learned that every episodic series wants secrecy. Some movies have several endings written, and some TV shows develop their own coded language to protect a major death in the story, or a major return in the movie.

Keeping it kayfabe is important to every evolving story, but I guess we in wrestling just go the extra mile.

Especially when you hear about people like Mr. Wrestling II and Mil Mascaras—who both wrestled in Lucha masks and kept their "characters" so well that many people they worked with had no idea what they actually looked like. Most wrestlers hid their real life from the fans to protect their personas, but these two guys even showered in their masks backstage to protect their work.

Back in Mid-South, we even had a heel entrance and a babyface entrance, so the good guys and bad guys were never seen entering, or exiting, the building together.

I remember when it leaked that Jake Roberts was leaving our territory, and word soon spread that you could expect Jake to lose in Houston because Jake was leaving to go to WWE. Watts and Houston promoter Paul Boesch got together and changed the finish to make sure Jake won. Houston was a big market for both bookers and they knew if their cards could be predicted ahead of time then they were dead in the water.

Keeping the secret, to all of us, was as essential as bringing your boots and tights; it wasn't choice, it was mandatory.

Some fans' desire to know what's going to happen in the wrestling business is more aggressive now than ever before, thanks to the explosion of the internet. Fans and "journalists" alike rake over things like interviews, rumors, social media posts (not just the wrestlers', but their friends' and family's, too), and anything else they can get their hands on just to try to piece together what wrestler is in what town, or to see if someone let something slip about an upcoming angle. Social media has made it more difficult to surprise and delight, as everything from backstage whispers to trademark applications are trawled through to get the next headline.

I guess I just don't understand why someone who calls themself a fan wants to know what the ending is going to be. I couldn't imagine wanting to have the ending of the movie I was planning to see spoiled for me. I just want to be surprised, as a fan, and as a commentator, too—which is why the Cena reveal was so impactful for the audience, and me, too.

As the fans counted down the arrival of the final entrant to the Rumble, the production team left a slight, dramatic pause before that iconic bass line kicked in. And then came the brass section that signaled the arrival of someone who was fast becoming one of the most polarizing Superstars in WWE history. Some loved Cena's kid-friendly, positive outlook, and some hated it. But *everyone* was vocal about it.

With his music blaring, John stood with his head bowed and his arms crossed in the narrower-than-usual Garden entranceway, as the fans all around him went absolutely crazy.

| *"John Cena is number 30!!"* |

He waited until his presence had sunk in with everyone in the building before exploding into life. The man had returned just four months after tearing his pectoral muscle off the bone, when doctors said it would take a year to heal. And you could see the real emotion of the moment running through his system as he made his way down the aisle.

When he hit the ring to eliminate several other wrestlers, you could hear a push and pull in the New York fans' voices; it was a wonderful mix of excitement, booing, cheering, and surprise.

And I believe that wonderful reaction was largely because they had no idea he was even in the building, much less that he'd be the last man to enter one of their favorite matches of the year.

In that instance, tight lips made the fans' night in the building better, it made the viewers' night at home better, and it made my job on commentary better because I had no idea either—and I couldn't have loved it more.

With the few remaining wrestlers down on the canvas, Cena and Triple H stood tall in the middle of the ring. And as they butted heads with the giant WrestleMania sign framed perfectly behind them, the arena was buzzing.

> *"This is all about the WrestleMania main event. Who is going to WrestleMania? Who's going to be in the main event?!?"*

As our returning hero went nose-to-nose with our potential villain, with the stakes of their conflict writ large in the frame as we drove it home on commentary, it was the perfect marriage between the wrestlers, the crowd, us broadcasters, and the production team.

And after a flurry of eliminations, it came down to Cena, Triple H, and Bautista as the final three combatants.

> *"It's down to three! It's down to three!"*

As the final action played out before the New York masses, Big Dave Bautista was thrown over the top rope and eliminated, leaving the stage set for Cena and Triple H to take this one home.

> *"It's psychological warfare here . . . It's physical warfare! As it's every man for himself. Who's going over the top rope? . . . The winner goes to WrestleMania in the main event against the champion . . . John Cena shocking the WWE world, returning right here tonight at the Royal Rumble."*

So much of our business has changed for the better, since the old days. But as it came down to two, Cena and Triple H, I couldn't help but think of how much the business also still benefits from the old-school foundations that were laid right back at the start.

> *"This match continues until one man is thrown over the top rope and both feet touch the floor."*

And then John and H began their final battle to see who would come out on top. They brought the audience with them by throwing simple, fundamental punches in the middle of the ring, the audience booing Cena—who they had just blown the roof off for—and cheering Triple H as he laid his fists in. Both men played into the passionate, opposing reactions by taking turns punching each other, giving room for the crowd to alternate between BOO, YAY, BOO, YAY, depending on who was doing the punching.

> *"The physicality, the emotion in the Garden is scintillating."*

Then Cena ducked over and lifted Triple H up for a back suplex, planting the fans' favorite flat on his back in the center of the ring to massive boos from the New York faithful.

> *"The lightning rod, John Cena, able to counter 'The Game.'"*

Both men played on the emotions of the fans perfectly. Then, in the last few seconds, after near misses, power moves, and last-second reversals, Cena picked Triple H up on his shoulders and dumped "The Game" over the top rope to win a Royal Rumble that nobody expected him to even be in. And once again, the audience exploded in cheers for Cena.

> *"When we started this historic night, the last man I thought would headline WrestleMania would be John Cena, because I didn't think John Cena was physically*

able to return to combat in the WWE. And my, oh my, how wrong I was! . . . A superhuman display of strength and toughness by John Cena. And John Cena has won the 2008 Royal Rumble in a huge, huge shocker!!"

An old-school mindset had just delivered a modern moment to remember.

"Mayweather has taken it to the street!"

March 30, 2008
Big Show vs. Floyd Mayweather, WrestleMania 24
The Citrus Bowl
Orlando, Florida

"Attraction" is a term we use in professional wrestling for someone or something that adds value and intrigue above and beyond what's normally expected in a match, but it's also a word you see used in the entertainment field more broadly. It is usually something that captures the imagination, something that's can't-miss, whether it's a new ride in a theme park, a signature animal in a zoo, a celebrated painting in a museum, or a "dream collab" (JR is hip) between musical artists.

Andre The Giant was wrestling's greatest ever attraction wrestler. Standing at over seven feet tall, weighing five hundred pounds, he had the size, strength, and natural charisma that meant you couldn't take your eyes off him. When "The Eighth Wonder of the World" was wrestling, nobody went to the concession stands, or took a bathroom break, because everyone wanted to experience watching him live. Andre The Giant stoked interest just because of who he was, and not just in fans, but in non-fans, too.

Attraction wrestlers—and attraction matches—have always been part of the fabric of what we do. It's easier to get people to buy in if there's something on offer that piques their interest above and beyond the norm. An attraction is a hook. Sometimes that hook comes in the form of a match, and other times it comes in the form of a person, like in 1995, when tattooed super heavyweight wrestler Bam Bam Bigelow wrestled NFL legend Lawrence Taylor at WrestleMania 11, or when Gorilla Monsoon took on Muhammad Ali in 1974. The "attraction" is so ingrained in wrestling that it can be traced all the way back to the main event of WrestleMania 1, which featured TV's biggest star at the time, Mr. T, teaming with Hulk Hogan against Roddy Piper and Paul Orndorff.

More recently, WWE landed UFC pioneer and former champion Ronda Rousey. I feel WWE did a wonderful job with her presentation at the beginning—keeping her fresh and intriguing—but faltered a little at the end when they overexposed her by putting her on TV every week. But it looks like WWE has learned from that mistake, as it has since used the hugely popular Latin star Bad Bunny and YouTube lighting rod Logan Paul sparingly on their shows to maximize their effect.

Because that's the thing about attractions—they cease to be just that if they become commonplace.

Arguably the biggest fumble of an attraction wrestler in history is "Big Show" Paul Wight. In my opinion, over the years, Paul has been the most consistently miscast and misused Superstar I've ever had the pleasure of working with. On the surface that might sound like I'm saying something negative about him, but I assure you Paul would tell you the same himself. Here we have a man who is a legitimate attraction, just due to the fact that he's billed at seven foot and 450 pounds. There ain't a lot of those kinds of people walking the earth, folks. And all that natural currency was wasted time and again by having him on TV every week, winning and losing like all the other "normal" guys.

And not only was he on WWE TV every week, but he was cast as a utility player instead of the obvious attraction that he was. It seemed anytime WWE was in a hole, they'd call on Paul to turn from heel to face, or face to heel, at the drop of a hat. They'd put him in a diaper and have him dance like a giant baby, or write him breaking a toilet after eating a spicy burrito, to name just two headshaking "storylines'" they had him in.

From a company that rightfully adored Andre The Giant, it was baffling to witness.

However, when WWE did get it right on the creative end, Big Show always killed it on the delivery—and never more so than when paired with what many consider the greatest boxer of all time, the undefeated Floyd "Money" Mayweather.

Now, this is the definition of an attraction.

Boxer versus wrestler.

Super heavyweight versus welterweight.

No holds barred.

Pinfall or submission, or . . . knockout.

Finally, all the stars had aligned and Paul would get his chance to shine—and at WrestleMania, no less. But first the build had to match the compelling contracts of both men. After all, watching a five-foot-four, 150-pound boxer square up to a seven-foot, 450-pound wrestler might give the impression that the contest will be fast, easy, and not worth your time.

So, on the Road to WrestleMania, Paul asked one of the best, if not *the* best, boxer in history to break Paul's nose for real, live on TV. "Show" knew that, to catch the casual eyeballs that Floyd would surely bring to WWE, he needed to make the contest look more realistic. After all, if the boxer punches the wrestler clean in the face, and there's no effects to be seen, then where's the danger going forward? Why should someone pay to see the match?

Being the veteran he was, Paul knew that the best way to kick-off such a potentially explosive story was to add more gas to the fire by adding a little "color" to the proceedings.

So, the month before WrestleMania, the two men faced off during an altercation in the ring, where Big Show dismissively taunted his much smaller opponent by getting on his knees and dropping his hands. The message was clear: the overconfident giant didn't feel threatened by Mayweather at all.

That is, until Floyd unleashed a rapid four-punch combination that broke Paul's nose cleanly and decisively.

When the giant saw his own blood, he sprang to his feet and charged, chasing Mayweather and his entourage out of the ring, over the barricades, and into the crowd like something from the Running of the Bulls.

As the giant fumed, the boxer taunted him from far away in the arena—and the crowd was now fully invested.

We all knew we had ourselves an attraction.

WWE marketed their bout as "The Greatest Fighter in the World Versus the Largest Athlete in the World." And six weeks later, at WrestleMania 24, under the hot night sky of Orlando, Florida, "Big Show" Paul Wight, and Floyd "Money" Mayweather met to put on a match that shocked many with just how great it was.

| *"Mayweather is in Big Show's world. A world of giants."* |

"Show" threw his opponent around like a rag doll, stood on him, tossed him over the ropes onto his entourage—and Floyd took it all. No shortcuts, no laziness, no bullshit.

For my money (pardon the pun), Floyd is the most talented and committed celebrity to ever step in our business—and that covers a lot of ground, because throughout history, the worlds of sports and entertainment have collided with professional wrestling many times.

> *"Mayweather showing the courage that made him the Greatest Fighter in the World. Not backing up. But Mayweather has never, ever been in the ring with anyone like the Big Show."*

Amazing names like Tyson Fury, Oscar De La Hoya, Lennox Lewis, and Muhammad Ali have all made appearances in our business, but when Mayweather came in, he went above and beyond to get his match right. He ran his mouth, accentuated his cocky persona, and exuded arrogance to get the audience to boo him. Usually, the size difference alone would have made Mayweather the babyface, but Floyd was so good at what he did, he managed to make "David" the hated guy in his battle with "Goliath."

And he just added to that when he began to use weapons, like chairs and brass knux, to cheat and gain the advantage.

> *"The chair is bending around the skull of Big Show . . . this has turned into a street fight . . . It looks like brass knux to me. Mayweather took off his glove . . . oh, right hand! A brass knux–molded right hand! Anything goes . . . the referee is counting . . . and . . . Mayweather wins the match!! I am absolutely astonished that Floyd Mayweather not only could win, but survive this night."*

And that's the attraction of the attraction. On the same card as the legendary Ric Flair's retirement from WWE, people still remember just how surprisingly great Floyd versus "Show" was. It had all the right ingredients, blended perfectly to make something that was of passing interest at the beginning into something truly great in the end.

It's just a pity from where I sat that Paul didn't get the opportunity in WWE to shine more.

"I just had an out-of-body experience!"

April 5, 2009
The Undertaker vs. Shawn Michaels, WrestleMania 25
Reliant Stadium
Houston, Texas

Oil and water might not mix, but they can sure have one hell of a wrestling match. Maybe even the best wrestling match of all time. And the road to that wrestling match was abundant in life lessons if you know the two guys involved as long as I have.

The thing that jumps out to me the most about Shawn Michaels and The Undertaker's journey is that they exemplify how none of us need to stay who we once were—and the road behind us doesn't need to define the stretch we're on right now.

People change and situations change all the time.

I guess I was experiencing that firsthand at the time, as my own situation had changed when I was drafted to *SmackDown* in 2008 without any notice live on-air—then demoted from lead announcer once I got there. I was in favor, out of favor, lead, not lead, fired, not fired, and moved between *Raw*, *SmackDown*, and *Main Event* over and over again. But without any real power to change anything, all I could do was watch my career bounce around. After a long time in the business, I guess I just had to accept that people and situations change all the time, and that mine might, too. Because any journey, no matter where you begin and end, involves change all the way along.

I saw it in the people I was entrusted to manage in the locker room all the time. Some start off unsure and reluctant, while others come in brash and cocky. Some of those people switch roles as the years go by, depending on how their careers are moving. But much like in any other high-pressure environment, the more time people spend with each other in the trenches, the more respect they can gain for each other—even if they're completely different personalities.

That's kind of the story of Shawn and 'Taker.

I was in Mid-South for Shawn's first televised match, and at Wrestle-Mania 26 for his last. In between those two points in time, Michaels became in my view either the number 1 or 1A wrestler who has ever lived. He was that damn good. But he was also that damn difficult and selfish at times, too. Which is why I think he and Undertaker didn't get on as people for most of their long runs in WWE.

Shawn liked to be outspoken; Undertaker kept to himself. Shawn liked to poke the traditions of wrestling; 'Taker liked to honor them. The two men shared the same locker room for a long time but hardly ever talked to each other. They were from two different dimensions in our business, and even to look at them—and their presentations on-screen—you could see that they were two different personalities who couldn't be more opposite.

Mark and Shawn, or The Undertaker and The Heartbreak Kid, as they were known to fans, were our oil and water.

Eventually the two men went through enough years, wars, and changes together that they learned to respect each other immensely. But respect isn't always needed to create art together when you're as talented as these men are.

And that's just what they did at WrestleMania 25—create art.

You know when you've seen something so perfect, something so truly extraordinary, that you want to live it again in your mind, just to try to re-create the feeling you had the first time you'd experienced it? Well, Shawn Michaels versus The Undertaker at WrestleMania 25 was like that for me. I'd seen almost forty years and thousands of wrestling matches, and I was sure that this one match was perfect.

Even as I write that last line, I think, "It couldn't have been." But then I go back and watch the match again for research, and it just reaffirms for me what I thought of it the first time I saw it: it's the perfect wrestling match.

It's the match I point younger wrestlers toward if they want to break down the ring psychology of a classic battle between light and dark. Shawn, a born-again Christian, was lowered to the ramp bathed in white light, while Undertaker rose up from under the ramp through smoke and fire. And that was just the start of the contrasts that made it so great. Then came the size difference, the speed difference, the character difference, and all the friction those differences naturally evoke.

From a storytelling point of view, the two men feel like they're from different genres, almost. Shawn came up as the flashy, handsome tag-team wrestler, while 'Taker arrived to the company eerie and methodical.

Backstage, Undertaker grew to be the loyal and levelheaded soldier coming up through the ranks, while Shawn was the brash, selfish loud-mouth climbing the same ladder. 'Taker mostly kept to himself and did whatever the business needed from him; Shawn had problems with creative and dropping titles when it came his time to lose—so much so that Undertaker waited at the curtain for the main event of WrestleMania 14 to make sure Shawn did business the right way. Either he dropped the title to Steve Austin, or there would be an ass-kicking coming old HBK's way.

Undertaker didn't care for Shawn back then, but they didn't need to be friends outside the ring to be great inside it.

One of 'Taker and Shawn's matches—the first Hell in a Cell—was so good and filled with so many memorable moments that it nearly killed Mick Foley, who wasn't even in the match. Worried that he couldn't possibly compete with what Shawn and Undertaker did in the first Cell match, Mick tried to top it in the next Hell in a Cell match by notoriously flying off, and through, the cage, as we saw earlier.

But it was on a WrestleMania night in Texas that Undertaker and Shawn put on an all-time classic in an otherwise middling kind of card.

And it couldn't have come at a better time for me, as, even though I was the lowest I'd ever been on the commentary pecking order, I was selected to call the show alongside Michael Cole and my old broadcast brother, Jerry Lawler. Honestly, getting that call was probably one of the greatest gifts I ever received.

> *"Look at the eyes of The Undertaker. Look at the eyes of Shawn Michaels. One is defiant. One set of eyes is destructive."*

At the start of the match, the speed and strength difference between the two was on display, with 'Taker trying to land bombs and Shawn firing off quick hits. And then came a little arrogant crotch-chop that fired up Undertaker to rain down right hands on Heartbreak Kid.

> *"Powerfully pulverizing right hands. Upstairs and the body shots from The Undertaker . . . Michaels upside down, then inside out. Elevated to the top floor . . . Powerful pace, a very destructive pace set by Undertaker. Not what Michaels wanted to deal with. So now The Undertaker put this match right where he wants it."*

Michaels was getting his ass kicked by the much bigger, much more aggressive Undertaker, while Jerry, Michael, and I went to work reminding the audience that Undertaker had never beaten Shawn in a one-on-one matchup before. And right on cue, Shawn used his quickness to turn the tide of the match again. I went right back in there, sowing some questions in the minds of the fans to help enhance the amazing presentation they were being served by two amazing athletes.

> *"We remember, King. You and I called the first Hell in a Cell match. Michaels able to use every trick in the book to win that contest. Maybe outmaneuvering The Undertaker. Was the Undertaker underestimating Michaels on that*

night? I don't know! And then Shawn Michaels got hurt.
Did he really win that casket match? The scoreboard says
yes, but Michaels was gone for four years. Is that a win?"

Minute on minute, the two men moved through the gears of what was building into a classic.

It can be hard to pull open-air stadium crowds with you when you are hours into a long production like WrestleMania. I've seen many top stars struggle with keeping the audience alive after they've already seen every move, over several hours—but Michaels and Undertaker were telling so perfect a story in that ring that every single voice rose with them.

Hold for hold, blow for blow, submission attempt followed by a counter submission attempt. It can't be called textbook because if it was, everyone could copy it. And let me tell you, the true greats are the hardest to copy.

"Somebody's gonna tap! Will Michaels tap at
WrestleMania 25?! . . . Michaels desperately, courageously,
with every fiber of his being, got to the ropes."

And out we went to ringside, where Undertaker continued to beat on Shawn with kicks, punches, and a leg drop from the apron . . . that missed. The two pros slowed it right down to take the audience to a lower gear before Shawn launched himself from the top turnbuckle with a backflip to the outside, only to find Undertaker moved out of the way.

"My God. The sickening thud of Michaels's missed moonsault."

It was a total wipeout . . . that I thought couldn't be beaten until I saw what happened next. The near-seven-foot Undertaker climbed back into the ring and hit the ropes with bad intentions. He sprinted toward the ropes where Shawn was standing on the floor outside, launched himself over the top rope, and torpedoed toward the concrete headfirst—until he managed to tuck his chin at the last second to save himself from legitimately breaking his neck. Undertaker was millimeters away from something going very badly wrong.

And the crowd went from cheering at the launch to gasping at the landing.

And then it got as quiet as a building with over seventy thousand can get.

Until the pros were ready to work again.

Shawn rolled out and grabbed the referee, insisting that he begin to count Undertaker out. With every number climbing to the ten needed for Michaels to win, the audience chanted along. Their voices became even louder as they saw the large, dark figure of The Undertaker begin to move to try to get back to the ring in time.

And in the ring, Shawn played his role perfectly as he prayed for The Undertaker to be counted out, which only made the audience chant even louder and harder to urge "The Deadman" to make it back inside in time.

> *"Undertaker was less than a second away from being counted out! Michaels has had a moment or two to regroup and tune up the band perhaps."*

The live audience saw exactly what I was seeing—Shawn Michaels striking the familiar pose he always struck, just before hitting his opponent with his finishing move, Sweet Chin Music.

But as Michaels's iconic kick flew out to end it all, 'Taker sidestepped the boot to the face, and instead lifted Shawn high into the Texas air and dropped him down in a finishing move of his own, the choke-slam.

1 . . . 2 . . . and Michaels kicked out of the pin just before the count of three.

> *"The resilience and the will of Shawn Michaels is unbelievable!"*

And then a machine gun–like series of finishing move, counter, finishing move that left Undertaker down after a Sweet Chin Music kick to the face. But it, too, was one second shy of finishing the match.

More attempted finishing moves, and more counters, until, eventually, Undertaker got Shawn up for his modified powerbomb, which damn near sent Michaels through the ring.

> "Michaels's head bounced off the canvas. His body is wracked [with pain] . . . Unbelievable— Michaels kicked out!! How in the name of all that's decent did Michaels kick out of this? Undertaker cannot believe that anyone can kick out of the Last Ride as we've just seen Shawn Michaels do."

I knew I was watching a piece of art. Reversal after reversal, neither man able to break the will of the other. Michaels tried to lure 'Taker into the rope, but the bigger, stronger man lifted Shawn into the Tombstone position. This was it. This was the move nobody gets up from.

> "Michaels is caught. Shawn is caught! Tombstone! The count! And . . . a kick out! I'm not believing this! I just had an out-of-body experience!"

The Undertaker sold the shit out of Michaels kicking out of everything he had. As The Deadman and The Heartbreak Kid lay on the mat, the camera zoomed in on the look of disbelief on The Undertaker's face—a sentiment that was written all over the audience's faces, too. Nobody could believe what they were seeing.

> "The Undertaker's eyes tell a better story than we could ever . . . Choke-slams, Last Rides, Tombstones, and a kick, and a kick out, and a kick out."

'Taker had been through it all over the years, with every top name you could imagine. But here, on this night, in this building, even his devasting arsenal of moves couldn't keep Michaels down for the three count. But as the now-incensed Undertaker rose to his feet, the people could feel the end was indeed near.

> *"Look at the eyes of this man. There is no emptiness;*
> *there is focus. There is evil intentions in the most*
> *dangerous entity to ever step into a ring."*

Until . . . *BOOM!* From out of nowhere, a barely conscious Shawn Michaels planted The Undertaker's head into the mat with a desperation DDT—and slowly dragged himself into an all-or-nothing climb to the top rope.

> *"It is that inherent quality that this young man has had*
> *since the first day I laid eyes on him. Shawn Michaels is*
> *special. He's extraordinary. And he's taking an amazing*
> *chance here to beat The Undertaker . . . And Michaels's*
> *elbow hits! What a collision. What a crash!"*

Then it was Shawn's turn to try put this match away, using his patented kick to the head that had previously beaten all the greats. Only, here in Texas, Shawn's finishing move yielded a barely-there kick out by Undertaker, causing the crowd to chant "This is awesome" at the two legends giving everything they had.

> *"Good God almighty, this match continues! This*
> *classic is continuing. Can you believe, ladies and*
> *gentlemen, what we are witnessing here together*
> *tonight?! The world is watching a classic."*

And as The Undertaker dished out the final Tombstone that sealed the match in his favor, I had goose bumps. I had tears in my eyes, I was so emotionally wrapped up in that presentation. And if I was that emotional, as a grizzled veteran, I can only imagine the impact it had on younger wrestling fans.

> *"As a fan of sports entertainment, I am honored to have the opportunity to sit at ringside and see this."*

I said it, and I meant it.
What a road they traveled.
What a story they told.
What friends they became.
And what fans we remain.

"I love being back on Raw. I watch you every week."

November 15, 2010
Return to Monday Night Raw
The GIANT Center
Hershey, Pennsylvania

The lead announcer is the mouthpiece of the company they represent.

In WWE they're the mouthpieces of Vince McMahon.

Sometimes that can lead to a conflict with what I believe the role of the lead announcer should be: a trusted voice within the show. If the announcer's credibility is in doubt, then everything they tell the audience will be doubted. In a storytelling medium like ours, to make your lead voice an unreliable narrator makes no sense.

And that's why my last few years with WWE were so frustrating. It wasn't that they were playing around with my position in the company, it was that they were playing around with the role's function. And that became very evident to me the night I was invited back to *Raw* for an Old School episode.

When you've spent decades in a relationship, it's always weird suddenly looking at it from the outside in. It's like seeing an old flame who you once knew everything about, and she about you, and you're now strangers again, back to small talk and niceties. That's what it was like for me in 2010, coming back to *Raw*, a show I was once the lead voice of, as a "legend."

As I'm sure the cool kids will remember, that was the year Lady Gaga wore the meat dress, *Avatar* became the highest grossing movie of all time, and Instagram was born.

It was also the year Bryan Danielson joined NXT, Bret "Hitman" Hart returned to WWE after a twelve-year absence after the Montreal Screwjob, Hulk Hogan debuted for Total Nonstop Action, and Shawn Michaels retired and went in the WWE Hall of Fame.

And it was the year that WWE offered me a new, long-term contract, even as I sensed my time in WWE was drawing to a close.

It was a weird, very WWE move, because while I knew they didn't want to use me all that much, they didn't want any other company to get me, either.

I guess I hoped back then that I could still turn it around, but I was being used less and less in a weekly capacity, and more and more in a "guest role" kind of situation where I'd show up for some of the bigger shows and then ultimately go away again. The lead announcer duties were now being handled by Michael Cole, a former news journalist with real-world experience in covering national politics and international civil war.

Now, I understand the need to build for the future, and in the future Vince saw Michael as the lead announcer for his brand. So, I guess the only way to put it was, I was being put out to pasture, and that's a position that I found very hard to handle at the time, because I felt like I had a lot more to offer the business, and specifically the broadcast position in WWE.

Monday Night Raw was such a huge part of my life, and I'd like to think that I was a big part of its life, too, up to that point. And here I was being invited back to the show, not as part of the main roster broadcast team, but as an "old school" broadcaster from the past. And if I'm being honest with myself, it hurt a little more to see my old colleague and longtime friend Jerry Lawler still working his job there. It was just the starkness of the signal it sent, that between what many consider to be the greatest announce team on *Monday Night Raw*, King was considered "current," and I was considered "the past."

As I've written about in this book, I love Jerry. He is, and was, untouchable in his role—but on that night he was the measuring stick I used to make myself feel worse about everything. If it wasn't an age thing (Jerry is a little older than me) and it wasn't a freshness thing (King was also there a little longer than me), then it was just a me thing.

And it hurt like hell when I was faced with it.

It stung even more that, when I went out there, Vince decided it would be "fun" to have Michael Cole berate me and my work for the one match I was booked to call.

Now, if you want to put me out to pasture, that's one thing. I understand that. But directing Cole to be obnoxious and overbearing toward me, while also being dismissive of the wrestlers working in the ring, that just burns his credibility as the lead guy, when you want him to be the trusted voice of your show.

So, instead of returning fire and berating Cole, I focused on the match, and the effort of the wrestlers Cole was instructed to denigrate while taking shots at me.

I cover this trying period extensively in *Under the Black Hat*, but let me just say here that I have nothing against Michael whatsoever. He has just crossed twenty-five years in WWE, was a phenomenal hire, and continues to be every single week on their broadcasts. Over the years, I've had people ask me time and time again if I dislike Michael because of all the mean things he said about me on the show—and nothing could be further from the truth.

I know that fans had to suffer, too, through this awful period where Cole was instructed to be obnoxious and boorish on-air. They even had to suffer through me and Michael "wrestling" each other and participating in "rap battles" and all kinds of other forms of torture, but it was never Michael's call to say or do any of that stuff. He was a man fulfilling the wishes of his boss, just like I tried to do when I was in his role. No hard feelings whatsoever.

So, in the few minutes I had back in position on my old show, I tried my best to work around the childish taunts that Vince fed Cole to say to me on-air.

Vince wanted a change. He wanted his audience, who still had good feelings toward me, to know that I was old and out of touch. He wanted them to move on from me, to let me fade into a corner of WWE without fuss. And he used his airtime and his lead announcer's credibility to convey that live on *Raw*.

Making Cole a heel was one of the dumbest things we had ever done, because you want everybody to trust this guy. If Michael is a heel and he's lying, exaggerating, then our audience begins to ask, "Do I believe that broadcaster or do I think he's bullshitting me?"

The intent was clearly to torpedo me, but the net effect was they were hurting Cole even more. And the fans hated it all. But that didn't really matter, because Vince and his circle loved the interaction between Cole and me—and were thrilled that fans were getting pissed about it.

Then, instead of cooler heads prevailing, they continued to further humiliate the two of us by completely taking us out of our comfort zone and putting us in the ring!

Somebody else could have used the TV time more, but that's not how the creative went. And I could see that Michael didn't like doing it either. That's why there were never any hard feelings between us—even though I blacked his eye and chipped his tooth in our in-ring tussle.

Now, I didn't go out there with the intent of hurting anyone, but I'm not trained in this area. The last thing Vince said to me before I went out there was, "Lay your shit in, JR." And when your adrenaline is pumping and you have no idea how to throw a working punch that's designed to not hurt, it's almost impossible to judge distance and power on the fly. Some of my punches went flesh-to-flesh, which only further added fuel to the gossip fire.

So, from the whole cluster, the guy they wanted to "sunset" was getting cheered more than ever, and the guy they wanted to lead their broadcasts was getting booed. He got a black eye, and I had to get a tetanus shot because my untrained ass hit him in the mouth, his tooth ran into my knuckles, and it bled like a hog.

But here's the positive news about that deal to me. Michael Cole endured it and survived it. It was as horrible a time for him creatively as it was for me, but he didn't break under the strain of it all. He survived it, and now he's got a title and he's making good money, so I'm proud as hell of him.

Michael is no different than us, folks. He's a wrestling fan. He's had a really good job in wrestling for years and years, and he's earned every moment of it—every accolade, every promotion, every raise, and all of his exposure. He's earned all of that, and in a very classy way. He's Mr. Reliability. I think he's one of the more underrated guys in broadcasting.

As for me, back then, I knew I had a lot left to offer. But it was starting to look like it might just be outside the golden-walled garden of WWE.

"It is the end of an era, and we are all going to be part of it!"

April 1, 2012
Triple H vs. The Undertaker, WrestleMania 28
Sun Life Stadium
Miami, Florida

The thing about branding a match as "the End of an Era," when it features three of your top names ever, is that you need to be pretty confident you've found the names to take over their roles first. And I don't just mean you've found someone who has been hot for a few months. I mean you can't replace Shawn Michaels (who was recently retired, but came back to referee the match), Triple H, and Undertaker with anyone less than a name who has proven he can carry the load of the company long term.

But even on a WrestleMania card that featured Daniel Bryan, Randy Orton, Cody Rhodes, CM Punk, and the returning Rock, there was one guy who was going to be the face of the company from there.

And that was John Cena.

When I first met with Cena in 2001, back when I was still head of talent relations, I was so excited to sign the guy that I went immediately to my office from the plane to draw up the paperwork. I told Vince that same morning that we were signing a WrestleMania main-eventer, who I knew could lead the WWE for a generation.

Vince at that time wasn't sold, but in 2012, at WrestleMania 28, the boss was so fully invested that he put Cena in a position to break box-office records that year by putting him against The Rock, in Dwayne's first match back in almost eight years.

For me, it was a bittersweet time. I had been fired on-air six months before from my *Raw* broadcasting duties, in my hometown, again without any prior knowledge it would happen live on TV. Even though it came wrapped in a story, being fired on-air still means you're not on-air anymore, so I'd been kinda just waiting around ever since, to see if I could get back in the game somehow.

Then Triple H, Undertaker, and Shawn Michaels lobbied Vince to use me for their WrestleMania 28 match, and suddenly I was back for one match, and one match only.

The boys going to McMahon to pull me out of the mothballs was such a heartfelt gesture to me. It's one I will never forget. And I intended to repay them with every ounce of passion and conviction I could muster. I might have been a little rusty, but once I hit that announce table, I knew I was ready to go to work again.

> "*This is, without question, the biggest honor, the biggest privilege, that I've ever had as a broadcaster. To be able to sit here and document this matchup between The Undertaker and Triple H, two men that are surefire Hall of Famers. It is the end of an era, and we are all going to be part of it.*"

It truly was the end of an era, and not just for the guys in the ring. I knew then, although I tried not to face it, that I had to move on. I was dying on the vine waiting for something to change in my favor in WWE. But the truth was, I was scared leaving the only game in town. So, in the meantime, I focused solely on delivering something truly special with three men who I had been through a lot with, both on-screen and behind the scenes.

> "I talked to 'The Game' earlier today and it was a very poignant conversation. I've been with him since he came to WWE, and at one time he lived for titles, he lived for gold. And he earned them. Thirteen-time world champion. Then he lived for the money. He wanted to make millions, and he's earned millions. But now there's only one thing left for 'The Game,' and that is to end the streak of The Undertaker at WrestleMania . . . We will find out if 'The Game' can do what his best friend, Shawn Michaels, could not do."

And then The Undertaker's signature gong sounded, marking his arrival. Smoke began rising from the ramp, and flames danced all around the man in black as he stalked his way to ringside. It was a helluva feeling to be sitting there watching this entrance unfold.

> "Through fifty-foot-high flames walks The Demon of Death Valley, one of the most intimidating individuals in the history of WWE. And without a doubt, ladies and gentlemen, simply looking at this man and what's at stake, any other human being on the face of the earth would be intimidated. Would be afraid of their career and mortality. But the one man that isn't is standing in the center of the ring waiting, and that's 'The Game.' The Undertaker, nineteen wins and no losses at WrestleMania. And remember, ladies and gentlemen, that the road to everlasting immortality runs through WrestleMania, and on this night it runs through Hell in a Cell."

Both men squared up. The audience chanted for The Undertaker, as the Cell came down over the ring. The stage was set. Could Triple H beat the man who had retired his best friend, Shawn Michaels, the year before? And could that same best friend, who was now their referee, not get emotionally—or physically—involved, and call the match down the middle?

> *"There's no doubt that Satan Structure is morally corrupt. It awaits its victims here tonight. We're looking at them: Undertaker, Triple H."*

And when all the pageantry was done, Triple H and Undertaker, both first-ballot Hall of Famers, teed off on each other with fists loaded with bad intentions—a flurry that The Undertaker came out on top of.

> *"How will we start this matchup? We're seeing it— physically, intimidatingly. This match can end at any moment with these heavy strikes by the most feared striker in WWE. Up and down, hard body shots, carcinogenic right hands of The Undertaker. So debilitating."*

With the scene set, I wanted to take that same energy all the way to the finale of the match. If we were going out, we were going out in style. And, boy, did these guys deliver! It was a slobberknocker of a match that tested both men's will and desire—and said to the rest of the card yet to come, *Follow that.* Backward and forward, one man in control and then the other—it was a masterclass of a performance that had the crowd fully invested. And it was done through the storytelling, with all three men playing their roles perfectly when the time came for them to shine.

Michaels, as referee and Triple H's best buddy, had been calling the match right down the middle—until near the end when he Superkicked Undertaker right in the face, dropping The Deadman where he stood.

> *"It looks like we've driven through the scene of a car accident; there's bodies everywhere . . . NO! SWEET CHIN MUSIC. SWEET CHIN MUSIC AND A PEDIGREE!*

> *They got the count . . . oh, they haven't got it! It's not*
> *over! It's not over! The streak lives!! . . . The Undertaker*
> *will not die on April 1, 2012. He will not die!!"*

Undertaker was down from Shawn and Hunter's finishing moves, and in Triple H's hand was now his trusty sledgehammer. The end was near and the audience could sense it.

> *"And now, sledgehammer in hand once again. The*
> *demolition continues. The carnage ensues."*

But then, like many times past, The Undertaker sat right up like nothing had happened—and began to beat the shit out of a stunned Triple H.

> *"Kick. Shot to the jaw. The Undertaker is in full assault*
> *mode . . . Look out, look out, look out . . . Tombstone!*
> *The Undertaker with a Tombstone! Can it be?! Can*
> *it be?! Oh my! Oh my God! I can't believe what I'm*
> *seeing! The perseverance and the heart on display by*
> *these men. Hell in a Cell changes careers. Tonight,*
> *it's changing lives; it's maybe destroying friendships.*
> *But it is, ladies and gentlemen, the end of an era."*

Pinfall denied, Undertaker and Triple H exchanged headbutts on the canvass as they both struggled to find their vertical base. Both men had given the other almost everything they had. Almost.

> *"The human anatomy cannot take much more. Whose will is*
> *greater? Whose heart is beating stronger? . . . I've never seen*
> *a display of courage and guts like we're seeing here tonight."*

And then The Undertaker's head was spiked into the mat by another Triple H Pedigree. And then another kick out by The Deadman! What a match, and what a reaction from the sold-out crowd. The pacing, passion, and the story being told dragged everyone in—including me.

> *"Hell, I'm just as excited as the fans—this is unbelievable . . .*
> *You can check out of Hell in a Cell, but after tonight, can*
> *you truly ever leave? The Undertaker stirring . . . Triple H is*
> *now reaching desperately, trying, clawing. The sledgehammer*
> *could now without question be the difference. With the streak*
> *of 19–0 on the line, in jeopardy . . . Who will execute who*
> *in this matchup? And The Undertaker has a weapon. Look*
> *at the foot! The Undertaker stepping on the sledgehammer."*

And then it was The Undertaker's turn to wear "The Game" down with chair shot after chair shot in the back and jabs into the rib cage. Triple H tried to stand, only to be dropped again by The Deadman. And a clothespin attempt failed to end the match.

> *"Does one really win in Hell in a Cell or does one*
> *merely survive? Triple H is fully aware of the danger*
> *he's in, 'The Game' writhing in pain. No human being*
> *should suffer in this manner. 'The Game' lunging, but*
> *there's not enough gas in the tank. Undertaker shaking*
> *his head. And 'The Game' defiant, courageous. Still*
> *his mind says, 'I will fight you! I will fight you!'"*

Hunter stood, and we could sense that this amazing match was coming to a close. It was the end of an era for sure, for all four of us. We could feel it, and the audience could feel it, too.

I knew the way my WWE bookings were going that I couldn't help but look at the bigger picture. And what a journey it had been, from debuting at WrestleMania full of hope in 1993, to winding down at WrestleMania full of gratitude and pride in 2012. I would come back to WWE for appearances few and far between. But as far as being considered their number-one announcer, or even a regular announcer, my time there had truly passed.

Hunter stood, his sledgehammer taken from him by The Undertaker. "The Game" wanted to go out on his shield, go out swinging, and I understood his thinking perfectly.

> *"And the shot heard round the world with that sledgehammer. And The Undertaker disposes of that. And is 'The Game' next on that disposal list? The way this one has gone, who knows?"*

Hunter tried to claw his way up, unable to stand on his own steam. The Undertaker looked down on "The Game" and ran his thumb across his throat like a blade, signaling the end for Triple H.

> *"A battered, a courageous Triple H tried to use The Undertaker's own legs to pull 'The Game' up to regain his virtual base."*

But Triple H just lifted himself right into a Tombstone pile driver.

> *"My God, we know what that means. The sign of disaster. And . . . the three!! God, what a war. I tell you, in four decades sitting at ringside, I can honestly say that I have never seen anything like we've just witnessed . . . Look, The Undertaker's back. He's just fighting to get back up. The era has ended. We will never see it again."*

But what an amazing, life-changing era it was.

"Keep punching, keep going!"

May 26, 2014
Rocky Juarez vs. Rene Alvarado, Golden Boy Live!
Fort Bliss Arena
El Paso, Texas

Sometimes the words I say are also the ones I need to hear. I guess it makes sense that thoughts rattling around in your head come out your mouth, too.

In 2014, the wrestling world revolved around WWE, but something exciting was beginning to happen at the grassroots level of our business. Smaller companies were just starting to gain larger crowds as internet-savvy, disenfranchised fans began looking for alternatives to Vince's product. And while their box-office numbers were comparatively small, the passion to support those fan-friendly, fast-paced, and match-heavy companies was large, and growing.

I'd been paying attention to it all, because I'd been "retired" by WWE the year before and was assessing my next moves. After twenty years with one company, I was out on my own again, and after a few months out, I was getting used to it. I was, luckily, beyond the point of needing to work, though I don't think I'll ever be past the point of wanting to work.

So I set up my podcast and began fielding other broadcasting offers that came my way. I knew I wasn't ready to leave the wrestling business, so

I found new ways to stay in the game and remain engaged with my fans. I took some time to write my first book, go on the speaking circuit, and just generally set my own pace and agenda for the first time in forty years.

I wasn't sure exactly what I wanted to do, now that I was free to explore other options, but I knew I had a lot of gas left in the tank—and Fox Sports and Golden Boy Promotions seemed to think so, too, as they offered me a deal to be their new boxing broadcaster.

Up to that point, I'd called Atlanta Falcons football, XFL, and an MMA card with UFC Hall of Famer Chael Sonnen—but this was the first time I'd been hired to sit in the booth for a boxing event, and I was very excited to try my hand in a whole new world, with a whole new machine around me.

I approached my debut in boxing the same way I did my job in wrestling, with respect, enthusiasm, and genuine appreciation for those who were in the ring—and in search of the human story underscoring the battle ahead. I was looking for why the audience should care beyond the hooks and the uppercuts. And for that night's main event, that personal reason people should care presented itself in the build-up to the battle.

Rocky Juarez, the challenger, a longtime contender but never champion, was going up against durable WBC Silver Featherweight Champion René Alvarado in a match that Rocky said would be his last if he didn't leave victorious.

It was all or nothing, and "The Rock" fought like it. He went out there to prove something to his opponent, the crowd, and maybe that little voice in his head that said he might be done. And the people in attendance traveled right along his journey with him, chanting, "Rocky! Rocky!" as the fight raged on.

| *"I think I've heard that chant before, somewhere."* |

Both men gave it everything they had, but Juarez was fighting for something more than just gold. He was fighting for what it represented to him: his career, and his legacy in a sport that he'd given his whole life to. The end was coming, and each of Rocky's punches was launched as a statement of intent. This man wasn't ready to bow out without the one thing that would bring him peace in his career—gold around his waist.

> *"His name is Rocky. He was born to be a fighter. But he also said to us quite clearly that if I don't win this I'm done."*

Where I was in my own life and career, I could see in this man's eyes. He wanted to go out on terms of his own making, knowing in his heart and soul that even though the clock was ticking, he had so much more to offer. Alvarado was a worthy champion, but he was up against a man who was fighting for much more than just a win or a loss. He was up against someone who had tied his career and identity to a ten count or the judges' scorecard.

> *"Rocky's corner succinct in telling 'The Rock': 'We know you're tired, we know you're tired, but keep the pressure on, keep punching, keep going!'"*

And the challenger kept driving forward, even though all the shots he landed on Alvarado bounced off the champion's granite chin.

> *"Twenty-five seconds left. 'The Rock' needs a flurry. He needs a flurry to build momentum. To score as much as he can to put this thing out of reach . . . Oh, oh, what a right hand! A right hand by Rocky Juarez. I don't know how Alvarado stayed upright, but he did. This crowd on their feet, and rightly so. We've just seen a hell of a fight!"*

The crowd sounded their respect and appreciation for the battle they had just witnessed. But the corner of the challenger had been on the wrong side of too many judges' decisions to take anything for granted.

Rocky, with his head bowed, waited for the result, and cracked a smile as his name was finally called out as champion. Much like his wrestling counterpart, "The Rock" was the people's champion that day, as the noise in the building rose significantly with mention of his name as the champion after all this time.

> *"Finally, the heartbreak ends for Rocky Juarez. The thirty-four-year-old has found new life in the game of the sweet science."*

I had an amazing time in the boxing world and truly loved getting the chance to prove myself in a new setting. And as my years away from WWE went on, I got to test myself in other ways, too. I called matches for New Japan Pro Wrestling live and in the studio; I got to travel to the UK to be lead announcer on the iconic *World of Sport* as they attempted a reboot.

My life was varied and interesting and moving just the way I wanted it to move—until, on March 22, 2017, my world was crushed in an instant when my wife, Jan, was taken off life support, two days after she was struck from behind by a vehicle while on her Vespa scooter.

The woman I was so proud and lucky to marry in 1993, the woman who stuck with me through everything—when the world thought I was somebody, and when it thought I was nobody—was taken from me just a couple of minutes from our home.

She'd stood by me in our first years of marriage when I got Bell's palsy and lost my job at WWE, and didn't know how I was going to provide for us. She was there when I became addicted to sleeping pills and fell into many bouts of depression.

She stayed with me. She saved me. She minded me. She guided me. She protected me. And she loved me. My little angel fought for the two of us when I was too down to help her out. And she won. She kept us together until I was able to get up and start swinging again. She could have left at any time when I was at my worst, but she was taken from me when we were at our best.

We were planning the rest of our lives together. Until we weren't.

And while she lay in a coma those two days, WWE called me.

They said that Vince wanted me to come back home.

Vince knew me well enough to know that if I lost Jan, I could have gotten lost pretty quickly, too. He wanted me to be around the business, around the fans and my colleagues, and not be alone at home.

At my worst time, wrestling was there to surround me, and shield me, and give me some purpose at a time when most other things in my life felt meaningless.

The unbearable pain that I felt, and still do, without her could have cut me adrift if I hadn't had that familiar place to go. That never-still, traveling circus—ever-changing, night after night, town after town, city after city— was the only place that ever felt like home.

And I was truly blessed to have it.

"How do you like AEW now?!"

May 25, 2019
AEW's Inaugural PPV, Double or Nothing
MGM Grand Garden Arena
Las Vegas, Nevada

Alternatives are good for everybody. The second someone has a monopoly on anything, that anything inevitably gets worse. And while wrestling has always had hot territories, and large players, there was never really one central player who cornered the wrestling business outright—until WWE.

Since WCW went out of business in 2001 and left WWE unopposed on top of the wrestling mountain, there had been other, much smaller players here and there, but our industry effectively went from thirty-ish territories when I started, to three nationally broadcast companies during the Monday Night Wars, to just one internationally recognized company.

And when that happened, the term "professional wrestling" became interchangeable with "WWE" in the vocabulary of the mainstream and the casual fan alike. There was one show in town, and everyone knew it. And that meant less variety for fans, fewer opportunities for talent, and less chance of any other company being able to rise up and make themselves a national force once again.

When WWE became the only real show in town, it didn't so much take something new for our business to redraw itself again—it took it going all the way back to the start. Just like what happened after the end of the "Golden Era" of the 1950s—professional wrestling went back to its small, territory-based roots, and began to build out small, exciting, independent companies where people could work and make a name for themselves. And from these small companies, wrestlers around the country (and internationally, too) began to understand the power of entrepreneurship and brand building. This grassroots effect was real and growing rapidly through social media, podcasts, YouTube, and online PPVs. Wrestling fans were finding their new favorite indie wrestler just like music fans were finding their new favorite song or new favorite indie band. The likes of The Young Bucks and Kenny Omega started making real money setting their own dates, selling their own shirts, and amassing their own fan bases.

The hunger for an alternative was clearly shining through. Thousands of wrestling fans, who just felt WWE was no longer for them, turned out night after night in smaller venues to support their beloved professional wrestling.

And they brought their cash and collective voices with them—so much so, that in 2017, when wrestling journalist Dave Meltzer bet one dollar online that the trailblazing Ring of Honor wrestling company wouldn't be able to sell 10,000 tickets to its latest card (something no company outside of WWE had done since the closure of WCW), indie wrestling fans sold out that event in thirty minutes, with 11,262 tickets purchased.

The sellout led people with product knowledge and contacts to notice the business opportunity numbers like this could lead to. There were a lot of lapsed wrestling fans who wanted to support something other than WWE. And there was one man in particular who knew that, if he could hire the right people, and bring the right resources, and convince the right talent to come aboard a brand-new wrestling company—then building that national alternative was all of sudden a real possibility.

That man was Tony Kahn, and his company was All Elite Wrestling.

After Jan died, and my two-year contract came to a close in WWE, I decided to not re-up, as they had their broadcast teams set and I wanted to do something to challenge myself full-time, instead of just here and there. I truly loved WWE, but Vince understood my need to keep going, and not languish on the sidelines while trying to deal with being alone.

I needed something more engaging, something more scary and risky, to help me not be in my head so much. So WWE and I parted on great terms, as I looked to the future once more.

When the offer to join AEW came in, I took it.

I'd first met Tony in Long Beach one night, after Tony came with his friend, as a fan, to a New Japan event there. Over the course of the night, he began to ask me questions about how to run a wrestling company, and I thought no more of it. Many people had floated and talked about new wrestling companies over the years—and a few had tried to get various companies off the ground—but nobody in North America could get all the variables needed to present an alternative to WWE. So, when my manager called me one day and said there was an offer, I was wary at first. But the more I learned, the more I could see that AEW had a shot.

With Tony's father being a billionaire and owner of the Jacksonville Jaguars and the Fulham Premier League soccer team, Tony had access to the financing and the TV relationships to make it happen. And as Tony himself was the Director of Football at Fulham *and* Senior President of Football and Analytics at the Jaguars, he uniquely understood the importance of talent acquisition and brand awareness in getting a sports franchise going. I have no idea if I was the first person hired to AEW, but I know I was one of the first five for sure. I signed a three-year deal and was excited to be the voice of the start-up brand because I believed in the talent, the mission statement, and the want to offer choice in our business.

Unlike so many of the start-ups that came before it, AEW seemed to find steady legs really early on. I knew from experience that the two biggest pillars of any new wrestling endeavor are talent and television. Well, AEW was knee deep in talks with Warner Brothers Discovery for the TV part, and one look down their roster showed me that they had enough talent to launch. If you have a locker room with New Japan Pro-Wrestling standout Kenny Omega, WWE veteran Chris Jericho, The Young Bucks, and Cody Rhodes in it, then you have a shot.

All any start-up can offer is an opportunity at success—no guarantees. And that's maybe part of what attracted me to their pitch in the first instance. Tony clearly wasn't messing around when it came to a vision for what the wrestling business needed: another company to make the business better for workers and fans alike.

And with the marquee names that made that impressive thirty-minute ROH sellout a reality now signed to AEW as both talent and co-executive vice presidents, AEW was ready for its inaugural PPV, Double or Nothing.

And I was onboard, too, and so grateful to be, so far into my career.

A new boss, in a new company, calling a new PPV. And I knew our intent was to finish that same raucous, inaugural PPV as hot as possible, to let the fans know that AEW had arrived.

I just had no idea what that hot finish would be.

I'd heard that we were in talks with former WWE Champion Dean Ambrose, but I had no idea that he'd shed his WWE skin and appear at Double or Nothing as Jon Moxley, where he blew the roof off with his last-minute entrance.

And I had a feeling, when I heard the fans' reaction to Moxley showing up in the final minutes of our broadcast, that AEW was on to something that was sorely lacking in our industry.

| *"Hey. Hey. Hey! What the hell?!"* |

Moxley was so full of passion and raw aggression that I felt it in my bones all the way from the broadcast position. It felt like a Stone Cold moment, and it made any tiny reservations that I might have had about jumping to a new company almost fifty years into my career disappear.

| *"Good God almighty, the roof just came off!"* |

The crowd, having already experienced everything the company had to offer, still had the energy to roar Moxley on as he entered the ring. They could feel that this moment was for them. And looking at Jon, I could see that this moment was for him, too.

Moxley had told the world about feeling restricted and tied down creatively in WWE, so when he appeared at Double or Nothing, newly invigorated, he brought with him an energy that lit up the MGM Grand Garden Arena.

He entered through the crowd, jumped the barricade, and rolled into the ring looking for a fight. Omega was down on the mat; Chris Jericho was in the corner, microphone in hand. And both Jon and Chris knew to milk the reaction a little longer.

> *"Jon Moxley has deployed on this squared circle in the MGM Grand Garden Arena with a twinkle in his eye, and Jericho is pissed!"*

The ensuing violent catharsis after he hit the ring brought back wonderful memories of the best nights during WWE's Attitude Era. With a DDT planting Jericho's head into the canvass, and then the same for the referee, the chaotic scene was alive.

> *"The thunder and lightning of Jon Moxley leaving its mark!"*

It felt like teamwork. Like all the staff and crew and wrestlers and the fans were working together to make something worth remembering. This was the night that wrestling got its second viable voice—and everyone in the building was pulling in unison to make it happen. Those people in the stands, they held up their end of the deal, and we should all be grateful for that, as fellow wrestling fans. There was so much riding on AEW having a hot first night that it lit a fire under us all.

Moxley and Omega began to fight through the ring, over the barricade, and into the crowd.

*"Moxley and Omega on the outside, beating the hell
out of each other. And here they come, right into the
front row. It is physical, it is intense, and these fans
are absolutely going crazy . . . It's a bar fight!"*

But we were essentially in a battle with ourselves. WWE was too big and too far down the road, with too many historical relationships and brand deals and too much international cachet to try to "topple."

That was never AEW's focus. We weren't trying to beat WWE, but to establish ourselves as an alternative to WWE. There's a whole lot of pie out there, and millions and millions of wrestling fans were no longer dining on the kind WWE was selling.

Moxley and Omega fought their way onto the giant poker chip staging we had in the arena, for a moment that was designed to be eye-catching and leave wrestling fans all over the world with a viral clip that could light up the internet.

The debuting Moxley hooked Omega's hands behind his back and spiked Kenny's head in the center of the giant stack they were both fighting on.

*"Moxley is out of control; he's so unpredictable. And now
look at this. Omega, Moxley on top of the stack of chips . . .
Oh, what a moment! How do you like AEW now?!"*

I knew the next time we had a major show, anything less than overwhelming success was going to make Double or Nothing feel like a fluke. And one thing you can't be, when you're the new kid on the block, is just lucky. You have to aim to be consistently great. That's what converts interest into fandom.

And I couldn't wait for the chance to convert more viewers into fans, over and over again.

*"What a night it was here at Double or Nothing. For
our whole crew, I'm Jim Ross saying thanks for being
with us, everybody. And so long till next time."*

"Bottom line, gentlemen, he's got the old man's blood in him. 'The American Dream' lives through the heart and soul of his son . . ."

October 3, 2019
Cody Rhodes vs. Sammy Guevara, AEW Dynamite
Capital One Arena
Washington, DC

There's a place in life and business for the new and the old to work side by side. Now, I know I'm saying this as a man in his seventies, and therefore might sound a little biased, but most things in life need those who have been there to guide those who are on their way.

And even though I'm older now, I love innovation—and I love it even more when it's tethered to tradition and legacy. We can, and must, all move forward in life—but that doesn't mean we ignore the well-trodden paths of the past. Thankfully, the more I move forward in this business, and the more I see it change, the more I hear the echoes of yesterday coming back in new and helpful ways.

AEW, to me, is a company that has that blending of *then* and *now* in its very DNA. And there seems to me to be a very clear path from *then* to explain why that's the case.

When I was a child, we didn't have cable, so I would drive thirty miles one way to my cousin's house to catch wrestling on Saturdays, only to come home and reenact the matches I'd witnessed in my room with my toy soldiers on my bed. I lived in a concrete blockhouse in East Oklahoma, dreaming of one day calling the matches and somehow being involved in the business I loved.

My story isn't unusual in that regard. A lot of wrestling fans that get hooked as kids imagine themselves being under those lights, or surrounded by those passionate crowds. One of those fans was Tony Kahn, who, like a lot of us, used all his spare time as a kid to consume everything he could when it came to professional wrestling.

Young Tony watched promotions from all over the world and memorized the dates, times, and participants on obscure and legendary cards alike. He was then, and is now, a walking encyclopedia on professional wrestling. While I used to simulate the matches when I was a boy, Tony, many years later, in another part of the country, and in a house many times removed from a brick farmhouse in Oklahoma, wrote wrestling shows in his spare time. And the name of the show he invented at that young age: *Dynamite.*

Cut to years later. A thirty-six-year-old Tony Kahn, fresh from the huge success of AEW's inaugural PPV, was about to bring AEW's first-ever weekly wrestling show to TNT—and I was right there to guide it on its way.

> "All Elite Wrestling Dynamite *is on the air! Live from the sold-out Capital One Arena from Washington, DC, our nation's capital. Fourteen thousand, one hundred twenty-nine fans jammed this joint!"*

It was fresh, it was nostalgic, it was the future and the past coming together on the same night as TNT hosted its first wrestling show since

WCW closed down almost twenty years before. And it wouldn't be long before we ended up going head-to-head with WWE's "third brand" NXT on Wednesday nights, after they decided to move opposite us to give wrestling its first true head-to-head battle since the Monday Night Wars.

Again, everything new was echoing the old.

We embraced that theme on our show immediately, as I introduced the world to my new masked partner, Excalibur, *and* my good friend, and former partner from my Crockett/WCW days, Tony Schiavone.

It felt great walking that live-TV high wire again, on a new show that was ironing out all its wrinkles live on-air—like we were building a plane as we were flying it.

| *"We're going to kick this off with a major matchup!"* |

And the first wrestler to make his entrance for the newly minted company and their flagship show was "The American Nightmare," Cody Rhodes, the son of my dear, departed, white-shirt/red-blood-loving friend, Dusty Rhodes.

> *"Man, what an ovation! What an atmosphere here tonight.*
> *Ladies and gentlemen, wherever you are watching around*
> *the world, whether it be here in the States on TNT, in*
> *Canada on TSN, the United Kingdom on ITV, or worldwide*
> *through the FITE app, we thank you for being with us!"*

The delivery system that boomed during the TV era, and expanded during the PPV era, had now metastasized into a patchwork quilt of legacy TV networks, international partners, and live-streaming services that covered the globe. That meant that, even as an alternative brand, we were able to welcome any wrestling fan, from almost anywhere in the world, that wanted to join us.

And who better to represent the mission statement of the company than a second-generation, present-day star like Cody? A man who chose to leave WWE, to go to the indie wrestling market to charter his own course, which concluded with him banking on AEW.

> *"Bottom line, gentlemen, he's got the old man's blood in him. 'The American Dream' lives through the heart and soul of his son Cody, and this is a huge matchup."*

And if Cody was the fresh link to the past, his opponent in *Dynamite*'s first-ever match was a surefire rocket to the future: Sammy Guevara.

> *"Very talented young man is Sammy Guevara. Win, lose, or draw in this matchup, he is a great signee for the AEW group."*

Right out of the gate, AEW had to take risks on a lot of young guys, because WWE began to sign anyone and everyone who had any name value—which I can only guess was to slow down AEW's progress. So our guys were having to learn to wrestle a main event live, on national TV, in prime time. This wasn't access television or even cable, and there were no do-overs, no take-backs if things went south. And the company put their faith that first match not only in Cody, but also in a guy with far less experience, but all the potential in the world.

Sammy Guevara was a young, athletic, cocky heel, who knew already how to get the audience to dislike him. Veterans backstage like Cody and Jericho pinpointed Guevara as having unlimited ability if given the right opportunities. Well, here in his first big TV match, he was proving his high-profile supporters correct, in the highest-pressure situation he'd ever encountered.

Cody was hitting Sammy with all he had, but still the match raged on.

> *"What the hell is it going to take? What the hell is it going to take to beat Sammy Guevara here tonight?! . . . Sammy is having trouble maintaining his equilibrium. His balance has been affected. Good Lord, he's been resurrected!"*

After several close calls for Guevara, Sammy decided to climb the top rope and let fly. And as he rotated through the air, the more experienced Rhodes waited to get his knees up and roll Guevara into a pin.

> *"Knees up! Inside cradle! Inside cradle hooked.*
> *And . . . locked in the three count! Cody beats*
> *Sammy Guevara in a helluva match!"*

But it was much more than that. It was a mission statement, a clear signal to the fans watching live and all around the world. It was the opening salvo from a company that wanted us to talk about the past, to not be ashamed of our history. To remember and credit the pioneers who popularized certain moves and mastered certain matches.

WWE made the strategic decision to ban the word "wrestling" from its broadcasts, even though it's literally in their name. And clearly whatever decisions they took along the way helped grow them into a multibillion-dollar company. But AEW started out as they meant to continue: standing on the shoulders of the giants that came before them.

Tony and I grew up in different generations, in different circumstances, in different parts of the country, but the communal nature of being a fan of something bigger than us brought me, him, and a team of hundreds before an arena of thousands to present his vision for a new worldwide audience of millions.

And that night he used the new and the old, the fresh and the classic, to get it done.

"It's Wednesday . . . and you know what that means."

December 30, 2020
Brody Lee Celebration of Life, AEW Dynamite
Daily's Place
Jacksonville, Florida

The welcoming line to AEW's flagship show, *Dynamite*, wasn't of my creation, although I was the one with the honor of first using it to greet our audience. "You know what that means" was a line often repeated by a wrestler beloved in our business, one who left us far too soon.

2020 was a weird year in general because of the global pandemic that made a lot of the world stand still. The entertainment business mostly shut down, with musical tours grinding to a halt and movie productions shutting down. Nothing from our world was going on the road, so AEW had two choices: follow that path and close down just as it was heating up, or to take up an audience-less residence in the Jacksonville Jaguars' home of Daily's Place, and see what happened. Unlike most other touring or live productions, both AEW and WWE are reliant on live performances to fill their live TV slots every week. Britt Baker, our resident licensed dentist, had a breakout run in particular, after a rocky start, where she used the pandemic shows as a reset to focus on sharpening her character, and in-ring game, to the point where she became one of the shining lights of the whole company at that time.

Not having to live or die on the reactions of the in-house crowd, just having to focus on the cameras and the job at hand, helped several wrestlers come into their own.

So what seemed like a bad situation initially turned into a great situation, as AEW found their groove in this unique environment really fast. New stars were made, and the TV ratings began to rise. People were sitting at home, looking for new things to entertain them as they rode out the uncertainty of what was happening around the world. And what better way to take your mind off the awful scenes and headlines of the time than the over-the-top nonstop action of the professional wrestling world?

But that time wasn't all celebration and growth for AEW.

There was a huge loss mixed in there, too.

Now, I've lost many friends in this business; most of them were too young, with far too much road in front of them. A lot of those deaths seemed preventable, as I guess, looking back, it was some kind of substance misuse that took a lot our brothers far too quickly, and far too soon. It got to a stage in the '90s where every time somebody started a sentence with, "Hey, did you hear about . . ." I just assumed it was another needless, senseless death.

And a lot of times, unfortunately, I was right.

A lot has changed since then; talent now are looking after themselves outside the ring better than I can ever remember. By and large, they know more about the effects of certain kinds of lifestyles than any generation I've been a part of. As a whole, the touring lifestyle of our business just seems less chaotic than it did in the past; you're more likely to catch our guys gaming after shows than partying nowadays. And that to me is a great thing. I don't mind any person letting their hair down and blowing off a little steam in our line of work, but the hedonistic approach of past generations just had a Russian roulette kind of feel to it, where it wasn't a matter of when another wrestler's poor choices would cause them to be taken from us too soon. It was just a matter of who it would be.

But sometimes, when a young man goes, it's not because of his lifestyle, bad choices, or risky behaviors. Sometimes life just sucks. That's what happened with Jonathan Huber, who was hospitalized in late 2020 with idiopathic pulmonary fibrosis, a rare type of lung disease that took his life the day after Christmas that same year.

Jon was our TNT champion in AEW, but he lost that title on October 7 and was in the ICU by the end of that month. This was when most of us in the company first heard he was sick—but to everyone's credit, the news never leaked publicly. And then, just a couple of months after that, on December 26, the man who was loved and respected by everybody was gone at forty-one years old, leaving behind two young sons, Brodie and Nolan, and his wife, Amanda.

Four days after Jon's passing, AEW owner Tony Kahn turned the whole broadcast of *Dynamite* into a two-hour celebration of the life of "Brodie Lee," as he was known in AEW, where his friends and family could speak and grieve and remember their friend, husband, and father.

I was proud that WWE put aside the usual political tribalism in wrestling and let their talent appear on AEW's tribute to Brodie without any reservations. That man was beloved across the industry, and it warmed my heart to see people from both companies be given the time and freedom to express themselves. Because that's what they needed to do to make sense of their hurt and loss at that time.

> *"It's so great to hear the hearts being expressed,*
> *the feelings, real feeling, not TV persona feelings,*
> *but the feelings of human beings."*

In our business, it's very rare not to make enemies along the way, and it's more rare to find someone that nobody has a bad word to say about. But Jon was spoken about the same way The Boys would talk about one of the most universally beloved men in our business, Owen Hart.

Owen, like Jon, died far too young, after an accidental fall from the rafters during his ring entrance on PPV in 1999. It was one of the most harrowing things I've ever witnessed sitting ringside, and that night has never left me.

Owen, too, was beloved backstage as a great wrestler, an upbeat presence on the road, and a great father who didn't get involved in all the temptations that a lot of guys did back then.

To Owen, he was just doing his job for his family.

Jon was exactly the same.

I can only wish that someday I will be spoken about with half the love and respect that these great men are. I might not get there, but I'm trying to live a life that at least points me in their direction.

Both men were always smiling, and had a great sense of humor. They understood just how important it was in an industry like ours to keep it light on the road, and they took on responsibility for that. To put Brodie in the same sentence as Owen, in terms of just how much he was loved in every locker room he was in, is probably the best compliment I can give.

When Jon came to AEW, I had the pleasure of sitting with him and talking about how he's always been a talent that should have been given more. More time, more attention, and more thought. But this business doesn't get it right all the time. So, when he came in to AEW, we both knew this was his time to shine. We knew that Tony Kahn was giving "Brodie" his own ball to play with in the form of a directionless faction called Dark Order, and, boy, did Jon make that work.

I didn't realize it at the time, but Jon's death impacted me more than I wanted to acknowledge. I was focused on getting through the show without my voice breaking—and helping AEW tell the world what a great man Jon was.

Before we went on-air, I said to the young guys that it doesn't hurt to laugh because that's how Jon made it through hard situations, and I'm sure he'd love to be remembered as that guy. After all, that was the rep he had across all the locker rooms he was in.

And while he'd won titles in WWE and AEW, and was an amazing worker in the ring, most, when they spoke about him, didn't focus on that at all—they talked about what a great father he was, and how much he loved his family.

You can see it in his son Brodie Jr., who idolized his father, and his father's business, so much that the two were inseparable on TV days at AEW's home arena in Jacksonville. A lot of the other wrestlers would show Brodie Jr. a thing or two when he came around, and between what his father showed him, and the interest the other talent showed in him, Brodie Jr. built up a wrestling acumen far, far beyond his eight years. So much so that, at our New Year's Eve gathering, young Brodie and one of his father's good friends, Adam Cole, did a little "spot" where Brodie Jr. threw a clothesline just like his father, pinned Adam—and, to my delight, hooked the leg while doing so.

It genuinely touched my heart. The boy was dealing with his grief through wrestling, and being around people who loved him and his dad.

I could relate to that feeling.

We began the night with a ten-bell salute as the AEW roster stood in silent respect on the ramp, surrounding Jon's wife, Amanda, and their young family. We continued with matches and personal recorded messages, and wrestlers respectfully mimicking Jon's in-ring mannerisms and moves. We ended with his boots laid in the middle of the ring by his son.

Jon "Brodie Lee" Huber wasn't engaging in risky behaviors; he didn't tempt fate or live close to the edge. He was a loving family man who got sick. And that sickness took him from his young family without much warning.

I've had the privilege of welcoming many audiences to many programs over the years, but no matter whose voice you hear on *Dynamite*, now or in the future, it's Jon Huber who welcomes you now.

"Game face on, ready for battle. There's never been anyone else like this man . . . It's clobberin' time!"

September 5, 2021
CM Punk vs. Darby Allin, All Out
NOW Arena
Chicago, Illinois

Just two years after AEW's launch with a primarily online fan base at 2019's All Out, 2021's All Out made over ten million dollars in PPV buys alone. That number made it the largest non-WWE wrestling event of all time, almost tripling the PPV buy rate of the previous two All Out PPVs. And the huge difference maker in 2021's All Out? The in-ring return of CM Punk.

Now, getting a *sense* of how a company is doing is important, but at the end of the day, it's the numbers that tell you whether you're going to survive or not. And, boy, was that 2021 PPV number encouraging, to say the least. It was a further sign that lapsed wrestling fans would tune back in to wrestling for something compelling—and that they were willing to pay in an "old money" way to get to see it.

In 2014, WWE had given up on the PPV model they helped pioneer in the early '80s, instead favoring a subscription streaming service where fans paid a monthly fee to access the company's "Premium Live Experiences," as they rebranded them.

Well, All Out told us squarely that PPV wasn't dead just yet, just abandoned.

AEW, with its internet heart and territory soul, reached its domestic PPV audience through cable and select multiplexes and theater showings, as well as being available domestically and internationally through a couple of different apps across all the streaming services. But it wasn't the PPV reach that got the number.

It was the headliner.

After all, you can make your show available everywhere, but for *any* company to get numbers like that, they need a star attraction that compels people to shell out their hard-earned money to see them. That "star on top" business model has been in effect in our business since the first day wrestling sold tickets. But when a company is just starting out, it needs that magic ingredient even more. AEW in 2021 was growing fast (still is, with an expanding presence on Warner Discovery networks) and pulling in impressive numbers, which tells me that Tony Kahn was (and is) making all the right moves to grow the company from an internet rumor to a bona fide long-term brand.

But like I found out when I was head of talent relations in WWE, you can never have too many top guys that the audience will pay to see. And in AEW that marquee name was still needed. But it was delivered, in my opinion, when CM Punk signed his name to a multi-year contract after being on the sidelines of our business for seven years, after being fired from WWE on his wedding day back in 2014.

Tension had been building between Punk and WWE for a while, and it all came to head a few months before his firing, after WWE's Royal Rumble PLE, when Punk got into a heated argument with Triple H and Vince McMahon about a myriad of issues ranging from his creative to his general health.

Feeling there was no resolution to be had, Punk left the arena WWE was appearing at that day and didn't come back. He stayed away until he was terminated, and both parties ended up in a messy legal battle. Still, Punk stuck to his guns and never wrestled for WWE again.

He never wrestled again, period, until AEW.

Rumors were floating around that he might show in AEW in his hometown of Chicago, in the most intentionally worst-kept secret of all time, and, with just hearsay to go on, the 15,000-seat building sold out in anticipation that the man who once walked away was indeed coming back.

Immediately upon Punk's arrival to AEW, we saw a movement in interest, ticket sales, and TV ratings.

Tony was able to attract Punk with AEW's much lighter schedule, and the opportunity to wrestle for his fans mostly on his own terms—a freedom, creatively, that he never got in WWE.

And I'm sure they offered him a nice stack of cash, too.

While it takes a cast of hundreds to produce the five hours of original content we air week in and week out, there need to be a name, or names, at the public apex of that effort. A name that can pierce through all the other options, opinions, and overwhelming number of choices people have for entertainment, and compel folks to tune in to see what they're going to do next.

CM Punk was, and is, as I write this, that guy for AEW. He is one of the most intelligent and gifted athletes to ever step into a pro wrestling ring. He's a very outspoken performer and is not afraid to speak his mind in the real world—but more importantly, he's a proven star who moves the needle wherever he goes.

And he moved it again in his hometown of Chicago on PPV, as Punk made his in-ring debut for AEW at All Out.

"What's he got left, ladies and gentlemen? What has CM Punk have left? That's a question he's asked himself many, many times."

The story Punk was telling in his comeback was one of a man who didn't know what he was capable of in the ring anymore. And we were all about to find out live, and in real time, as the Chicago faithful showered their hometown hero with adulation.

> *"The Best in the World getting ready for battle for the first time in seven years in a pro wrestling ring . . . Big-time feel here. Big-match feel. Where else would you want to be, ladies and gentlemen, than enjoying this phenomenal PPV?"*

As the lights came up, the crowd filled the arena with chants of "CM PUNK! CM PUNK!" as Punk's opponent, the intense, face-painted, up-and-coming daredevil Darby Allin, sat in his corner and soaked it all in.

> *"Darby has not taken his eyes off his adversary once. Same expression. Same focus. Same mindset."*

And then the bell rang.

> *"The most welcome bell I ever heard."*

I meant it. It's hard to articulate what a genuine name and draw like Punk does for a company who is out there making a name for itself. And in there with Darby, as they both went face-to-face in the middle of the ring, it was easy to see why he'd returned to wrestling. Punk had unfinished business to address in an industry that had left him feeling burned. He loves pro wrestling passionately—some might say too much—so the chance to write his last chapters in his own voice was a proposition too tempting to pass up.

As fans of AEW now know, the relationship between Punk and protocol has never been an easy one. He likes to walk outside the lines a lot, and if there's something on his mind, the world is probably going to know. But his value is in that mindset. As my old colleague Eric Bischoff likes to say, "Controversy creates cash." Punk is the walking embodiment of that statement.

And on this night, his first night back between the ropes, he proved once again that whatever friction he brings with him only adds to the bottom line.

As Punk and Darby battled to the finish of their match, it was apparent that Punk wasn't just viable on the posters of AEW, but in the ring still, too. The seven-year absence might have slowed his pace a little, but Punk was knocking out that ring rust and building momentum with every hard-hitting moment that passed.

| *"Fans loving this. As we all are! What a PPV we've had, folks."* |

It was a wonderful back-and-forth wrestling match that mixed the fundamentals with Darby's high-flying style. If Punk wanted to test his gas tank out there, then there was no better opponent for him. Darby is something else, and hasn't got an ounce of quit in him. But as the match hurtled toward the finish, Punk hit Darby with a knee to the jaw, his signature move, and as Allin went down, the audience counted along to Punk's pin: 1 . . . 2 . . . 3!

> *"Got it! What a match. One hell of a wrestling match . . . If you were wondering if he has anything left, I think CM Punk has definitely answered that question. You're damn right he's got plenty left."*

Punk set up his story, where he needed to address any talk of him being "past it" or "over the hill," and with that match gave his reply in front of an adoring hometown fan base.

> *"Darby put his heart and soul into the match. But on this night, September 5th, it just wasn't enough for the returning*

CM Punk . . . What is next for CM Punk? Best in World has got a lot left in the tank, and he's willing to prove it."

Numbers don't lie. You can divide opinions, you can walk out of one company and into another, and have all your strong opinions along the way. You can be seen as a hero for standing up, or a martyr for walking away. But what matters is the numbers. Some fans will love you for your principled stances, and some not so much. Some will love you for your righteous tone, and some not so much. The important part is that those fans are willing to pay to let the world know. Chant or boo, cheer or jeer. CM Punk brings it all.

People who can do that are rare.

And that's why we gravitate to them—fans and owners alike.

"Something is going to implode—I mean, really implode—here tonight. The intensity is too much."

September 4, 2022
CM Punk vs. Jon Moxley, All Out
NOW Arena
Chicago, Illinois

In anything that's living, that's growing, that's moving through this world, there are going to be challenging times. It's inevitable, and none of us are going to get from one end of this life to the other without facing that reality in some way. I think the people and places that thrive are the ones who handle those challenges the best.

As AEW was heading into its biggest annual PPV, All Out 2022, we were putting together some compelling broadcasts and cementing our place as one of the top-rated shows on our network—all while growing in all the other metrics that matter to a booming start-up, too.

With a stellar roster, and CM Punk on top, AEW was delivering both on the balance sheet and in the ring.

But as always, in life, things weren't rosy everywhere.

Not backstage, and not with me personally.

As All Out 2022 rolled around, I'd just been through a year of constant challenges as I recovered from skin cancer. After twenty-two radiation treatments in twenty-two days, I was sore and worn down, but I never missed work. Every day I went to the hospital, had the treatment, went home alone—and then once a week, continued to go live on-air with *AEW Dynamite*.

It was the "alone" part that was the hardest for me. I'm not going to lie, when I first got the news, I was scared to death. My age, and being many miles from family back in Oklahoma, meant I had to face whatever was coming down the line at me alone. My daughters have their own lives, their own families, and their own businesses to manage. I'm not the kind to roll up on them and expect they drop anything for me. As a matter of fact, I would hate to think I was a minute's bother to anyone, so despite their kind offers of support, I stayed in Florida, where I have a place just five minutes away from the Mayo Clinic.

Which is where, thankfully, I got word at the end of 2021 that I was cancer free.

But because of the intense radiation treatments, I still had weekly appointments there—still do—where they scraped away tissue that would allow the radiation burn wound above my ankle to heal. It hurt like hell, but I saw any dead cells they got rid of as getting me closer to being 100 percent. But because of where it was, and the lack of flesh around that ankle area, they had trouble stopping the bleeding, and getting it to heal up.

Somewhere between the visits, and the cross-country traveling with an open wound, I decided I finally needed to take a few weeks off. Just something to recharge my batteries a little. But even then, I didn't want to stay away too long, as I knew I had a great thing going with my old partner Tony and AEW's new and talented play-by-play guy, Excalibur.

Maybe I was a little worried that they'd move on without me.

I was a little weary on my return, but Excalibur made me tear up when he said his father asked him if he knew how lucky he was to be getting the education he was getting working with JR. His words hit me at the right time to make me immediately emotional because, after what I'd been through, and was still going through, I'd never felt older or more beaten down. Excalibur's words made me feel useful, and let me know that I'm still contributing to the business that I've poured my whole life into.

But education is a two-way street, and Excalibur has been a huge asset to me, too, educating me on other styles of wrestling that he is proficient in and that I'm not as familiar with, such as the Japanese Strong Style or the Mexican Lucha style. I might be in my seventies, and known as "the voice of wrestling," but I'm still excited to learn. I'm still excited to be a part of a team, part of a cohesive locker room.

When I managed the talent in WWE, I did it like we were a sports team. And as we've seen in our favorite leagues time and time again, the morale of the locker room can dictate the results on the field. Many great teams have fizzled because of locker room disharmony, and many not-so-great teams have triumphed because they played as one unit.

Vince used to love when there was tension with The Boys. He saw it as a competitive thing, so nothing made him happier than when the locker room was on edge. Well, nothing except maybe a fart noise. He loved those more than anything else.

I've always taken the opposite approach (on the locker room, not fart noises). I want talent that's hungry for success; I want them to strive to be the best they can be. But there's no success to be had from letting tensions build and whispers spread. Wrestling is a team game, and everyone needs to pull in the same direction or the ship goes off course very quickly. And that's something that'll always be true, at least until someone can figure out how to go out there and wrestle by themselves.

In a business full of tough people with big egos, I've seen and heard all kinds of finger-pointing, violence, spats, brawls, and death threats. And those were just directed at me. I guess that's why I didn't really get too animated when I heard there was a backstage altercation after the All Out 2022 PPV between CM Punk, Kenny Omega, and The Young Bucks.

I called the main event of that show, where Punk challenged Jon Moxley for the AEW world title, and there was something in the Chicago air that night.

> *"I have a gut feeling, maybe from sitting out here so many*
> *years, something is going to implode—I mean, really*
> *implode—here tonight. The intensity is too much."*

Little did I know that the real fireworks would ignite after the match, away from other people, and between AEW's top stars.

Punk took over the after-show press conference, to squash some rumors and to pour a little gas on others. And after Punk recounted his version of events, Kenny Omega and The Young Bucks went to his dressing room to discuss what was said—and a scuffle occurred.

The fallout left AEW with division in the locker room, threatened lawsuits, and an internal investigation that sidelined Punk for months.

Now, I have no idea who was right and who was wrong. And because I don't run talent relations in AEW, it's not my business to know. What I do know is AEW is growing rapidly, and it needs all its main event guys working with each other.

I heard Kenny, in an interview, describe what happened as a blowup not dissimilar to what you'd find in any locker room across any other sport. I think his take, as someone who was involved, is a sober, rational way to handle an issue that blew up into something massive in our business, and in our company in particular.

For any issues that risk spilling out into the public, you want to get all the involved parties into a room and settle it as quickly after it happened as you possibly can. Wrestling is a genre where there's always been a right way and a wrong way of "doing business." I've seen some guys and gals get heat in the locker room because they're acting in a way that's frowned upon, but it's because they're so new that they have no idea what the protocols are. Other times, people have been assholes, and they're being ostracized for good reason. But most of the time, problems arise because people feel disrespected, or they're angry, or they have an issue they feel isn't being addressed.

And in my view, the only way to find out what the issues are between all parties is to talk it out. Talk it out, and make sure none of what's being discussed is leaking online and adding gas to the fire.

Expanding any rapidly growing business is challenging, and we need cool heads to prevail. We need people to communicate as professionals. Professionals who are on the same team.

And if at the end of the talking and listening there's no way forward, the person responsible for the whole locker room should voice their take on it. And mine always was: if we can't solve this problem, then I'll have to eliminate it, as my responsibility is to the collective.

The company has to come first.

I've said this many times to talent. We have to take care of the goose because the goose lays the golden eggs that we deposit in the bank. So, to me, that's the bottom line.

After the altercation, it seems that all the people involved have handled it internally, and Punk has come back to headline AEW's new show, *Collision*. It was a challenging time, but one that got resolved, and all parties decided to move on for the good of the goose.

AEW's goose is getting bigger and bigger, and so will the challenges that come with that growth. However, I feel that there's talent enough at the top to deal with whatever new dilemmas and rewards are sure to come down the road.

In a business that's run on friction, everyone doesn't have to be friends, but they do all have to pull for the same team.

"God, I love this drama! This energy!"

June 17, 2023
Debut of AEW Collision
United Center
Chicago, Illinois

I arrived to the venue that day with a black eye, and more frustratingly for me, a voice that kept coming and going all day. The doctor said it was a reaction to my body fighting against what was happening to me. I was in Chicago to lend my voice to the debut of AEW's new show, *Collision*—but I really shouldn't have been there at all. My eye was swollen shut, I'd flown in from Florida with a concussion, and I was, for lack of a better term, shaken.

The night before, I'd gotten up to use the bathroom, tripped over the CPAP machine in my room, and knocked myself out when I fell. When I woke up on the bedroom floor, I crawled into bed with my face bloodied. In my confused state, I got back under the sheets instead of calling for help, which could have been real bad for me, if things had gone sideways.

I'm not going to lie, I got a fright when I woke up, my vision blurred, my sheets covered in blood. But I wanted to make my flight to Chicago even though my head was hurting so bad it made me ill. I suspected then I had a concussion (which was later confirmed), but I didn't want to let anyone down by not being where I gave my word I'd be. I wanted to do what I had always done, and be what I'd always been, which is reliable. Anyone who has been hired by me in the past knows that being reliable is the first thing I ask of the talent, so I always felt I needed to model that same trait, too. And I have. Sometimes to my detriment.

So I caught my flight.

But the more the minutes passed, the more I knew the shot to my head had shaken me up pretty bad. I was weak, unsteady on my feet, but I still wanted to be the man my parents raised, the man The Boys would admire, the man who wouldn't let anyone down. I guess even though I'm seventy-one, and five decades in the business, I'm still trying to be the man that shows everyone he's meant to be there.

I also knew this would probably be the last new debut show I'd ever work.

Over the course of my career, I have been blessed to be heard on all of the big shows that wrestling fans today hold dear. I have worked across the world in tiny halls and massive arenas. I have been cued in by some of the best minds that have ever been a part of this business. I have pulled myself back up onto the horse after all kinds of sicknesses and personal tragedies, but as I arrived in Chicago, I felt my world was crumbling around me.

I'm writing this only a few weeks later, and my kids and grandkids are worried about me living alone, worried about me working so hard after my cancer battle this year and last. I know I've run myself dangerously low in trying to travel to the shows every week. But I convinced myself that I'm John Wayne, that I know what I'm doing, because I have been happy, I have been sick, I have been hurt, and I have been on top of the world—and I've done it all while sitting in a black seat, wearing a black hat, and talking to the wrestling world. I have been lead, I have been color, I have been host, and I have fired and hired, in and out. And looking back on it all for this book has meant the world to me.

But it's also made me rethink my life, now that I'm moving toward the inevitable.

I have this dream I can't shake, and it's me being found dead, alone, in a Marriott. I've always been concerned about dying on the road, but the older I get the more prevalent the dream becomes, because I feel drawn to the road, because I never really learned to stay at home. Especially now that there's nobody waiting for me when I get there.

So I travel and fill up my calendar with things to do and places to be. Places where I feel useful. Places where I know people who are just like me will be waiting to put on a show.

And my dream of being found out there, instead of at home, grows stronger, looping over and over in my head. I try to forget it, but it's in there on replay.

Then I book into yet another Marriott.

I don't want to let anyone down.

I don't want to look weak.

So I make my way out to call the main event of the new show—guided down the ramp by a stagehand so I don't fall again. And then as I open my mouth, trying not to get sick from my concussion, my voice trembles out, hoarse and weak. The second I hear myself, I know something has to change in my life. I am not going away, but I know my time is shorter than longer here, and I need to do something to extend my time.

> *"I'm under the weather, I apologize for my voice. I'm under the weather, but I wouldn't miss this for the world. I love this."*

Along this journey I have been forced to change, been glad to evolve. I took orders I didn't like, and I passed on life-changing news that I loved. I have been the good guy and the bad guy, and even when—maybe especially when—I felt out of my comfort zone, I went at the job at hand even harder, with more tenacity than I thought possible. I'm a small-town boy who's seen more of the world than most people alive. I came from a farm surrounded by nobody, and ended up engulfed in seas of people. I am flawed, I've been wrong, but I promise you I've learned, and relearned, all the hard lessons a person should. I know what I am, and I'm finally okay with what that entails.

But I knew after I had to be helped to the back, and I found it hard to lift my head, that something had to change. So I made the call to take myself off the road.

Now, anyone who knows anything about me knows that if I'm tagging out, it means there's something very wrong. To Tony Kahn's credit, he told me to take all the time I need. For once, I checked my ego and did what was right for my well-being.

Well, I'm writing this a couple months after that debut *Collision*, and strangely, I'm also currently in contract negotiations with AEW to see what might happen next. Whatever they want to do is fine by me. I've never been in contract talks before where I was so relaxed about whatever the outcome might be. I've enjoyed my time with AEW, and would like it to continue in some way, but do I need to be out on the road every week at seventy-one?

The first few weeks after the fall were rough. I wasn't able to walk without pain, and even getting out of bed has been pure misery for me. My eye didn't open for a fortnight, and the open wound from my cancer surgery was sore as hell after, too. So I guess I was just lying there, in a really dark hole mentally, in plenty of pain physically, and thinking about my life more broadly.

Whatever happens in my contract (you guys will know when you read this, but I don't as I write this), I'm okay with doing less, traveling less, and living a little more. Airports are stressful nowadays, and having to navigate the tension, the noise, the delays, and the overcrowding isn't something that appeals to me on a week-to-week basis anymore. I think I've done enough of that over my five decades on the road. Maybe it's time for me to take a more part-time approach. I will never leave wrestling, as I love it too much, but maybe I will give less of my time to it. I have no idea. All I know is I just want to live longer, and that I'm at the crossroads of my life.

I've done everything I can do in wrestling, but have I done everything I can do with my daughters or grandkids?

I know that wrestling fans will understand when I make the adjustments that I feel I need to make in my life and maybe come back and see them less. When I do show up again—and I will—I might stumble a time or two, like I always have, and I might misspeak a couple or three times, like I always have. But those words and sentences they hear will come from a man who has always had passion for his job that drove him through the hardest times, and carried him through the greatest.

"Wouldn't want to be anywhere else in the entire world than right here!"

August 5, 2023
Return to AEW Collision
Bon Secours Wellness Arena
Greenville, South Carolina

Like in much of my journey over these last five decades, whenever I was faced with a debilitating low, a new high was right around the corner. And I guess I was so low this time that the high came just from knowing that I was still needed.

After weeks and weeks of physical pain and just-as-persistent mental turmoil, I was contacted by AEW and asked if I was ready to make my return. My assignment, straight from Tony Kahn, was to call the main event of *Collision* once again. I was feeling a lot better, but more than that, I was feeling like I had something to prove. I wanted to get back and do better for the audience who I felt I'd let down with my previous appearance.

With one phone call, I noticed a whiplash of emotion between how I felt leaving *Collision* on its debut and how I now felt about coming back. Just a few weeks before, I was ready to pull back from the business because,

273

if I'm being honest, I was trying to mentally pull back from it, before it pulled back from me.

I was trying to control matters that were, and still are, out of my hands.

But I know deep down that through the self-doubt and the protective posturing, anytime I can come in and make a difference in professional wrestling, I will be there.

As I packed another bag and caught a glimpse of myself in the mirror—older now and a little more beaten up—I wished I didn't love it so much. Wished I didn't need it so much. But then I caught that stupid way of thinking and remembered a couple of things that set me straight.

I thought of what Tony Soprano tells his nephew when Christopher is moaning about having a hard night working out in the rain: "You chose this life."

And I chose this one.

I am what I am, and what I am is a professional wrestling broadcaster. It's what I was when it wasn't cool to say that at dinner parties. It's what I was when it wasn't paying my rent. It's what I was when I drove for two cents a mile and packed wrestlers and ring gear into my car to drive hundreds of miles each way just to make the next small town. I have been who I am on regional TV, broadcast, satellite, cable, pay-per-view, online, and in streaming.

I was a professional wrestling broadcaster then, and I still am now.

And I have come to understand that the luckiest find I ever made in my life—after my angel, Jan—was purpose. That reason to get up in the morning, that North Star to move toward when you have nothing else in life guiding you. Take away the money, the fame, the accolades, the ovations, and purpose is what pulls us along. I started doing this when there was nothing in it, only hardship, struggle, and money worries. And yet, I'm so happy that I did do it. I'm so happy that I continued to make that next mile, that I learned my next lesson, that I called that next match. So, after fifty years, if I'm not doing that, it's not that I don't have any idea what to do, it's that I have no idea who I am.

And that's why I flew to South Carolina, to a building that was buzzing as I walked backstage once again. I soaked in the atmosphere, let myself remember and feel again just how much I loved this.

| *"This should be compelling, compelling television, AEW style!"* |

We were building toward the biggest wrestling show ever staged. And it wasn't WWE who was staging it—it was us. It was the start-up, the company that many thought wouldn't make it. We were heading toward London where 81,035 had paid to see us, making it the largest paid gate in wrestling history.

I had to be there.

I wanted to be there.

And AEW wanted me there, too.

So, like many times before—filled with purpose again—the weeks on the road began to blur into one another. We soon went from South Carolina to our record-breaking London PPV the following month. And all the feelings I felt about slowing down began to fade once again.

The call of the road is always going to be too much for me.

Even with the Marriott dream following closely behind me.

I chose this life.

And I rechoose it every day I wake up.

Wrestling is hot again, and the business as a whole is as exciting and electric as I've ever felt it, packed with broken records, new opportunities, names leaving and joining, and more great wrestling product on our TVs than ever before.

I've seen a lot change, and seen a lot stay the same over the years, but one thing I know for sure is that wrestling is in a great place now, on the national and international stage. We have come a long way from shady deals, the "only one per show," the lack of opportunities for our women's division, and the ignorance around the health and well-being of our talent. Wrestling now is in a much better place than any time I've been in it.

I started this journey with the call "ATTENTION, WRESTLING FANS!" and it's been my goal to keep you engaged ever since. Because I am a fan who walked through the looking glass and spent the last fifty years of his life narrating the journey back to you. And I will continue to talk to you all, and I will continue to be a part of professional wrestling, as long as I'm a part of this world. But whatever happens from here, we'll have to wait and see. I've learned enough to know that I never want to know the finish—not even mine.

I am proud that I survived all the craziness and greatness to get to call myself a lifer who continues to live and work and strive and have purpose in this business. I wasn't meant to be here. I wasn't meant to last here. And I wasn't meant to thrive here.

But I did, and I will again.

And I hope that, along the way, I've made your day a little better at some point, or I've made your fandom a little greater, or given you pause, or a reason to bust out a "BY GAWD!!" randomly in your life.

I've had a hell of a run, and I'm glad you came along with me.

We're not stopping, folks, but I've finally learned there's nothing wrong with slowing down, either.

I can't wait to see you all again, and as always—so long, everybody, and thank you for letting me into your homes.

INDEX

ABOUT THE AUTHOR AND WRITER

Jim Ross has been involved in professional wrestling for fifty years and is considered the Voice of Wrestling. In addition to calling matches for Mid-South, NWA, WCW, WWE, AEW, and other entities, JR has also served as a key executive across those companies. Elected into the WWE, NWA, and National Wrestling Halls of Fame, Ross is also a *New York Times* best-selling author, a BBQ guru, and the co-host of his own podcast, *Grilling JR*. He is a central weekly voice for All Elite Wrestling, which airs on TBS and TNT. In addition to *Business Is About to Pick Up!*, he is the author of two memoirs, *Under the Black Hat* and *Slobberknocker*, and two cookbooks, *J.R.'s Cookbook* and *Can You Take the Heat?*

Paul O'Brien is an award-winning filmmaker and bestselling author. His stage plays have been commissioned or staged in his native Ireland by the National Theatre of Ireland, Red Kettle Theatre Company, and the National Theatre School of Ireland. His independent movie, *Staid*, was awarded Best Foreign Feature Film at the Los Angeles Independent Film Festival. In addition to co-writing Jim Ross's previous memoirs, *Slobber-knocker* and *Under the Black Hat*, Paul also wrote the acclaimed trilogy of organized crime novels, *Blood Red Turns Dollar Green*, *A Shoot*, and *The Hurting Circus*, which are set in the professional wrestling territories.